From
Wollstonecraft
to Stoker

From Wollstonecraft to Stoker

Essays on Gothic and Victorian Sensation Fiction

Edited by MARILYN BROCK

McFarland & Company, Inc., Publishers
Jefferson, North Carolina, and London

LIBRARY OF CONGRESS CATALOGUING-IN-PUBLICATION DATA

From Wollstonecraft to Stoker : essays on Gothic and Victorian
sensation fiction / edited by Marilyn Brock.
    p.   cm.
    Includes bibliographical references and index.

ISBN 978-0-7864-4021-4
softcover : 50# alkaline paper ∞

    1. English fiction — 19th century — History and criticism.
2.   Gothic fiction (Literary genre), English — History and
criticism.   3. Horror tales, English — History and criticism.
4. Literature and society — Great Britain — History — 19th
century.   I. Brock, Marilyn, 1969–
PR878.T3F76   2009
823'.087290908 — dc22   2009016894

British Library cataloguing data are available

On the cover: *The Nightmare,* Henry Fuseli, oil on canvas, 1790-91
(Goethe-Museum, Frankfurt)

Manufactured in the United States of America

*McFarland & Company, Inc., Publishers
  Box 611, Jefferson, North Carolina 28640
   www.mcfarlandpub.com*

Acknowledgments

I would like to thank my dissertation chair, the writer Michael Griffith, for all the support and compassion he showed me during my long and arduous tenure as a University of Cincinnati doctoral student; as well as Joyce Carol Oates, Michael's former professor at Princeton, and my authorial heroine. I'd also like to thank my dissertation committee members Brock Clarke and Jim Schiff, both wonderful writers and critics. I can't thank Tamar Heller enough. She is my mentor in Victorian Gothic, the woman who sparked my insatiable interest in literature with her endless intellectual capability and knowledge. Thanks to Jana Braziel for all her wisdom and scholarship in French feminism, psychoanalysis, and postcolonial theory.

Thanks to all those supportive along the way: my beautiful son Darren, my family, my friends, my loved ones, the brilliant Richard Fantina and each of this edition's contributors: Julie M. Barst, Saverio Tomaiuolo, Laurence Talairach-Vielmas, Stephanie King, Judith Sanders, Maria Granic-White, Jennifer Beauvais, Kate Holterhoff, Elizabeth Anderman, and Nicholas Harris. Julia Kristeva deserves mention for her immortal contributions to the study of Gothic literature, and of course, so does Victorian author Emily Brontë, who began all of this for me with *Wuthering Heights*.

Table of Contents

Part Three — Fallen Woman, Fallen Man in the Victorian Novel

Introduction

From Wollstonecraft to Stoker focuses on issues of gender, class, and imperialism in Gothic and sensation narratives in the nineteenth century. One goal of this collection is to show that Gothic and sensation fiction have much in common as literary genres that represent experiences inexpressible in literary realism by providing access to a dark, unconscious mode of knowledge. Gothic conventions are often defined by tropes of confinement, burial or immurement in mysterious, convoluted castles and mansions, and often feature dark secrets and protagonists (often female) who have been degraded, misidentified, or imprisoned. Anne Williams' *Art of Darkness: A Poetics of Gothic* relates, "The Female Gothic creates a Looking-Glass World where ancient assumptions about the 'male' and the 'female,' the 'Line of Good' and the 'Line of Evil,' are suspended or so transformed as to reveal an entirely different world, exposing the perils lurking in the father's corridors of power" (107). The feminine experience easily finds a home in Gothic convention because the metaphor of confinement captures so well the historical female experience of being marginalized and undervalued.

The experience of abjection represents a primary concern of several of the authors here. In *Powers of Horror*, Julia Kristeva defines abjection in a sense that suggests an emotional affinity with literary terror or horror; it is "the place where meaning collapses" (2). The subject in Gothic literature often occupies a psychic borderline where identity momentarily collapses, an experience both horrifying and pleasurable. Simultaneously, the reader occupies a similar position. Kristeva views the experience of reading the Gothic novel as a way to work through difficult psychological processes. According to Kristeva, experiencing the horrible or the unknown through reading helps prevent the subject from enacting these unhealthy impulses in real life:

> Hence also its being seen as taking the place of the sacred, which, to the extent that it has left us without leaving us alone, calls forth the quacks from all four corners of perversion. Because it occupies its place, because it hence

> decks itself out in the sacred power of horror, literature may also involve not an ultimate resistance to but an unveiling of the abject: an elaboration, a discharge, and a hollowing out of abjection through the Crisis of the Word [208].

Additionally, the subject can project unresolved drives onto the characters, villains or otherwise, which provides an outlet for the cathartic release of the psychic energy caught up in repressing these drives. The psychology of the Gothic novel is to find one's self while purging the unwanted, the "Other"; the genre rearranges the borders of the self and what the self thinks it should be.

Part One—The Instability of Identity: Character, Class, and Gender

The Gothic genre arose at the end of the eighteenth century, a time of troubled national and domestic politics. Written in the French Revolutionary period, Mary Wollstonecraft's literary work testified to the need to change the way women were viewed in British society. Her Gothic novel *Maria, or the Wrongs of Woman,* published in 1797, presents a litany of nightmarish female experiences within home and society to provoke change for women's rights. The focus on family in Wollstonecraft's writing and other Gothic novels by her contemporaries reveal emerging ideologies that identify the woman's place as the home, defined as the private sphere, which she mainly found unfavorable. Male dominance was associated with the public sphere, or the workplace. *Maria*'s narrative depicts feelings of isolation and imprisonment that accompany the female experience in the context of these domestic ideologies.

My essay "Desire and Fear: Feminine Abjection in the Gothic Fiction of Mary Wollstonecraft" explains connections between anti-feminist cultural forces, the development of female identity, and how this influenced Wollstonecraft's *Maria* during the Gothic's first wave of popularity in Britain. Wollstonecraft's work to empower women reflects her own experience of feminine abjection in the socio-historical environment described in her political text *A Vindication of the Rights of Woman.* Didactic in nature, Wollstonecraft's *Maria* represents in fictional form the political perspectives espoused in *A Vindication of the Rights of Woman.* By ingeniously combining Gothic technique with feminist doctrine, Wollstonecraft helped spark what would grow into the feminist movement. The synthesis of the Gothic with feminism was a crucial development during the Romantic period, and the popular Gothic became one of the few venues in which women might express, in a form intense and distorted on the one hand but readily accessible on the other, their perception of the restraints on feminine experience. The Gothic and its mid– to late–nineteenth century counterpart, sensation fiction, might be said to have become a kind of private language of solidarity among women.

Wollstonecraft, like all the authors of Gothic novels of the late eighteenth century, followed the style set forth by Horace Walpole, whose *The Castle of Otranto* (1764) inaugurated the genre which grew in popularity until it sparked a literary mania and flourished throughout the 1790s. Walpole described his fiction as a blend of romance and adventure. Fanciful representation was a means to project, in symbolic form, the primal desires, hopes and terrors in the depths of the human mind. Bestsellers like *The Monk* by Matthew Lewis and Ann Radcliffe's *The Italian* and *The Mysteries of Udolpho* made the Gothic genre the most lucrative and popular form of narrative literature in English (Miles 41). Readers devoured stories that combined the sublime and the terrible, losing themselves for hours as they turned the pages to find out the identity of a killer or what would happen to the pretty-but-helpless heroine. During the 1790s, Gothic fiction constituted about forty percent of all books published in England (Miles 43). The genre also precipitated arguments about the propriety of reading such fiction as the primary audience for Gothic novels were women; consequently, the style became associated with "low" literature because of its relatively open portrayal of sexual themes and its potential to corrupt women's minds.

Richard Fantina's essay "'The Maiden Felt Hot Pain': Agency and Passivity in the Work of Letitia Elizabeth Landon" responds to the codification of gender in the designation of the "poetess." Victorian critics generally considered the "poetess" distinct from the "serious" male poet because she focused on the domestic realm, romantic love, and the sublime. Though Landon cannot be considered a feminist like Wollstonecraft, she grants her heroines an unprecedented agency within women's supposed secondary and submissive position. Landon lived on the cusp of the Romantic and Victorian periods and became one of the most famous female poets in England in the 1820s and 1830s. Her immense body of work included narrative and short poems, four novels and many short stories, several of which (e.g., "The Bride of Lindorf") are fine examples of Gothic fiction. Deeply influenced by the late

Romantic poets, especially Byron, her poems celebrate erotic passion while depicting the violent deaths of her characters that often result from it. Fantina focuses on her poetry, discussing it in conjunction with Kristeva's theory of abjection.

The pairing of femininity with the Other, an issue central to abjection, reflected Victorian anxieties that can be argued as a response to British imperial conquest. The domestic ideology that stabilized British national identity was dependent on definitions supported by the colonial regime, which was conducive to a fear that patriarchal dominance could easily implode. This threat, which is often represented through the conflation of a "racial Other" and the female in Gothic-influenced narratives, is characteristic of the fear of "reverse colonization," a term defined by Stephen Arata in *Fictions of Loss in the Victorian Fin de Siècle*. Writers like Charlotte Brontë who produced novels that combined realism with elements of the Gothic such as *Jane Eyre* offer a storyline that depicts the relationship between the domestic realm and imperialist interests. In Brontë's novel, Rochester, Jane's eventual husband, returns from the West Indies with a non–English wife named Bertha Mason. Bertha's character figures a revolutionary racial and female "Other" by her associations with revolutionary rage in several instances (she burns Rochester's house down after being locked in the attic due to her insanity; she attacks her brother Richard Mason, biting him like a vampire; she rips Jane's wedding veil; and so on). She is paired with Jane to become the image of an alternative self to enact Jane's gender- and socio-economic class-related rage (Hoeveler 206). The narrative is able to cast off Jane's revolutionary tendencies in the form of another character (Rochester's first wife) to assimilate her story into British norms. Therefore, Bertha represents the other in many forms: the return of the colonized; the impotence of the British male as a result of "going native"; the repressed female. Bertha is literally incarcerated, the rage of the former slave as *Jane Eyre* was written just over a decade after slavery was abolished in the colonies, and her anger is a threat to domestic security. She mutilates Rochester while burning down Thornfield Hall, his English manor, and the English male is therefore scarred from the revolutionary passions of the racial and female Other, Bertha, while his second wife, Jane, is absolved of them through Bertha's acts. Domestic ideology is supported by Brontë's demonic racial Other as Bertha destroys herself and allows Jane to civilize Rochester through middle class love. In *Gothic Feminism: The Professionalization of Gender from Charlotte Smith to the Brontës*, Diane Long Hoeveler defines Jane Eyre the character as another figure for ressentiment; she is a revolutionary female whose quest for a satisfactory identity within the paradigm of the Victorian social order is completed by redeeming Rochester rather than acting out her rage (188). Later, in the Victorian period after Wollstonecraft first combined the Gothic and feminism during the Romantic era, Gothic and sensation fiction protagonists still found themselves constrained, confined, and with limited choices. Charlotte Brontë's *Jane Eyre* (1847) depicts a young governess suffering from a conflict between her true nature and the social world. In "'Portrait of a governess, disconnected, poor, and plain': Staging the Spectral Self in Charlotte Brontë's *Jane Eyre*," Laurence Talairach-Vielmas looks at the way the author deals with the feminine ideal in her foundational novel. As Brontë plays upon a heroine comparing herself to other models of femininity, the novel brings to light the significance of visual culture in the construction of the romance between Jane and Rochester. However, Brontë's use of Gothic stereotypes ultimately discredits images of ideal femininity.

As previously noted, Victorian critics were concerned with the alleged negative effects that depictions of female sexual transgression in Gothic literature might have on female readers. Emerging some two generations after Gothic fiction, sensation fiction was highly influenced by its predecessor. Frank depictions of transgressive behavior in sensation fiction gave rise once again to fears of the potentially harmful effects of literature that questioned or misrepresented the accepted domestic ideology. In *Dead Secrets: Wilkie Collins and the Female Gothic*, Tamar Heller explains that the labeling of fiction as "sensation" is an attack on the genre, separating it from highbrow literature (59). Heller explains how sensation fiction (and Gothic fiction) often represents members low in the rankings of the "body politic," and that the plots typically allude to problems with the Victorian dispersal of ideological and legal power, such as women's legal rights within marriage or gender roles that prove problematic or contradictory (59). Attacking the genre links sensational narratives to cultural issues related to gender and class, such as transgressive sexuality and behavior, criminal activity, and fallen reputations. Victorian critic Margaret Oliphant linked ideas in sensation fiction with frustrated revolutionary aspirations (87), which was a craving for fundamental change in the working of society. These types of sensational narratives were also criticized by writers like Matthew Arnold who asserted that literature should be highbrow, exemplifying Greek and Classical literature, as to improve the character of society by providing a sense of meaning in life in response to waning religious influences in British culture.

Reaching the height of its popularity in the 1860s, sensation fiction caught the ire of critics when one of the genre's foremost authors, Wilkie Collins, authored bestsellers like *The Woman in White*, *No Name*, *Armadale*, and *The Moonstone*. *The Woman in White* ignited popular phenomenon that included new fashion trends inspired by the characters in the novel. In *Victorian Sensations: Essays on a Scandalous Genre*, Richard Fantina and Kimberly Harrison define sensation fiction "as 'novels with a secret.' Involving mysteries, murders and social improprieties usually within the respectable middle class or the aristocratic home, the novels capitalized on the Victorian public's appetite for scandal" (xii). The sensation novel contained a realistic narrative that included Gothic elements, similar to those in Brontë's novel, yet was labeled sensational because it elicited a bodily response. *The Woman in White* (1863) features a narrative that shows characters engaged in a series of disruptive ambitions precariously contained within a social and legal framework. Judith Sanders's essay, "A Shock to the System, a System to the Shocks: The Horrors of the 'Happy Ending' in *The Woman in White*," discusses the presence of Collins's narrative consciousness through the circulation of heterosexual passions that rally with institutional forces like marriage and madhouses. Hartright, the novel's hero, in particular, serves to enact the process of working masculine heterosexual desire into the conventional framework of marital stability. Collins's work continued to be described as "low" due to his transgressive depiction of domestic arrangements, even as *The Woman in White* ends with Hartright living with both Laura Fairlie and Marian Halcombe in domestic bliss.

Elizabeth Anderman's "Hysterical Sensations: Bodies in Action in Wilkie Collins's *The Woman in White*" explores the combination of the physical experience of reading this sensation novel with the intellectual process of figuring out the narrative's mystery, which causes a kind of hysteria. Readers can actually gauge how to respond to the narrative by monitoring their physical response while reading. Anderman defines reader hysteria as the result of a breakdown in narrative voice, and compares the Victorian ideology surrounding feminine hysteria and the reading of sensation fiction. Feminine hysteria was associated with women who exerted too much mental energy and therefore starved their wombs, causing mental illness. Freud elaborated upon this by suggesting that a repression of a sexual event causes hysteria. Anderman describes how hysteria is related to the repression of a sexual event in the narrative of Collins's sensation novel.

Part Two—The Colonial Context of Gothic and Sensation Fiction

The British Empire was a source of vast colonial power. Domestic life was supported by British interests abroad in economic terms (foreign trade, import of goods) and in social terms. Imperial conquest was significant to definitions of British masculinity, and this was depicted in Victorian literature by images of male heroes reinforcing their patriarchal mandates by their travels abroad. The colonial adventure was often depicted as a rite of manhood and featured in narratives about upper and middle class enterprisers conquering uncharted territories and dark continents, such as Rochester in *Jane Eyre*, who traveled to the West Indies to discover true manhood, and, in his case, bring back a colonized wife. Victorian homes were often adorned with exotic collectibles from other lands. Conflated with this depiction of the home (as supported by empire) were images of women, also colonized by the British domestic regime. British national identity was defined, in Hegelian terms, against racially Othered signifiers. Racially associated characteristics, ranging from dark skin, dark eyes, conspicuous teeth, devouring emotional passions, non–Christian practices or contagious diseases, were used by England's bourgeois culture to define what was (and wasn't) English; therefore, imperialistic conceptions of race helped to determine and maintain who went where in the social order. This concept of subject as defined against Other caused anxieties in that the necessary contact with the racial Other provoked concern about an atavistic or miscegenistic blending of identity that could deracinate an English nationality as easily as it supported it. Questions such as "What makes one English?" could similarly be ideologically translated as "Who are the savages?" or "What makes men civilized?" when Western "truisms" became suspect as a result of the intersection of Eastern and Western discourses. Growing Victorian concerns with the effects of "going native" led to questions about the effects of imperialism, such as "Does this enhance masculinity or dilute Englishness?" The Victorian novels represent these concerns so frequently that it becomes obvious that the Empire was by no means uncontested. The concept of a triumphant imperialism unveiled its Gothic underside — a fear of the Other as representative of a possible collapse of the (British) self, which was the seat of the fear of the resistance of those colonized, both outwardly in terms of an invasion by others, and domestically, as in a collapse of society through the resistance of British females.

Domestic literature often used the colonial experience to depict contrast and tension with the daily activities in the English home, as in Charlotte Brontë's *Jane Eyre* or Charles Dickens's *Great Expectations*. Mid-Victorian fiction's depiction of a link in the British socio-cultural hierarchy between the position of the roles of women and racial others were influenced by publications and discourse about the taxonomies of origin, most famously in Darwin's *On the origin of species* in 1859, which increased a generalized perception that human beings were inherently stratified beings and belonged to racial, sexual and economic categories. Appearances and behaviors associated with these categories were enforced by the circulation of beliefs, social norms and legal translations of power. Collins's *The Woman in White* prefigures these beliefs that emerged more forcefully throughout the latter part of the nineteenth century while imperialism expanded. Social applications of scientific investigations of bodily evolution reflected the Victorians' ideologically-based form of social control through the internalization of normative societal restraints. Those designated as marginal within the body politic, namely fallen women and racial others, are often associated with the Gothic narrative that gave voice to a so-called narrative of exile. While Gothic novels developed as a response to contradictory politics from the late eighteenth century and onward, the narrative method was continually being reconfigured as an extension of the subjective experience and ongoing discourses within the existing order of Victorian society.

Charles Dickens's *Great Expectations* (1861) represents London as a metropole, a city whose ideas must be "read" and interpreted to understand relationships of power. It is through interpretation of secrets, laws, debates on women's bodies, and histories that social hierarchies are established and maintained. Dickens endorsed British imperialism but was cautious about its effect on the domestic front and its effect on the family. His tendency was to show that the regulation of English social power and order is enforced through definitions of what distinguishes roles in society, and attempts to expose the mire of problems and contradictions about female sexuality and society at large — and the unfairness of these signifiers. Julie M. Barst's "Sensations Down Under: Australia's Seismic Charge in *Great Expectations* and *Lady Audley's Secret*" discusses how Pip is disappointed when it is the convict from Australia who has funded his rise to gentlemen status, not the wealthy Miss Havisham or her daughter Estella. This corresponds with the manner by which England has derived wealth from colonial holdings in Australia, a land associated with economic advancement, yet there are negative feelings about the dark and sensational character of Magwitch. Magwitch is a transgressive bachelor, a characterization to match Miss Havisham's transgressive bachelorette.

The status of the family continued to assume paramount importance in mid–Victorian literature's conversations about conflicts between the social world and the natural world. Like *Jane Eyre*, Dickens's *Great Expectations* illuminates the problems between Miss Havisham's natural state and that which is demanded by the social order. Her attitude toward Estella depicts how female sexuality serves as a venue by which to appropriate value, demonstrating a capitalistic system of exchange by associating commodities with the female body. Dickens exemplifies the Victorian dialectic of natural versus social order and the pathologies associated with the conflict and excesses of these ideologemes. As a result, the female position secures the British domestic arena in the same manner Britain imperial conquest secures land and capital, the colonization of women and figures of marginalized races, such as Count Dracula, depict a common theme of subjugation on both fronts, which support the British domestic and economic system. The health of the family, as Foucault points out (123), was dependent on respectable female sexuality while the racial other was to be marginalized due to a fear of miscegenation (119).

Authors such as Mary Elizabeth Braddon of "Good Lady Ducayne" (1874), J. Sheridan Le Fanu of *In a Glass Darkly* (1872) and *Uncle Silas* (1899) and Bram Stoker of *Dracula* (1897) and *Jewel of the Seven Stars* (1912) found great success with horror stories in the late nineteenth century and the early twentieth. In Victorian ideology, the family is meant to serve as a protective apparatus for society; however, these authors' fiction exposes the problems with the effectiveness of the role of the family and the associated issues concerning the threats to domesticity through foreign ideas introduced by imperialism and wayward sexuality.

Anxieties concerning the defining elements of female gender roles that dominated mid–nineteenth century Victorian fiction evolved into fears concerning the corruption of these same ideals by the follies associated with imperialism at the end of the century. By late Victorian culture, twenty-five percent of the world was under British rule. The British's increasing fear of the racial other is shown through depictions of demonic characters with racially associated characteristics deracinating victims through sexually aggressive acts, such as vampire lust or a mummy curse. The idea of a dominant race was taking shape in response to Darwin's evolutionary theories and as a result of the emphasis on scientific taxonomy and categorization. The fear of the Other is depicted at its most potent in relation to female sexuality as the uncertainty of the imperial project in the late Victorian era was reflected in a sense of decline in patriarchal potency around the world and at home. Saverio Tomaiuolo's "Reading Between the (Blood)lines of Victorian Vampires: Mary Elizabeth Braddon's 'Good Lady Ducayne'" discusses the significant connection between the circulation of blood and the circulation of commodities and a vampire-like desire to prolong one's life by any means. Themes in "Good Lady Ducayne" represent a sense of decayed female sexuality and procreation in the late nineteenth century which recalls Dickens' depiction of Miss Havisham as an unproductive figure who symbolizes a dysfunction in the economy when she utilizes Estella as a commodity and is not Pip's benefactor.

J. Sheridan Le Fanu, an Irishman like Stoker, was the conservative author of *In a Glass Darkly*, a collection of stories that included the vampire tale *Carmilla*. Le Fanu features the vampire in a context where feminine sexuality and knowledge is represented as a threat. My essay "The Vamp and the Good English Mother: Female Roles in Le Fanu's *Carmilla* and Stoker's *Dracula*" discusses how Le Fanu's vampiric depiction of Laura and Carmilla's friendship Others their relationship into a homo-social rewriting of gender boundaries associated with racial Otherness that is similar to the themes in *Dracula*. *Carmilla* is narrated as a case study of Dr. Hesselius. Eastern mysticism is associated with the loss of rationality and represented by Carmilla's inexplicable powers over Laura, a young British girl living in Styria who is rendered lethargic and senseless. Laura acts like she doesn't know Carmilla desires her, even though Carmilla expressly makes statements like, "I live in you; and you would die for me, I love you so" (270). This conflation of sexual language and Othering demonstrates a fear of reverse-colonization in response to signs of aggressive female sexuality.

Kate Holterhoff's "Liminality and Power in Bram Stoker's *Jewel of the Seven Stars*" explores the relationships between liminality and gender politics. Liminality is related to the experience of a dream and is a state that can reveal what women most desire. Consequently, Stoker's narrative symbolizes the jewel as a horror of women's empowerment for society, similar to the Gothic associations of transgressive females with empowered feminine sexuality in the Victorian era. This is also related to concerns about motherhood and images of birth trauma that Stoker depicts in the novel and the feelings of impotency that men face when women are considered the ideal.

Part Three — Fallen Woman, Fallen Man in the Victorian Novel

In Elizabeth Gaskell's *Ruth* (1853), the circumstances of the heroine's fall power the narrative. In a society in which morality was built upon an ideology of honor and shame, women were held to a standard of chastity that did not exist for men. Women, it was thought, needed to remain chaste to keep Victorian society pure. In *Woman and the Demon: The Life of a Victorian Myth* (1982), Nina Auerbach defines four primary roles for women — the angel, who is the sacred and respectable Victorian mother; the fallen woman, who has committed some sexual transgression; the old maid or spinster; and the demon, who has social self-knowledge and is "about no good" (90). All of the categories are dependent on each other and inform what the other means; "together they place women at the junction between the social and the spiritual, the humanly perishable and the transcendently potent" (64). By choosing the fallen Ruth as her heroine in a novel with highly critical representations of mid–nineteenth century London, Gaskell challenges challenging ideas about predetermined fate as defined by social norms and drawing on one of Dickens's classic frames of references for contrasting what is wrong with society — the use of the innocent, victimized child. Pre-Raphaelite painters of mid–Victorian portraits often depicted fallen women as enigmatic icons, symbolic of the kind of unseemly power unleashed by sexual defiance within British culture. The power associated with fallenness involved ideologies about contagion as Judith Walkowitz has shown in her discussion of the Contagious Diseases Acts in *Prostitution and Victorian Society: Women, Class, and the State* (1980). This ideology was, in part, a continuation of Milton's ideas about the "power of the fall" in *Paradise Lost*. Hence, fallen women were banished, often to the Thames River among the poor. Elizabeth Gaskell's *Ruth* reveals the artificiality of separation between the fallen woman and the angel by her angelic characterization of the title character and her depiction of the fallen woman as moving against possession by societal forces. Maria Granic-White's "*Ruth:* An Analysis of the Victorian Signifieds" argues that the artificially constructed values of Ruth's society changed the meaning of their linguistic symbols and that "Gaskell questions the absolute nature of the two concepts of the pure and the fallen and exposed the complex problems of Victorian society." Gaskell's novel is ordinarily described as a non-gothic narrative about a fallen woman, but it imagines a tragic ending in which Ruth dies while nursing her former lover back to health, a rather Gothic ending to an otherwise realist narrative. Mr. Bellingham, who seduces Ruth at age fifteen and abandons her while she is pregnant, eventually develops typhus, and Ruth, having redeemed herself from sin, nevertheless ends up dying while nursing him. He views her "beautiful" corpse and laments her death, exclaiming "Poor Ruth!" (Gaskell 453). The image of her corpse evokes the Gothic in that Ruth's power appears to be stronger after her death, much like Catherine Earnshaw's ghost who haunts Heathcliff in Emily Brontë's *Wuthering Heights* (1847), another narrative combining realism and Gothicism to exhibit social wrongs. Gaskell's Gothic finale depicts the author's inability to describe a happy ending for her fallen victim, similar to the textual endings Emily Brontë in *Wuthering Heights* and Mary Wollstonecraft in *Maria*. Death in the Gothic functions as the most common resolution for female characters that sexually transgress feminine boundaries and are preternaturally possessed by cultural male dominance.

Stephanie King's "Violence as Patrimony in Le Fanu's *Uncle Silas*" conceptualizes the character of the fallen man, a neglected counterpart to the widely-depicted fallen woman. Le Fanu's novel describes the fallen man as weak, morally corrupt, and violent. He is, as King states, a male predator who "mocks the hierarchical system on which patriarchal lineage and masculinities are built." Le Fanu's narrative links drug use and violent crimes in British Victorian culture as it is the addiction which allows Silas to commit crimes, and without much remorse, because he has been medically prescribed the opium. Like Stoker's Count Dracula, a vampire who can pass as a gentleman at will, Uncle Silas is a drug addict who can pass as a British gentleman within society.

The genial bachelor is ubiquitous in Victorian literature. But Collins occasionally creates bachelors who threaten others, such as the brutal Geoffrey Delamyn in *Man and Wife* (1870). We can see other traits of the villainous bachelor in the work of Robert Louis Stevenson. In her essay "In the Company of Men: Masculinity Gone Wild in Robert Louis Stevenson's *The Strange Case of Dr. Jekyll and Mr. Hyde*," Jennifer Beauvais discusses the 1886 novel's depiction of masculinity in the private and public spheres as something akin to a male double consciousness. Hyde becomes the essence for the *fin de siècle* bachelor who incorporates masculine and feminine characteristics to move between public and private spaces. He flourishes in Stevenson's male community as he violently questions the benevolent image of Victorian masculinity and creates a frightening new understanding of the late century bachelor.

In "Ghostly Absence and Sexual Presence in 'Owen Wingrave' and 'The Jolly Corner,'" Nicholas Harris discusses two ghost stories by Henry James. The stories contain many elements of the Gothic but rather than presenting innocent young women as the protagonists and victims, they feature wayward young men haunted by patriarchal expectations. Drawing on Kristeva, Susan Sontag, and Roland Barthes, Harris suggests an anti-interpretive reading of these texts. In addition, following the lead of other critics, such as Eric Haralson (2003) and Neil Matheson (1999), Harris suggests a queer subtext in these stories.

The Gothic tradition provides a set of tropes and modes that are useful in undermining established ideologies, especially in areas like gender and domestic traditions, and provides avenues for carnivalesque representations of desire, such as the vampire stories, and desire's responses to authority, especially by undermining the body and bodily response. Gothic's ambiguity opens the space for dominant social myths to be tested and decentered, as it is an artistic system of languages. The use of multi-layered elements leaves the dominance of certain social voices in Gothic and sensation fiction unresolved and the narrative becomes a participant in the social struggle, its subversiveness depending on the position from which text is read. The genre uses mechanics that evoke the subconscious, which bursts out of conscious restraints as repression causes the imagination to rebel, and retranslates social problems such as the sublime versus industrialization, which is predicated on Victorian discourse about nature and science, and deconstructs and dismembers the real. It is a rebellion against restraint of neo-classicism and reason and a hybrid between novel and romance that was originally the result of a haunting by the decline of feudal aristocracy to state when the style first commenced. The use of the fantastic and other intense psychological states allows the high emotional tide associated with the Gothic and sensation to be presented in fiction at a level of subjective intensity not found in other forms of writing. Depicting the swirling emotions hidden within any regulated society, the Gothic demonstrates that cultural assumptions about identity, sexuality and the circulation of power require ongoing challenge and reformulation.

Works Cited

Arata, Stephen. *Fictions of Loss in the Victorian Fin de Siècle.* Cambridge: Cambridge University Press, 1996.

Auerbach, Nina. *Woman and the Demon: The Life of a Victorian Myth*. Cambridge: Harvard University Press, 1982.

Darwin, Charles R. *On the origin of species by means of natural selection, or the preservation of favoured races in the struggle for life*. London: John Murray, 1859. 1st edition, 1st issue.

Fantina, Richard, and Kimberly Harrison, eds. *Victorian Sensations: Essays from a Scandalous Genre*. Columbus: Ohio State University Press, 2006.

Foucault, Michel. *The History of Sexuality: An Introduction, Volume 1*. New York: Vintage, 1991.

Haralson, Eric. *Henry James and Queer Modernity*. Cambridge: Cambridge University Press, 2003.

Heller, Tamar. *Dead Secrets: Wilkie Collins and the Female Gothic*. New Haven: Yale University Press, 1992.

Hoeveler, Diane Long. *Gothic Feminism: The Professionalization of Gender from Charlotte Smith to the Brontës*. University Park: Pennsylvania State University Press, 1998.

Hogle, Jerrold E., ed. *Cambridge Companion to Gothic Fiction*. Cambridge: Cambridge University Press, 2002.

Kristeva, Julia. *Powers of Horror: An Essay on Abjection*. New York: Columbia University Press, 1982.

Le Fanu, J. Sheridan. *In a Glass Darkly*. Stroud, Gloucestershire: Alan Sutton, 1993.

Matheson, Neil. "Talking Horrors: James, Euphemism, and the Specter of Wilde." *American Literature* 71.4 (1999): 709–750.

Miles, Robert. "The 1790s: The Effulgence of the Gothic." *Cambridge Companion to Gothic Fiction*. Cambridge: Cambridge University Press, 2002.

Walkowitz, Judith. *Prostitution and Victorian Society: Women, Class, and the State*. Cambridge: Cambridge University Press, 1980.

Williams, Anne. *Art of Darkness: A Poetics of Gothic*. Chicago: The University of Chicago Press, 1995.

Wollstonecraft, Mary. 1797. *Maria*. New York: Norton, 1975.

_____. *A Vindication of the Rights of Woman*. New York: Broadview, 1999.

PART ONE

The Instability of Identity: Character, Class, and Gender

Desire and Fear

Feminine Abjection in the Gothic Fiction of Mary Wollstonecraft

Marilyn Brock

The Gothic is an important genre for representing female experience, and Romantic-era author Mary Wollstonecraft uses it to depict female subjugation in late eighteenth century culture. Wollstonecraft was critical of women's internalization of male-dominating perspectives. In her political text *A Vindication of the Rights of Woman* (1792), she asserts that women suffer from being guided by their emotions and experience as a consequence an inferior educational, political and social status. Wollstonecraft's ideas were a response to the key concepts associated with the Enlightenment and influential writers that were her contemporaries such as Jean-Jacques Rousseau, whose liberal texts *The Social Contract: Principles of the Political Right* and *On Education* influenced the philosophies that ignited the French Revolution, and Edmund Burke, British author of the conservative essay *Reflections on the Revolution in France*. Although she did not agree with his views on women, like Rousseau Wollstonecraft agreed with liberal concepts regarding the renunciation of aristocratic and otherwise conservative traditions that had institutionalized unnatural dominance. Her views contrasted with Burke's, who believed cherished traditions preserved social stability. In *Dead Secrets: Wilkie Collins and the Female Gothic*, Tamar Heller states, "Writing from a conservative viewpoint, Edmund Burke, in his *Reflections on the Revolution in France*, likens the French constitution before the revolution to a castle that, though it has suffered 'waste and dilapidation,' is yet a 'noble and venerable' castle on whose traditions, or 'foundations,' the French might have built rather than destroying them" (13). Furthermore, Heller states, "Conservatives, like Burke, meanwhile, expatiated on the 'horrible consequences of taking one half of the species wholly out of the guardianship and protection of the other,' seeing the liberation of women as the deathblow to a paternalistic order in which state and family are both ruled by benevolent father figures" (14).

Seeking to counter the influence of conservatives like Burke, Wollstonecraft examined the structure of relations between men and women. In particular, Wollstonecraft criticized the sexual objectification of women. In *A Vindication of the Rights of Woman,* she states that "the woman who has only been taught to please will soon find that her charms are oblique sunbeams, and that they cannot have much effect on her husband's heart when they are seen every day, when the summer is passed and gone. Will she then have sufficient native energy to look into herself for comfort, and cultivate her dormant faculties?" (136). She asserted that, in reality, women were like helpless queens, lacking intelligence and virtue, and internalizing beliefs taught by their mothers: "Women are told from their infancy, and taught by the example of their mothers, that a little knowledge of human weakness, justly termed cunning, softness of temper, outward obedience, and a scrupulous attention to a puerile kind of propriety, will obtain for them the protection of man" (126). Wollstonecraft thought that women were depicted and treated like infants, rendering them dependent, merely decorative creatures. For her, as for twentieth century French critic Julia Kristeva, women were "others": "What we designate as feminine, far from being a primeval essence, will be seen as an 'other' without a name" (58). Wollstonecraft sought to improve women's social status through an emphasis on rationality. She believed female value was essentially a commodity in a male-dominated market, and women had a stake in their own abjection in order to be valued and taken care of by society's men. Her writing thus sought to define for women some real value of their own.

I will discuss Wollstonecraft's views on women through the lens of Kristeva's theory of feminine abjection. Kristeva defines abjection as a "heterogeneous flux marks out a territory that I can call my own because the other, having dwelt in me as an alter ego, points it out to be through loathing ... I experience abjection only if an other has settled in place and stead of what will be me" (10). Wollstonecraft's association of women and otherness parallels Kristeva's theory of feminine abjection because Kristeva emphasizes abjection's association with what is socially devalued and marginalized; Moreover, she associates abjection with a reaction to bodily fluids, some of which are suggestively feminine, like breast milk and menstrual blood: "Neither tears, nor sperm, have any polluting value.... Menstrual blood, on the contrary, stands for the danger issuing from within the identity (social or sexual); it threatens the relationship between the sexes within a social aggregate and, through internalization, the identity of each sex in the face of sexual difference" (71). Similarly, she states that "abomination seems to proceed from another flow that mingles two identities and connotes the bond between the one and the other; milk" (105). For Kristeva, female subjugation in western society is a projection of the process of maternal abjection that occurs when the infant is born and responds with the burgeoning development of a self that is separate from the mother; as she quotes, "The attempt to establish a male, phallic power is vigorously threatened by no less virulent power of the opposite sex, which is oppressed (recently? or not sufficiently for the survival needs of society?). The other sex, the feminine, becomes synonymous with a radical evil that needs to be suppressed" (70). Traditionally, it has been the female's role to function on the margins of society in response to an unconscious need to reject the mother as abject, whether the infant be male or female. Kristeva states that "it is not lack of cleanliness or health that causes abjection, but what disturbs identity, systems, order" (4).

Wollstonecraft's version of Gothic narrative in her unfinished novel *Maria* (1798) depicts women's social marginalization and exile to a realm of abjection in its depiction of its heroine's subjugated female body. In the opening chapter, Maria, whose husband has incarcerated her in an insane asylum so he can seize her fortune, laments her inability to breastfeed her daughter.

> What effect [Maria's memories] must they have produced on one, true to the touch of sympathy, and tortured by maternal apprehension! Her infant's image was continually floating in Maria's sight, and the first smile of intelligence remembered, as none but a mother, an unhappy mother, can conceive. She heard her half speaking, half cooing, and felt little twinkling fingers on her burning bosom — a bosom bursting with the nutriment for which this cherished child might now be pining in vain. From a stranger she could indeed receive maternal aliment, Maria was grieved at the though — but who would watch her with a mother's tenderness, a mother's self-denial? [7].

The references to Maria's burning bosom depict the abject relationship between Maria's maternal need to breastfeed and her uneasy role as a mother as her daughter will likely develop poorly because she was born female. Significantly, she experiences the bodily frustration of being unable to breastfeed while locked in an insane asylum.

19

Western social hierarchies tend to assert legitimacy by repressing narratives about injustices; therefore, narratives by women like Maria might not be taken seriously. However, Wollstonecraft's Gothic novel depicts what is necessary for an acceptable sense of self, society, system and order; it is to transfer unacceptable individual and communal psychological reasoning and drives into obsessions, such as the haunted thoughts Maria narrates about her daughter and her social status. Furthermore, in *Maria*, women's repression is represented through images of confinement in order to indict male domination. Such literary forms of projections redirect uncomfortable energy from the unconscious into exterior images of monstrous agencies, such as the beastly character of Maria's husband, the insane asylum or her prison-like marriage, which are illustrations of situations that individuals attempt to avoid. Wollstonecraft therefore used her Gothic fiction to examine feminine oppression and resist the masculine presumption of moral authority.

Wollstonecraft clearly defines that her purpose in writing *Maria* is to depict feminine oppression, or, as she states in the preface, "That is what I have in view; ... To show the wrongs of different classes of women, equally oppressive, through, from the differences of education, equally various," while showing Maria, the novel's protagonist, as an "ordinary woman," a mortal, instead of a pre–Victorian Angel in the House that has either fallen from grace or is sexually corrupt (6). Like *A Vindication of the Rights of Woman*, *Maria* shows how conventional marriage degrades the female mind and condemns the bride to imprisonment; she is a creature, animal, object of her husband's possession. The novel begins with a third-person voice, proclaiming "abodes of horror have frequently been described, and castles, filled with specters and chimeras, conjured up by the magic spell of genius to harrow the soul, and absorb the wandering mind" (7). The list of representative Gothic conventions shows how the Gothic narrative, in which Maria resides, serves as catharsis for Maria, who is unhappily married and suffering. According to Kristeva,

> Suffering speaks its name here, "madness" — but does not linger with it, for the magic of surplus, scription, conveys the body, even more so the sick body, to a beyond made-up of sense and measure. Beyond the narrative, dizziness finds its language: music, as breath of words, rhythm of sentences, and not only as metaphor of an imaginary rival where the voice of mother and death is hiding [146].

Wollstonecraft demonstrates her resistance toward the late-eighteenth-century social constructions that oppressed the development of healthy female subjectivity in *A Vindication of the Rights of Woman,* when she claims that women are socialized from birth to become ornamental playthings inexperienced with reason: "She was created to be the toy of man, his rattle, and it must jingle in his ears whenever, dismissing reason, he chooses to be amused" (144). Wollstonecraft asserts that women need more than romantic love, and men need more than affection from women; they need rationality: "Pygmalion formed an ivory maid, and longed for an informing soul" (33). In *A Vindication of the Rights of Woman,* Wollstonecraft claims that conventional marriages lack friendship and reason because of the sexual objectification to which women submit.

Wollstonecraft's diagnosis of women's inequality recalls Kristeva's theory of how the subject is first compelled to formulate a distinctive self-definition. Abjection is the basis for the development of insight as a distinct being that is separate from the mother, and it is experienced as a feeling of revulsion or an act of expulsion from what can no longer be contained as part of the boundaries of the self. Prior to birth, Kristeva theorizes that the psychic experience is a wholly "semiotic" one, which is defined as a state of mind that exists prior to the development of the linguistic system of signs associated with language, judgment and position, where all drives and impulses are met organically and do not experience disruption from the outside world's "symbolic" order, which chronologically follows the semiotic state in psychological development, but is never completely eclipsed by it. In Western culture, the semiotic processes are associated with the feminine realm, because they are dominated by the symbolic processes that are associated with patriarchal systems, such as language and law. Wollstonecraft's narrative that describes Maria's infant "half cooing, half speaking" might illustrate the developmental point at which the semiotic type of cooing is becoming transferred into the symbolic realm which designates speaking (7).

The maintenance of the borders of self are kept vigilant by the fear of collapse into death, and therefore, there is pleasure in the experience of reading Gothic narratives that enable us to experiment in an imaginary sphere with the definitional boundaries of selfhood. Social laws, which privilege the patriarchal, define the subject as discreet from the threatening, feminine realm, so that psychological tension continues to exist between the contradiction of the excluded, but sanctified, mother. This excluded otherness, associated with mysterious femininity, is rendered Gothic when it is aligned with rage against symbolic order and patriarchal institutions.

In *Maria,* the heroine's pre-occupation with the plight of her infant daughter is an image of feminine rage against the dominating patriarchal system. Heller states, "Although Maria's written account of her childhood illustrates Wollstonecraft's claim that women are taught to assume an unequal place in society by the example of their mothers, it also represents at the same time an attempt to reverse this negative example by instructing one daughter to avoid her mother's errors" (27). Heller illustrates how Maria's narrative empowers women. According to Kristeva, fiction about abject women, such as characters like Maria, enact revolutionary tendencies in order to reject the symbolic order and jettison parts of the self that are unacceptable or contradictory into a unified sense of self, because for women, the process of being always involves abjecting part of oneself as a feminine being. Maria's character embodies this impulse in that she laments the feminine sex of her child because it dooms her daughter to social and emotional slavery. Maria's daughter, therefore, is a figure for repression of the abject feminine self enslaved by social circumstances.

Maria's Gothic environment is a literal translation of Wollstonecraft's critique of women's position political writings in *A Vindication of the Rights of Woman,* and also illustrates her theories on what women must do to improve society. Maria reflects on socially revolutionary impulses: "And to what purpose did she rally all her energy? Was not the world a vast prison, and women born slaves?" (11). She is wondering why she should bother pursuing the purposes of women's rights, when patriarchal society is depicted as a tyrannical boundary between Maria and her child while she is in prison, put there by her husband, George Venables, so that he can seize her fortune. As Kristeva might say, "A spiritualization of both the purity/ impurity distinction and the outside/ inside division of subjective space is thus effected" (119). Maria's narrative privileges Maria's voice over her husband's in order to demonstrate the legitimacy of feminine experience and shows how society, at all levels, is in decline because women are not intellectually developed enough to uphold ideologies of virtue and reason in the home or through employment (15). As her husband George goes from bad to worse — gambling, having affairs, drinking, having increasing debts — he illustrates how women cannot develop their husbands' morality without better minds and that women must be developed as more than mere ornaments or objects of possession for men in order for society to progress. In *A Vindication of the Rights of Woman,* she describes this situation with the metaphor "confined then in cages like the feathered race, they have nothing to do but plume themselves, and stalk with mock majesty from perch to perch. It is true they are provided with food and raiment, for which they neither toil nor spin; but health, liberty, and virtue are given in exchange" (171).

Wollstonecraft's anger toward patriarchal domination is evident in the *A Vindication of the Rights of Woman*, and she uses Maria as her image for the woman who learns to become an agent for political change: "Maria wished to pass the threshold of her prison, yet, when by chance she met the eye of rage glaring on her ... She shrunk back with more horror and affright" (17). The eye of rage refers to the prototypical lunatic in the asylum, whose anger recalls that of the lower-class women Burke describes as threatening the life of Marie Antoinette in *Reflections on the Revolution in France*. Wollstonecraft's sympathetic portrayal of the character of Jemima, a working-class woman employed at the asylum, shows that she is clearly interested in improving the plight of the poorer classes, and also senses its power by depicting Jemima as an authority figure over Maria; therefore, it is evident that *Maria's* narrative searches for answers to help all classes of women. Jemima is a prime example of woman-as-abject with her degraded class position which enhances the abuse she experiences as a woman. In Jemima's narrative about her past, she describes an experience where she asks a tradesman to turn out his pregnant mistress, so that Jemima may be taken in with him instead; this provokes the mistress to drown herself in a watering trough for horses. In response to the suicide, Jemima states,

> I happened that morning to be going out to wash, anticipating the moment when I should escape from such hard labour. I passed by, just as some men, going to work, drew out the stiff, cold corpse — Let me not recall the horrid moment — I recognized her pale visage; I listened to the tale told by the spectators, and my heart did not burst. I thought of my own state, and wondered how I could be such a monster! [50].

Jemima's story gives voice to the nature of female degradation and depicts connections that Kristeva explores between abjection, maternity and death. Jemima calls herself a monster, which illustrates the internalization of feminine abjection, even though she is only trying to survive; this internalized experience of oppression is demonstrated even more dramatically by the "other" mistress's self-destruction.

Jemima's narrative reflects an interest in empowerment for all types of women, including Jemima and the ill-fated trademan's mistress, in order to improve the development of society. In Maria's account of her biography, she explains that she is born innocent but society betrays her, "born in one

23

of the most romantic parts of England, an enthusiastic fondness for the varying charms of nature is the first sentiment I recollect" (59). This is reflective
of Rousseau's views on how harmful societal institutions and mores corrupt
children and create criminals out of victims of society, such as how Jemima's
describes herself as monstrous in response to her abject status. Wollstonecraft
applies Rousseau's theory to the specific situation concerning innocent
women developing in a society that considers the female abject. While
Jemima is considered fallen because she is a mistress, as is Maria because she
has been imprisoned and is considered insane, their narratives indicate that
the problem with fallen women is not an individual one but demonstrative
of greater problems in western culture and its treatment, views, and laws
concerning women (165).

In particular, Maria illustrates how patriarchal dominance denies the
importance of mothers and allows children to die, such as is illustrated when
the tradesman's mistress kills herself when she is with child and Jemima herself aborts an out-of-wedlock pregnancy. Moreover, this point is depicted
in a later scene when a woman says to Maria's husband, "'The child is very
weak, she cannot live long,'" and he replies, "'So much the better ... and pray
mind your own business, good woman'" (81). Jemima, who herself has been
denied proper nutrition as a baby, later finds out that Maria's infant has died
without Maria's maternal care. George's character illustrates how patriarchal
tyranny denies women the ability to nurture their children, an inability
which increases their abjection in society (81). The abject woman, particularly a fallen woman, as represented by Maria's character, is evocative of Kristeva's ideas on the borderline patient, which she defines "powerless outside,
impossible inside" (48). The fallen woman is similar to the borderline patient
because of the rupture in identification between the self and society, similar to the uneasy canyon between the self and other that renders the borderline individual fragile. Therefore, the fallen woman illustrates these same
characteristics and is battered by similar mechanisms, such as the need for
a catharsis of unreleased drives that are locked in the semiotic realm, causing unnecessary fear and desire and an emptiness in signification. In *Maria*,
Wollstonecraft restores linguistic authority to her narrator in order to enable
her to escape her abject state, both as a fallen woman and a victim of maternal abjection and patriarchal tyranny. Maria's narrative illustrates the Gothic-
styled therapy implicit in granting narrative authority to the marginalized
and oppressed, as Maria's speaking eases psychic tension caught in unconscious mental territories. Similarly, Kristeva argues that a positive effect

of symbolic-realm intervention, such as reading or speaking, mediates the harmful effects of repressed semiotic rage that often surfaces as a melancholy state.

To put it bluntly, a community will get the monster it deserves, and Wollstonecraft's monster of madness is a synthesis of competing discourses and ideologies symbolic of her time. Madness in literature is associated with the narrative of those who have little power, and Maria's confinement to an insane asylum renders her voice powerless until she chooses to write her own narrative. Maria's voice is thus the fictional representation of a ghostly miasma of oppressive ailments haunting women. Disassociated historical events and conditions such as female oppression are expressed in Maria's voice, and this depicts the release of repressed psychic pain from past experiences that affects the novel's narrative of the present. For Maria, her daughter's death is symbolic of the power females have lost in society, but the process of a disassociation with a traumatic event and the denial of something that is too painful to assimilate is a pathway to obsession, which is one of the defense mechanisms, defined by Sigmund Freud in the late nineteenth century, that individuals develop in order to survive within an ordered society.

Wollstonecraft's daughter, Mary Shelley, depicts more of this phenomena in her famous novel *Frankenstein* (1819), a text which is a successor to the type of Gothic narrative *Maria* exemplifies. For instance, Shelley's lead character, Victor Frankenstein, creates an immortal monster to ease his fears about death after his mother dies, but the creature becomes a doppelganger-type figure when Victor rejects it and the creature relentlessly followed him like an insidious shadow wanting to possess and dominate him, illustrating the legacy of maternal abjection. Kristeva explains, "Mother and death, both abominated, abjected, slyly build a victimizing and persecuting machine at the cost of which I become the subject of the symbolic as well as the other of the Abject" (112). Victor scientifically develops a way of reanimating dead bodies, and collects body parts from charnel houses to create his resurrected figure (83). The use of material from charnel houses recalls Wollstonecraft's images of slavery and the oppressed because the stacked, anonymous bodies, revived from death resemble the kind of unmarked, mass graves of bygone slaves and otherwise "unheard" individuals that are being brought forth to speak through the monster due to Victor's genius. Victor picks the body parts from these dead people, and puts together a hysterical figure while evoking associations with motherhood and death; he essentially gives birth to a hysterical vision — a creature resurrected in place of Victor's dead mother, who also becomes entwined with his love interest, Elizabeth, in the following dream sequence:

> I slept indeed, but I was disturbed by the wildest dreams. I thought I saw Elizabeth, in the bloom of health, walking in the streets of Inglostadt. Delighted and surprised, I embraced her; but as I imprinted the first kiss on her lips, they became livid with the hue of death; her features appeared to change, and I thought that I held the corpse of my dead mother in my arms [85].

The dream symbolizes the two-faced mother, defining the horror imbedded in abjection's double-bind of possession and lust for separation. Elizabeth, the monster and Victor's dead mother are all Victor's projected symbols from his psyche that is best illustrated during descriptions of liminal states which mirror his psychological unbalance, such as this dream sequence or the harsh, Arctic setting Frankenstein's monster escapes to. Shelley's monster embodies the semiotic impulse in that he is a motherless outcast who kills a child in a response to his father's rejection combined with his working class status, which illustrates an example of patriarchal system and law.

Suppressed (by death, imprisonment, or oppression) female voices represent the plight of abject women in a society ruled by a masculine symbolic realm. Maria experiences this in the final phase of her narrative, when a judge overrules her in the courtroom when she is pleading her case against her abusive husband. The last paragraph of the part of the novel Wollstonecraft completed before her death is in the judge's voice, not Maria's. He "alluded to 'the fallacy of letting women plead their feelings, as an excuse for the violation of the marriage-vow'" (133). This passage shows how female voices are silenced by patriarchal law, and thus rendered powerless. The narrative continues, describing the judge,

> For his part, he had always determined to oppose all innovation, and the new-fangled notions which encroached on the good old rules of conduct. We did not want French principles in public or private life — and, if women were allowed to plead their feelings, as an excuse or palliation of infidelity, it was opening a flood-gate for immortality. What virtuous woman thought of her feelings? It was her duty to love and obey the man chosen by her parents and relations, who were qualified by their experience to judge better for her, than she could for herself [133].

Obviously, the final line is in opposition to Wollstonecraft's goals for feminine power in *A Vindication of the Rights of Woman* and antithetical to the feminist discourse in *Maria*. The judge clearly desires to uphold traditional patriarchal values at the expense of feminine empowerment and voice, as the early part of the passage alludes to the revolutionary spirit associated with the perils in France and connects it with the potential uprising of British women. He defines Maria's testimony as abject in response to the dominant narrative in society, thus diluting the value and influence of her words. This part of the text illustrates the process of repressing female voice in response to masculine borders which override them. The female voices in *Maria* are thus countered in the ending by the judge's voice, and the act of legal silencing shows the reality of feminine marginalization, abjection, and the moral condemnation of women.

Through depictions of an unhealthy female experience, Wollstonecraft's Gothic narrative examines the paradox of a society that discredits the female role by dehumanizing women and taking away their rights. Maria's writing simultaneously explores a re-definition of female identity by depicting a mother forcibly separated from her daughter, while she attempts to escape her own historical conditions entrenched in institutionalized feminine abjection.

Obviously, for Wollstonecraft, reading, and other symbolic discourse, was not enough; political change was necessary to actualize her feminist goals in society. Filling in the lost and repressed stories of women, enables cultural transformations to occur. Wollstonecraft's quest to reevaluate the definitions of women embedded in patriarchal law, as indicated in the novel's courtroom scene, attempts to restore feminine voice and power.

Because history may be seen as a series of fictions which informs identity, Gothic literature questions all the intersections of human knowledge by transgressing symbolic codes and exploring repressed material. Therefore, because psychological properties are nonlinear, individuals and historical narratives are unreliable, but it is in their processes that one can understand the mechanisms of being. In order to understand these processes, that which has been suppressed in society needs to be uncovered in order to relieve society of its hauntings and ailments. In other words, what is uncanny and what is monstrous is what has not been resolved, and is what Wollstonecraft's novel investigates by illustrating repressed female voices in *Maria*.

Maria thus defamiliarizes conventional ways of perceiving definitions of gender in order to transform established labels and boundaries for the construction of female identity. The process of reading a Gothic novel is a therapeutic one, one which can show the elastic nature of the ego in the subject by the process of identification, collapse and resurrection, illustrated in Kristeva's theory on abjection, and by enabling the subject to adapt to the environment in new ways and/or confront conflicting mental discourses, particularly those which are labeled dangerous. The technique in these novels work in terms of identity by retranslating the fear of an unstable sense of self, though maternal abjection, into textual symbols that free up the anxiety created by what is left unsaid in women's experience and to be reidentified in text by decoding obsessional projections evocative of feminine abjection.

Works Cited

Bahktin, Mikail. *The Dialogical Imagination: Four Essays*. Austin: University of Texas Press, 1981.

Berebaum, Barbara. *The Gothic Imagination*. Durham: Duke University Press, 1987.

Botting, Fred. *The Gothic*. Cambridge: The English Association, 2001.

Burke, Edmund. *Reflections on the French Revolution*. New York: P.F. Collier, 1937.

Butler, Judith. "Desire." *Critical Terms for Literary Study*. Ed. Thomas McLaughlin. Chicago: The University of Chicago Press, 1995.

Byron, Glennis. *Spectral Readings: Toward a Gothic Geography*. New York: St. Martin's, 1999.

Cixous, Helene. "Laugh of the Medusa." *Modern Criticism and Theory*. Ed. David L. Lodge. London: Longman, 1988.

Foucault, Michel. *The History of Sexuality*. New York: Columbia University Press, 1976.

Freud, Sigmund. *The Uncanny*. 1919. New York: Penguin Classics, 2003.

Geary, Robert. *The Rise of the Supernatural*. Lewiston, NY: Edwin Mellen, 1992.

Gilbert, Sandra M., and Susan Gubar. *The Madwoman in the Attic: The Woman Writer and the Nineteenth Century Literary Imagination*. New Haven: Yale University Press, 1979.

Heller, Tamar. *Dead Secrets: Wilkie Collins and the Female Gothic*. New Haven: Yale University Press, 1992.

Hoeveler, Diane. *Gothic Feminism: The Professionalization of Gender from Charlotte Smith to the Brontës*. University Park: Pennsylvania State University Press, 1998.

Howard, Jacqueline. *Reading Gothic Fiction: A Bakhtinian Approach*. Oxford: Clarendon Press, 1994.

Kant, Immanuel. *The Critique of Judgment*. Trans. J.H. Bernard. New York: Hafner, 1951.

Kilgour, Maggie. *The Rise of the Gothic Novel*. New York: Routledge, 1995.

Kristeva, Julia. *Desire in Language*. New York: Columbia University Press, 1980.

_____. *The Kristeva Reader*. New York: Routledge, 1999.

_____. *Powers of Horror*. New York: Columbia University Press, 1982.

Levine, David. *Subjectivity in Political Economy*. New York: Routledge, 1998.

Moretti, Franco. "The Return of the Repressed." *Dracula*. Ed. Nina Baym. New York: Norton, 2000.

Popkin, Jeremy D. *History of the French Revolution*. Englewood Cliffs, NJ: Prentice Hall, 1995.

Sedgwick, Eve. *The Coherence of Gothic Conventions.* Durham: Duke University Press, 1997.

Shelley, Mary. 1792. *Frankenstein.* New York: Broadview, 2003.

Thurschwell, Pamela. *Sigmund Freud.* New York: Routledge, 2000.

Wollstonecraft, Mary. 1797. *Maria.* New York: Norton, 1975.

_____. 1792. *A Vindication of the Rights of Woman.* New York: Broadview, 1999.

"The Maiden Felt Hot Pain"
Agency and Passivity in the Work
of Letitia Elizabeth Landon

RICHARD FANTINA

From 1824 until her mysterious death in 1836 Letitia Elizabeth Landon, better known by her initials, L.E.L., was arguably the most celebrated female poet in England. Her rise to fame occurred as rapidly as Byron's a decade earlier. Like so many young poets of the time, Landon inevitably fell under the influence of Byron and she self-consciously employs Byronic themes such as passionate love and exotic locales. Germaine Greer identifies one of the reasons for the popularity of L.E.L.:

> She was obsessed, like all those of the generation which clutched at the Byronic hero. She took the psychic process begun by the general love affair with *Childe Harold* and took it one step further. The speaker was now not the Childe himself, but the woman he was making love to, a being every bit as combustible as himself... [264].

Landon certainly admired Bryon, Shelley, and Keats, all of whom died in the early years of her career.

Landon's poetical work (she also wrote novels, essays, and short fiction), with its emphasis on the passion inspired by physical love, has more in common with the canonical male poets than with many of the women poets of her era. While Landon may be compared to contemporaries like Felicia Hemans as examples of the phenomena of the "poetess," with the passivity that the term implies, her work yet exhibits an assertiveness — a quality that I refer to as a passive agency — that belies this. In a critical appraisal, Anne K. Mellor (1997) notes that a "poetess" such as Landon accepts "the hegemonic doctrine of the separate spheres" (64). However, Greer notes that "no other woman of her time had anything like her vigour in imaginings, and few men could equal her headlong kaleidoscopic rush through scene after scene to her almost unfailingly tragic conclusion" (265). While Landon's poetry reflects some essentialist notions of the separate spheres, it challenges the norm of women as docile and chaste. We might refer to her position as almost a strategic essentialism, for Landon worked to expand choices for women, especially in her portrayals of physical love. Mellor finds that the work of L.E.L. ultimately reveals "hollowness" in its conception of feminine beauty, suggesting that "Landon undermined the very femininity upon which her poetry was grounded; ideologically, her poetry implodes upon itself" (120). Yet Landon's heroines present themselves as vastly superior to the men they love. Stephenson answers the same critique by noting that in Landon's work "the emphasis on unhappy love ... provides her with a means of investigating culturally-determined concepts of the inherent distinctions between the love of men and of women" (80). Landon's overt celebration of female passion represents both the reason she succeeded in transcending the confines of the "poetess," and the probable cause for the decline in her reputation with the advent of the Victorian era. This paper will explore Landon's work with an emphasis on examples of her deployment of a passive agency as both the primary cause of her immediate success in the late Romantic era, and as the reason her work deserves continued recovery in the twenty-first century.[1]

The Tradition of the Poetess

Mellor (1997) discusses the distinction between the "poetess" and the "female poet" of the Romantic era, maintaining that the true female poet, such as Charlotte Smith or Anna Laetitia Barbauld, is "explicitly political and insistently occupies the public sphere" (64). In contrast, the work of the poetess is characterized by "the insistence that love and the domestic affections are primary to woman's happiness" (64). Landon and Felicia Hemans were the two most famous "poetesses" of the 1820s and 1830s. Yet, on the surface, the work of these two women could hardly be more different, as Hemans wrote pious, pastoral, poetry celebrating nation and motherhood, while Landon, a distinctly urban author from London, concentrates primarily on love between women and men. Despite their differences, Stuart Curran suggests that for both Hemans and Landon, "There are darker strains in their voluminous production — a focus on exile, a celebration of female

31

genius frustrated, a haunting omnipresence of death ... [that] invite a sophisticated reconsideration of their work" (189). Both "poetesses" were child prodigies but, while Hemans lived in relative comfort, Landon's precarious financial situation compelled her to negotiate the demands of the literary profession.

Laura Mandell notes that the term "poetess" was used patronizingly, condescendingly, but approvingly of women poets if they respected the doctrine of the separate spheres and dwelt on sentimentality and other "feminine" qualities ("Introduction," par. 4).[2] The use of "poetess" became common in the late eighteenth century in reaction to the writings of women such as Mary Wollstonecraft who advocated gender equality and supported the French Revolution.[3] Mellor notes that as male poets began to reject some of the rational tenets of the Enlightenment in favor of sensibility, many women poets were embracing rationalism that was, in part, a reaction against the wayward sensibility and "faults of the fathers and brothers and lovers" (1993: 64). The pragmatic "feminine Romantic ideology," writes Mellor, "urged its heroines to develop sound moral principles" and "virtuous thought and prudent behavior" to avoid "the temptations of sexual desire, excessive sensibility, or immediate personal gratification" (64). Landon's protagonists, on the contrary, display overt sexual desire, an almost morbid sensibility, and a view of Sappho (the original "poetess") as a model of exalted femininity for both her artistic achievements and her willingness to die for love. Many of Landon's heroines die from the exquisite pangs of love and while their male tormentors often go unpunished.

Mellor finds that Landon's work "appropriates the traditional Western cultural identification of Nature as female, of the female as body rather than mind" (118). Certainly, an impossible standard of female beauty and the compulsory abdication of the intellectual realm to men, described by Mellor, led inexorably to the ideal of the Victorian "Angel in the House." Landon inherited the informal rules governing the poetess and, apparently, accepted them. However her work complicates what Isobel Armstrong refers to as "the gush of the feminine" (15). Landon sought to grow within, and to expand, the confines of this role without embracing the pragmatic "feminine Romantic ideology" that Mellor has identified. As Stephenson notes, Landon "frequently took the opportunity to subvert the very limitations with which she appeared to comply" (4). From her earliest writings, it becomes apparent that Landon represents a departure from the "rational woman" identified by Mellor.

32

Sense and Sensuality

Landon first came to the attention of a broad public when William Jerden, editor of *The Literary Gazette*, began publishing her poems in 1820. Thrust into prominence at a young age in a period of great literary transition in one of the cultural capitals of the world, Landon's career appears to have been one of breathless production. Landon's poetry formed an integral element in the success of *The Literary Gazette*. The public quickly became fascinated by the mysterious and melancholy poetess who signed her work with the mysterious initials "L.E.L." Landon's popularity crossed gender boundaries. Cynthia Lawford writes that the poetry of L.E.L. "used to fire the minds and bring tears to the eyes of men and women alike" (2003: par. 4). Edward Bulwer-Lytton, a student at Cambridge during this period, writes that, in his circle of friends, "all of us praised the verse, and all of used to guess at the author. We soon learned it was a female, and our admiration doubled, and our conjectures tripled. Was she young? Was she pretty ... was she rich?" (329).

Landon's poetry began to appear in volumes, beginning with *The Improvisatrice, and Other Poems* (1824). Inspired in part by Germaine de Stael's *Corinne, or Italy* (1802), the heroine of "The Improvisatrice" is a Renaissance Woman from Florence, described by Landon in a prologue as "entirely Italian,— a young female with all the loveliness, vivid feeling, and genius of her own impassioned land" (51). The Improvisatrice writes poetry, paints on canvas, and plays the lute and the lyre. She is widely famous (like her creator) for her skills and relates:

> My power was but a woman's power;
> Yet, in that great and glorious dower
> Which Genius gives, I had my part [52: 25–28].
>
> ...
>
> Oh, yet my pulse throbs to recall,
> When first upon the gallery's wall
> Picture of mine was placed, to share
> Wonder and praise from each one there! [33–36].

The Improvisatrice, like Landon herself, works in a very public sphere.

In this poem, Landon celebrates a desperate and intensely carnal female passion for love and devotion that borders on obsession. The narrator of "The Improvisatrice" states candidly:

33

> Alas! that man should ever win
> So sweet a shrine to shame and sin
> As woman's heart!—and deeper woe
> For her fond weakness, not to know
> That yielding all but breaks the chain
> That never reunites again! [63: 600–05][4]

"The Improvisatrice" is replete with scenes of seduced and abandoned women. "Sappho's Song," one of the shorter poems within the longer narrative records the exquisite pleasure and the pain of love that give rise to the poetic impulse:

> It was my evil star above,
> Not my sweet lute, that wrought me wrong;
> It was not song that taught me love
> But it was love that taught me song [56: 148–152].

Such sentiments led Landon's audience, and even her friends, to speculate about her private life. How, they wondered, could a solitary young woman conjure up such emotions? Or had she experienced the kind of love her poems describe?

Several of Landon's narrator behave almost as priestesses of Art who hold public performances in which the audience enthusiastically interacts. In "The Improvisatrice," the poet-narrator relates that among the crowd:

> Youths and maidens with linked hands,
> Joined in the graceful sarabands,
> Smiled on the canvass; [47–49].

These lines recall the passage in John Keats's "I Stood Tip-toe Upon a Little Hill":

> Young men, and maidens at each other gaz'd
> With hands held back, and motionless, amaz'd
> To see the brightness in each other's eyes;
> And so they stood, fill'd with a sweet surprise,
> Until their tongues were loos'd in poesy [231–35].

In both Keats and Landon, artistic or poetic beauty comes to be communally enjoyed and it communicates its erotic possibilities from artist and poet to audience. Joel Hafner refers to Landon's "audience-centered vision of writing" (269) in "The Improvisatrice" and in other poems such as "The History of the Lyre" and "Sappho." In "Erinna," from *The Golden Violet* (1826), the poet expresses the hope that "I should be loved / For the so gentle sake of those soft chords / Which mingled others' feelings with mine own" (90: 50–52). Despite Landon's communal impulses, her work remains intensely individual and idiosyncratic.

Martyr to Love

Landon has been faulted for her over-reliance on depictions of female suffering, certainly one of her major themes. As the narrator of "Erinna" states, "I have told passionate tales of breaking hearts.... Of women's tenderness and women's tears" (96: 347, 350). Mellor and others have criticized Landon's apparent embrace of the idea of woman as masochist (117), well illustrated by the following lines in "The Improvisatrice":

> I would have rather been a slave,
> In tears of bondage, by his side,
> Than shared in all, if wanting him,
> This world had power to give beside! [71: 985–88].

Just before this passage, the poet speaks of loving "in open shame" (984). Yet if these lines present woman as passive victim, the poet also presents an audacious agency in the earlier lines, in which she says, "I loved him as young Genius loves" (959) and "I loved him, too, as woman loves / Reckless of sorrow, sin or scorn" (963–64), implying a readiness to engage in physical acts of love without a second thought to propriety. Mellor writes that in another narrative, *The Troubadour* (1825), the poet delivers "three versions of female love, all self-destroying ... in each case, the woman who loves is rejected, abandoned, or merely forgotten by her cruel lover" (1993: 115). While this analysis is undeniable, certainly such one-sided love is not exclusive to women. Goethe's *The Sorrows of Young Werther* (1774) presents a classic example of a young man suffering for love. Landon's heroines are quite emphatic in their abjection. In *The Golden Violet,* the narrator asks:

> For what is genius, but deep feeling
> Waken'd by passion to revealing?
> And what is feeling, but to be
> Alive to every misery
> While the heart too fond, too weak,
> Lies open for the vulture's beak? [225–30].

As Mellor notes, Landon's "The Proud Ladye" (1825) presents a female version of Keats's ballad "La Belle Dame Sans Merci" (1819) who holds the knight-hero "in thrall." McGann and Riess suggest that Landon's "The Fairy of the Fountains" (1835) is yet another revisitation of the same poem by Keats as well as a take on his "Lamia" (1819) (26). Landon's passive agency suggests an affinity with Keats's "negative capability" in that both privilege the recipient of experience rather than the actor.[5] In "The Fairy of the Fountains," the human-fairy hybrid, Melusina, hungers for human love and sacrifices immortality. She refuses to heed her mother's warning of her "mingled dower, / Human passion — fairy power" (220: 141) as, through an act of will, she abandons herself to "Three sweet genii, — Youth, Love, Hope, — " (229: 169). Melusina suffers both physical and spiritual pangs as an exile from her fairy state:

> Then the maiden felt hot pain
> Run through every burning vein
> Sudden, with a fearful cry,
> Writhes she in her agony;
> Burns her cheek as with a flame,
> For the maiden knows her shame [232–33: 275–80].

It takes an enormous effort for Melusina to engineer the circumstances certain to result in her powerlessness. Such active pursuit of danger and risk of defeat characterize Landon's driven women who consciously choose to leave themselves vulnerable. McGann and Riess, suggesting that Landon's use of passivity may be one of her greatest strengths, write: "Landon's imaginative authority rests in what she is able to fashion from her experience of passivity" (24). They further suggest that in her work "the dynamic of love and courtship ... supplies the (female) object of the enchanted (male) gaze with special insight" (24). It is this "special insight" by Landon that constitutes her passive agency. Mellor claims that because she was "working *within* an essentialist construction of the female as the beautiful and the loving, Landon's poetry uncovers the emptiness, the self-defeating consequences, of such a construction" (12). Yet, as Armstong notes, "Landon exacts critique from the essentialist category of woman" (27). One of the ways in which Landon so successfully exacts this critique is through her presentation of an assertive female subjectivity even as it reveals its surrender in the face of passion.

Julia Kristeva's theory of "abjection" can account for some of the psychological forces that inform Landon's poetry. While she does not discuss Landon, Kristeva captures some of the poet's reactions to the terrifying power of an obsessive desire: "There looms, within abjection, one of those violent, dark revolts of being, directed against a threat that seems to emanate from an exorbitant outside or inside, ejected beyond the scope of the possible, the tolerable, the thinkable" (1). Landon's central characters find themselves possessed by an intolerable, almost unthinkable, desire. The male love object often provides merely the incidental occasion for the heroine's passion to become stimulated. As Stephenson notes, "The individual male lover is always rather unimportant for Landon's women; it is the feelings he elicits from the women that are most valued" (61). Since so many of Landon's heroines are fully realized individuals, accomplished in the arts and with obvious and apparent sensitivity, their need for a lover seems almost an extension of their own singular achievements, a crowning touch to an imaginatively lived reality. Yet the will to abjection continues to assert itself for, as Kristeva writes, "That impetus, that spasm, that leap is drawn toward an elsewhere as tempting as it is condemned ... a vortex of summons and repulsion" (1). In "The Charmed Cup," one of the poems within "The Improvisatrice," Julian abandons the heroine Ida whose psychic pain at this loss becomes physical as "Upon her temple, each dark vein / Swelled in its agony of pain" (63: 592–93). Ida shambles, apparently aimlessly, through a windswept forest as

> Her hair is wet with rain and sleet,
> And blood is on her small snow feet.
> She has been forced a way to make
> Through prickly weed and thorned brake [63: 612–16].

Finally, as "Her heart lay dead, her life-blood froze" (64: 636), she arrives at her destination, the den of a "dark sorcerer" with whom she conducts a fateful transaction.

> He heard her prayer with withering look,
> Then from unholy herbs he took
> A drug and said it would recover
> The lost heart of her faithless lover [64–65: 650–53].

Shortly after this, Ida and Julian arrange a tryst: "It is the purple twilight hour, / And Julian is in Ida's bower" (656–57, p. 65). Julian has come voluntarily and apparently sincerely for a reconciliation. Yet to be sure of his renewed affection, Ida administers the sorcerer's potion and watches as it takes deadly effect.

> He drank it. Instantly the flame
> Ran through his veins: one firey throb
> Of bitter pain — the gasping sob
> Of agony — the cold death-sweat
> Is on his face — his teeth are set —

His bursting eyes are glazed and still
The drug had done its work of ill [65: 678–84].[6]

Julian's death returns Ida to abjection. Ida has been deceived, first by Julian and then by the sorcerer, as the device that was intended to restore her lover to her, kills him instead.

Landon's heroines derive strength, as McGann and Riess note, from their very submission, not so much to an external force but to their own resident desires. Kristeva notes that abjection "is experienced at the peak of its strength when the subject, weary of fruitless attempts to identify with something on the outside, finds the impossible within; when it finds that the impossible constitutes its very *being*, that it *is* none other than abject" (5). Landon's poetry presents exhibitionist displays of abjection and self-debasement, typical of sexual masochism. She speaks with her greatest authority when she reveals what Kristeva refers to "the eroticization of abjection" (55) and "the pangs and delights of masochism" (5). Writing of the male masochist, Gilles Deleuze notes: "The pain he suffers is an ultimate pleasure [and] it confirms him in his inalienable power and gives him a supreme certitude" (39). A similar process is at work in Landon's poetry.

Historically, psychoanalysis has viewed masochism as an essential component of female subjectivity and has been justly condemned by feminist critics for decades. Freud famously claimed that masochism is "characteristically female" (1961: 277); and Krafft-Ebing asserted that the male masochist "considers himself in a passive, feminine role" (237). Such views reflect what Carol Siegel refers to as a "touting of female masochism as essential femininity" that she finds "nonsensical" (16). This is especially so because the overwhelming majority of cases described by psychoanalysis deal with masochistic men. However, because of the general criticism of psychoanalysis in this regard, it has become controversial to speak of *any* woman who may share some of the characteristics of masochism, a topic hotly debated in the feminist "sex wars" over lesbian sadomasochism in the 1980s and '90s. Gayle Rubin (a veteran of the "sex wars"), along with other critics — such as Cealia R. Daileader, Giovanna Montenegro, and Anita Phillips — contend that one can categorically reject the finding of traditional psychoanalysis that masochism is an essential component of femininity, yet still allow for the psychodynamics of sexual submission and surrender in individual women.

Commenting on the fiercely passive quality of Landon's poetry, Greer writes:

> No female poet before L.E.L. had ever written of women's passion as she did. It was not like the love plaints of men, but the fierce, impotent, inward-turning tumult of a woman's heart, the agony of a creature unable to speak or act, forced to wreak her vengeance upon herself, to refuse to live [275].

While much of this is true, Landon's protagonists are seldom at a loss for words. Her heroines do not suffer physical violence from the men they love. On the contrary, they sometimes inflict violence in revenge as in the novel *Ethel Churchill* (1836). Occasionally, these women murder the female rivals for the affections of the lover, as in *The Venetian Bracelet* (1829) and the gothic short story *The Bride of Lindorf* (1834), only to commit suicide or die in madness in the end.[7] They suffer emotionally, and if physically injured, their wounds are usually self-inflicted. When in *The Venetian Bracelet*, Amenaïde learns of her betrayal by Leoni, she:

> Mutter'd "alone!" and dashed her on the ground.
> Corpse-like she lay,—her dark hair wildly thrown
> Far on the floor before her; white as stone
> As rigid stretch'd each hand,—her face was press'd
> Close to the earth; and but the heaving vest
> Told of some pang the shuddering frame confess'd,
> She seem'd as stricken down by instant death.—[lines 378–84]

After her raging and self-destructive energy has spent itself and she has slept, Amenaïde awakens as if from "some frightful dream" (438) and ponders herself:

> Her eye has caught a mirror,—that pale face,—
> Why lip and brow are sullied by the trace
> Of blood; its stain is on her tangled hair,
> Which shroud-like hides the neck that else were bare [lines 440–44].

These passages, like many in Landon's work, convey an acute awareness of corporeality, rare in women's poetry of that era. Yet Landon remained a readers' favorite for fifteen years. Greer comments on the popular acceptance of L.E.L.

> Woman's love was seldom if ever expressed before the proprieties had been satisfied, and then it was modest and tremulous. These willful creatures were a new species, and their creation was to cost Letitia Landon dear. Their immediate popularity was little more than a thoughtless response to novelty [276].

Some of Landon's contemporaries may simply have misread the intensity of her poetry and their dismissive or prurient reactions merely indicate that she was out of step with the attitudes of an emerging Victorian society. which may help explain why her body of work was consigned it to oblivion shortly after her death. Many critics appear to have underestimated the passionate quality of L.E.L.'s verse, mistaking her tortured characters for the fantasies of love-sick daughters of the middle class.

The Venetian Bracelet presents Landon's deployment of a passive agency. Amenaïde conforms to Kristeva's view that abjection "places the one haunted by it literally beside himself" (1). The poet creates a narrator who relates extremes of passion that do not conform to the public persona that Landon wished to project. Unlike Byron and other male poets, a female poet could not safely project herself as a sexual subject. Yet Landon's poetry places her literally outside, or beside, herself. Landon fills her poetry with her own sense of abjection. As Kristeva writes, "The abject is perverse because it neither gives up nor assumes a prohibition, a rule, or a law; but turns them aside, misleads, corrupts; uses them, takes advantage of them, the better to deny them. It kills in the name of life" (15). Amenaïde represents a prime example of this.

In *The Venetian Bracelet* when an itinerant peddler offers her a poisoned bracelet, Amenaïde cannot pass up the purchase and the opportunity to wreak vengeance upon her lover as "her memory traced / Her galling wrongs, and many an evil thought / Envy and hatred in her bosom wrought" (39). She proceeds to poison Leoni's blue-eyed and fair-haired English bride. (Landon's heroines are raven-haired, dark-eyed beauties.) Leoni is accused of the crime and sentenced to death. But so strong is Amenaïde's love for him that she cannot let him die and, after allowing him to languish in prison for a time, she confesses to the crime and then poisons herself. Greer writes of this remarkable poem that it "deals with an attachment so pure and deep and spiritual that it ends in murder and suicide" (307). Greer continues:

> L.E.L. is arguing that obsession is more ennobling than affection guided by common sense. Purity means for her not freedom from any taint of carnality but from any sordid considerations of convenience or social utility.... What is truly perverse about L.E.L.'s avowed position is that ... she insists on dragging herself into the poems in such a way that she invites discussion of her own emotional experience [307–8].

Clearly, Landon was not the vapid poetess that critics have considered her from the time of the Victorians until very recently.

Sex and the Single Poet

Lawford, who is preparing a literary biography of Landon, reveals that L.E.L. had a long affair with her editor, William Jerden, a married man twenty years her senior, and that they became the parents of three illegitimate children. As Lawford reconstructs the life of the poet, Landon fell in love with her first mentor and quickly developed a physical relationship with him. There was never any question that Jerden would leave his wife and family and this is part of what gives Landon's poetry such an air of melancholy and despair. Unlike many critics who see Landon's poetry as superficial and conformist, Lawford finds that the poet successfully brought the passion she felt in her own life to her published work. Lawford suggests that the couple usually met in the evenings which she finds revealed by the lines in "Song," published in the *Literary Gazette* (March 29, 1823): "I'll meet thee at the midnight hour, / When the light their stars are weeping." Lawford suggests that Landon describes a sexual climax in the lines:

Or with thy heart so near to mine
That I feel its every motion
Many wild tales shall be thine
Of the wonders of the ocean.

The narrator then records the sadness of parting upon daybreak: "But when the morning comes I fly, / Like the stars, away from heaven" (203–04, qtd. in Lawford, 2003: par. 58). However, in the scenario that Lawford presents, it would be Jerden, who must "fly" "when the morning comes," abandoning Landon.

Katherine Montweiler suggests that Landon's use of the suffering woman in *The Improvisatrice and Other Poems* serves to provide a site of identification for the audience. Just as the improvisatrice is inspired and sexually aroused by reading the poems of Sappho and Petrarch, Montweiler suggests that the poem has a similar effect upon its readers. Landon deploys a "onanistic poesaphilia" (par. 25), suggesting that the Improvisatrice "experiences autoerotic pleasures" (par. 21) through reading that serve to excite the erotic sensibilities of the reader. This view implies that Landon, while careful to avoid depicting overt sexuality, consciously deploys the erotic through textual suggestiveness and encourages masturbation in her female readers, an act that became increasingly proscribed as the nineteenth century progressed (see Foucault 42, 153).

41

Montweiler's suggestion is reinforced when we consider Landon's loving depictions of the female body that appear to relate as much to a narcissistic impulse as to same-sex desire. While Landon does not depict homoeroticism among women, she alludes to it in her choices of heroines such as the original Lesbians, Sappho and Erinna, as well as in her poem "Poppy." The latter poem, in the collection *Flowers of Loveliness* (1836), accompanies a picture of two woman caressing, and contains the lines:

> But a rosy lip has kissed her,
> With that kiss she wakes;
> Pale she gazes on the sister,
> Who her slumber breaks ["Poppy"].[8]

While Landon's female characters undoubtedly feel intense passion for their male lovers, these men usually receive relatively brief description compared to the detailed portraits of the women's skin, eyes, teeth, arms, necks, and especially their luxurious hair.

Stephenson notes that in Landon's work the "particular sensitivity traditionally ascribed to women, the gift of feeling rather than thinking ... makes the woman, in this respect, the only 'true' and 'natural' poet" (104). The title poem from *The Golden Violet* features a poetry competition in which the women poets hold a festival during which they provide the songs to entertain the guests, then sponsor a contest for deserving male poets (which strikes one as a type of affirmative action), emphasizing again Landon's privileging of women.[9]

Mellor writes that in all of Landon's poetry "the narrator refuses to tell the story of happy love," a comment that appears to support the necessity of a happy ending (116). Landon's refusal of a positive closure can be seen as an implicit critique of gender inequality. Many men in her poems are inconstant and practice a double standard that never receives the narrator's endorsement. If Landon accepts an essentialist definition of gender, she does so to assert female superiority both emotionally and intellectually as her brainy and hard-loving characters demonstrate. To Landon, women love more passionately, suffer more deeply, and create more spontaneously, than men.

Lawford has established that Landon was not sexually innocent. Long before new information was revealed concerning Landon's descendants, Mellor had written that L.E.L. "remained a virgin until seven months before her death," suggesting that all the sentiment in her poetry was artificial (120). Greer appears to have agreed that Landon lacked sexual experience, and suggests that "most of her heroines died virgins, as it is very probable their creator did" (264). Lawford has provided convincing evidence that Landon did not live a chaste life.[10]

Several scholars (e.g., Montweiler, Adriana Craciun) have commented on L.E.L.'s use of innovative narrative techniques to connect mind and body. Stephenson notes that "in 'The Improvisatrice,' for example, Landon accepts, and exploits the convention that a woman and her text are one: verbal expression of frustrated desire is confirmed with the language of the body" (96). Stephenson's remark suggests that Landon's work anticipates *l'écriture féminine*, as elaborated by Hélène Cixous and others. Stephenson's words convey the idea of L.E.L. "writing with the body." Of Landon's heroines, Stephenson writes that

> they are shown sensuously drawing out the moment following abandonment, slowly lingering over the deliciousness of their own words, over the twisting of their own bodies.... Men are shown to be nowhere near as exciting, or as satisfying, as words; the delights of language and the delights of the body are eventually fused [99].

Stephenson's remarks reflect Kristeva's theory of abjection. Landon's identification with her abused female creations leads to a cathartic rush of words. As Kristeva notes, "In abjection, revolt is completely within being. Within the being of language," adding that "abjection is eminently productive of culture" (45). Commentators from Freud (1977: 44) to Gilles Deleuze (134) to Leo Bersani (101) have suggested the link between passive sexuality and creativity.

As Landon became increasingly well-known in London, she inevitably made enemies. Early in her career she had written scathing book reviews for *The Literary Gazette* that, though anonymous, were nevertheless correctly attributed to her (Stephenson 28). Several contemporary gossip magazines wrote (essentially truthfully according to Lawford) of Landon's extra-martial relations with Jerden. In 1826, one of these, *The Wasp*, suggested that a pregnant Landon left London to have an abortion. The column mentions a "young lady" who, once so thin, "in the course of few months acquired so perceptible a degree of *embonpoint,* as to induce her kind friend Jerden to recommend a change of air," and after a "two months absence" she returned "as *thin* and poetical as ever" (qtd. by Stephenson 36). Lawford suggests that rather than an abortion, Landon went to the country to give birth (2003: par. 40–41). Similar rumors reported Landon engaging in sexual affairs with Bulwer-Lytton, yellow journalist Robert Maginn, and the artist Daniel Maclise. These rumors haunted L.E.L. when she became engaged to John

Forster, an editor and later biographer of Dickens. Forster, however, confronted Landon with the rumors and she was able to satisfy him that they were false. But the ordeal of being accused by the person she had planned to marry soured Landon on Foster and she broke off the engagement, explaining in a letter to Bulwer-Lytton that "I cannot get over the entire want of delicacy to me which could repeat such a slander to myself" (qtd. by Stephenson 48). As someone who spent most of her adult life celebrated as a poet but often reviled as a woman, Landon returns often in her poems to the rewards and pitfalls of celebrity.

The rumors continued to follow Landon even to the man she eventually married, George Maclean, a British officer stationed on Cape Coast off present day Ghana. Maclean had fought in the colonial wars against the Ashante and met Landon while on a leave in England. Maclean, too, nearly backed out of the marriage, apparently having heard the rumors of Landon's affairs. So strong was the double standard that Maclean's earlier acknowledged affair with an African woman was not considered important enough to render him ineligible for marriage but the unproven allegations of Landon's affairs represented a taint upon her character (Greer 340). However, the wedding took place and the couple moved to the African island where Landon died a few months later under mysterious circumstances. The four suggested causes of death are: 1) an accidental overdose of Prussic Acid, which Landon was taking for a malady; 2) suicide by a deliberate overdose; 3) murder by Maclean's enraged African mistress; 4) an epileptic seizure. The coroner's report concluded that the death was accidental and historically most commentators have agreed. Lawford however finds suicide more plausible.

Greer subtitles her chapter on Landon "The Sad Tale of L.E.L." Certainly, Landon's life appears often to have been unhappy. For all her celebration of the joys and sorrows of love, she seems to have found it rarely. One of the reasons for this, as Greer notes, is that Landon, living on the cusp of the Romantic and Victorian eras, was out of place in each (332). She was too cautious to fit comfortably into the Romantic era and unable, because of financial necessity, to abandon herself in Byronic fashion to the single-minded pursuit of the sensual pleasures she celebrates in her work. Yet she was not nearly staid enough to be acceptable to the Victorians. Her abjection was far more active and extreme than the pert and submissive requirements of the Victorian Angel.

Landon's work celebrates individual sensual experience and this places it more comfortably in the company of the writings of such male poets as

Byron and Keats — and, as Craciun suggests, the work of female authors like Bannerman and Dacre — than with many of the women poets of the era. Armstrong suggested in 1995 that canonical rigidity may "justify a one-sided study of women's poetry in isolation from male poetry" but calls for "the next step [which] will be to look at the interaction of the two" (32). The time has come to take that step and recognize that the work of L.E.L. represents the interactions that Armstrong suggests.

Notes

1. Despite her popularity with the public, Landon received severe criticism in her own time and in the Victorian period. Charles Lamb said of her: "If she belonged to me I would lock her up and feed her on bread and water till she left off writing poetry" (qtd. by Stephenson 8). In *Middlemarch* (1871–72) George Eliot invokes L.E.L.'s name to characterize the alleged vapidity of the poetry by women in the recent past (253–54). By the time of Eliot's novel, Landon was nearly forgotten and she remained in obscurity until quite recently. Since the last decade of the twentieth century, Landon's work has been increasingly discussed by scholars such as Greer (1995), Mellor (1993, 1997), Jerome McGann and Daniell Riess (1997), Glennis Stephenson (1995), Cynthia Lawford (2000, 2003) and others.

2. For a comprehensive introduction to the tradition of the poetess, see the work of Mandell, especially her website, *The Poetess Archive* (http://www.orgs.muohio.edu/womenpoets/poetess/) and the special issue she edited, *The Transatlantic Poetess,* of *Romanticism on the Net* (http://www.erudit.org/revue/ron/2003/v/n29/).

3. The blacklash against the female rationalist poetic output finds expression in Richard Polwhele's 1798 poem, "The Unsexed Female." In a note, Polwhele speaks for many as he laments the sympathy of the "unsex'd females" for the French Revolution: "The female advocates of Democracy in this country, though they have had no opportunity of imitating the French ladies, in their atrocious acts of cruelty; have yet assumed a stern serenity in the contemplation of those savage excesses" (9–10).

4. Except for *The Venetian Bracelet, The Golden Violet,* and "Poppy," all citations of Landon's work refer to *Selected Writings,* edited by Jerome McGann and Daniel Riess (Peterborough, Ont.: Broadview, 1997), and are indicated by page and line numbers in the text. References to the *The Venetian Bracelet* and *The Golden Violet* are taken from *The Chadwyck-Healy English Poetry Full-Text Database,* and "Poppy" from *The Letitia Elizabeth Landon* website by Glenn T. Himes <http://www.people.iup.edu/ghimes/miscpoem/flowers/poppy/popread.htm>.

5. In a letter John Hamilton Reynolds, Keats writes, "It is more noble to sit like Jove than to fly like Mercury" and "let us open our leaves like a flower and be passive and receptive" (Feb. 9, 1818).

6. These lines have much in common with a later poem by Emily Dickinson:

> I like a look of agony,
> Because I know it's true;
> Men do not sham convulsion,

> Nor simulate a throe.
> The eyes glaze once, and that is death.
> Impossible to feign
> The beads upon the forehead
> By homely anguish strung [113].

While Landon's narrator reacts with horrified fascination and Dickinson's appears more bemused at the spectacle of death, the impulse of the attraction appears to derive from a similar source in the psyche, an appreciation of corporeal reality in its extremes.

7. Scholars such as Adriana Craciun, Ellen Moody, and others have noted the similarities between Landon's work and that of Charlotte Dacre and Anne Bannerman. In a review of *Fatal Women of Romanticism,* Moody writes: "Craciun's goals are to make us remember the crippling circumstances these women had to negotiate and their courage, to lead us to understand them, to include them in the new canon, and to enjoy their texts" (201).

8. From L.E.L., *Flowers of Loveliness; Twelve Groups of Female Figures, Emblematic of Flowers; Designed by Various Artists With Poetical Illustrations* (London: Ackermann and Company, 1838). At the *Letitia Elizabeth Landon* website by Glann T. Himes <http://www.people.iup.edu/ghimes/miscpoem/flowers/poppy/popread.htm>.

9. The heroine, Clemenza, promises:

> The Golden Violet shall be
> The prize of Provence minstrelsy.
> Open I'll fling my castle hall
> To throng of harps and festival,
> Bidding the bards from wide and far
> Bring song of love or tale of war,
> And it shall be mine own to set
> The victor's crown of Violet [269–276].

10. See Lawford's "Diary," *London Review of Books,* 21 September 2000. Patrick Leahy comments on what he calls "the astonishing case of L.E.L.," crediting the worldwide web for creating the circumstances that led to the discovery (13). Leahy's remarks and existence of Landon's illegitimate children are confirmed by Michael de L. Landon, a distant relative and a former professor at the University of Mississippi, in a post to the geneaological website rootsweb.com (September 13, 2000) <http://listsearches.rootsweb.com/th/read/LANDON/2000-09/0968861248>.

Works Cited

Armstrong, Isobel. "The Gush of the Feminine." *Romantic Women Writers: Voices and Countervoices.* Hanover and London: University Press of New England, 1995.
Bersani, Leo. *Homos.* Cambridge: Harvard University Press, 1995.
Bulwer-Lytton, Edward. Review of *Romance and Reality. New Monthly Magazine* 32 (December 1831): 545–51. Reprinted in *Letitia Elizabeth Landon: Selected Writings.* Ed. Jerome McGann and Daniel Riess. Petersborough, Ont.: Broadview, 1997. 329–335.
Craciun, Adriana. *Fatal Women of Romanticism.* Cambridge Studies in Romanticism. Cambridge: Cambridge University Press, 2002.

Curran, Stuart. "The I Altered." *Romanticism and Feminism*. Ed. Anne K. Mellor. Indianapolis: Indiana University Press, 1988.

Deleuze, Gilles. "Coldness and Cruelty." *Masochism* (1969). Trans. Jean McNeill. New York: Zone Books, 1991.

Dickinson, Emily. "I Like a Look of Agony." Part IV, Poem 12. *The Complete Poems of Emily Dickinson*. Boston: Little, Brown, 1924; Bartleby.com, 2000. <www.bartleby.com/113/>.

Eliot, George. *Middlemarch*. Oxford and London: Oxford University Press, 1996.

Foucault, Michel. *The History of Sexuality: Volume 1, An Introduction*. Trans. Michael Hurley. New York: Vintage, 1979.

Freud, Sigmund. "The Economic Problem of Masochism." *The Standard Edition of the Complete Psychological Works of Sigmund Freud, Vol. XIX*. Trans. James Strachey. London: The Hogarth Press, 1961.

_____. *Five Introductory Lectures*. Trans. James Strachey. New York: Norton, 1977.

Greer, Germaine. *Slip-Shod Sibyls: Recognition, Rejection, and the Woman Poet*. London: Viking, 1995.

Haefner, Joel. "Romantic Scene(s) of Writing." *Re-Visioning Romanticism: British Women Writers 1776–1837*. Ed. Carol Shiner Wilson and Joel Haefner. Philadelphia: Pennsylvania University Press.

Himes, Glenn T. *Letitia Elizabeth Landon (L.E.L) 1802–1838*. <http://www.people.iup.edu/ghimes/index_landon.html>.

Keats, John. "I Stood Tip-Toe Upon a Little Hill." *The Poems of John Keats*. Ed. Jack Stillinger. *An Electronic Concordance to the Keats's Poetry*. Ed. Noah Comet. *Romantic Circles* <http://www.rc.umd.edu/reference/keatsconcordance/index.html>.

Krafft-Ebing, Richard von. *Psychopathia Sexualis*. New York: G.P. Putnam & Sons, 1965.

Kristeva, Julia. *Powers of Horror: An Essay on Abjection*. New York: Columbia University Press, 1982.

Landon, Letetia Elizabeth. "The Bride of Lindorf." *The Vampire and Other Tales of the Macabre*. Ed. Robert Morrison and Chris Baldick. Oxford and New York: Oxford University Press, 1997.

_____. *The Golden Violet* (1827). *The Chadwyck-Healey English Poetry Full-Text Database* at the University of New Brunswick <http://dev.hil.unb.ca/Texts/EPD/UNB/view-works.cgi?c=landonla.708&pos=5>.

_____. "The Improvisatrice." *Letitia Elizabeth Landon: Selected Writings*. Ed. Jerome McGann and Daniel Riess. Petersborough, Ont.: Broadview, 1997. 51–80.

_____. *Letitia Elizabeth Landon: Selected Writings*. Ed. Jerome McGann and Daniel Riess. Petersborough, Ont.: Broadview, 1997.

_____. "The Poppy." *Flowers of Loveliness; Twelve Groups of Female Figures, Emblematic of Flowers; Designed by Various Artists With Poetical Illustrations*. London: Ackermann and Company, 1838. At the *Letitia Elizabeth Landon* website by Glenn T. Himes <http://www.people.iup.edu/ghimes/miscpoem/flowers/poppy/popread.htm>.

_____. *The Venetian Bracelet* (1829). *The Chadwyck-Healey English Poetry Full-Text Database* at the University of New Brunswick <http://dev.hil.unb.ca/Texts/EPD/UNB/view-works.cgi?c=landonla.708&pos=9&keywords=Venetian+Bracelet>.

Lawford, Cynthia. "Diary." *London Review of Books*. 21 September 2000.

_____. "Thou shalt bid thy fair hands rove': L.E.L.'s Wooing of Sex, Pain, Death and the Editor." *Romanticism on the Net*, "The Transatlantic Poetess," guest editor Laura Mandell. No. 29–30, Feb.-May 2003. <http://www.erudit.org/revue/ron/2003/v/n29/007718ar.html> 25 Feb. 2005.

Leahy, Patrick. "Googling the Victorians." *Journal of Victorian Culture* No. 103 (Spring 2005): 72–86.

Mandell, Laura. *The Poetess Archive.* <http://www.orgs.muohio.edu/womenpoets/poet ess/>.

_____. "Introduction: The Poetess Tradition." *Romanticism on the Net,* "The Transatlantic Poetess," guest editor Laura Mandell. No. 29–30, Feb.-May 2003. <http://www.erudit.org/revue/ron/2003/v/n29/007712ar.html>.

McGann, Jerome, and Daniel Riess. "Introduction." *Letitia Elizabeth Landon: Selected Writings.* Petersborough, Ont.: Broadview, 1997.

Mellor, Anne K. *Romanticism and Gender.* London: Routledge, 1993.

_____. *"Distinguishing the Poetess from the Female Poet." Approaches to Teaching British Women Poets of the Romantic Period.* Ed. Stephen C. Behrendt and Harriet Kramer Linkin. New York: Modern Language Association, 1997.

Montweiler, Katherine. "'Laughing at Love: L.E.L. and the Embellishment of Eros." *Romanticism on the Net,* "The Transatlantic Poetess," guest editor Laura Mandell. No. 29–30, Feb.-May 2003. <http://www.erudit.org/revue/ron/2003/v/n29/007717 ar.html> 25 Feb. 2005.

Moody, Ellen. "A Review of Josephine McDonagh, *Child Murder and British Culture, 1720- 1900* and Adriana Craciun, *Fatal Women of Romanticism." Keats-Shelley Journal,* LIV (2005): 199–202. Revised and reprinted at <http://www.jimandellen.org/ Reviewers.Corner.McDonagh.Craciun.html>.

Phillips, Anita. *A Defense of Masochism.* New York: St. Martin's, 1998.

Polwhele, Richard. "The Unsexed Females," *Electronic Text Center,* University of Virginia Library. <http://etext.lib.virginia.edu/etcbin/toccer-new2?id=PolUnse.sgm&images =images/modeng&data=/texts/english/modeng/parsed&tag=public&part=all> 26 Feb. 2005.

Siegel, Carol. *Male Masochism, Modern Revisions of the Story of Love.* Bloomington and Indianapolis: Indiana University Press, 1995.

Stephenson, Glennis. *Letitia Landon: The Woman Behind L.E.L.* Manchester and New York: Manchester University Press, 1995.

"Portrait of a governess, disconnected, poor, and plain":
Staging the Spectral Self in Charlotte Brontë's Jane Eyre

LAURENCE TALAIRACH-VIELMAS

[A]ppearance should not be mistaken for truth.... The world may not like to see these ideas dissevered, for it has been accustomed to blend them; finding it convenient to make external show pass for sterling worth — to let white-washed walls vouch for clean shrines. It may hate him who dares to scrutinize and expose — to rase the gilding, and show base metal under it — to penetrate the sepulchre, and reveal charnel relics: but hate as it will, it is indebted to him (Brontë 1).

Charlotte Brontë's preface to *Jane Eyre* may perhaps have surprised Victorian readers used to trusting appearances and finding in the codes of physiognomy and phrenology very reliable methods for reading the inner self. Her words become even more confusing as the novel does foreground physiognomy and phrenology as valuable tools for reading character. In fact, Brontë's condemnation of "external show" is far more blatant in the novel's allusions to visual culture and the glamorous world of fashion which can turn toads into princesses. Indeed, the influence of print culture on the narrative, as we shall see, points out the gap between the inner self and outer appearance: the beauties of Thornfield — though dressed as angels in pure white — are selfish and self-centered maidens. Moreover, Brontë's construction of the inner self as a "shrine" or a "sepulchre" hosting "charnel relics" reveals how she relies upon Gothic terminology to shape inner space, turning the macabre or the spectral into so many reflections of the private self.

Feminist criticism has long argued that the Gothic enabled women to investigate "the problems of the boundaries of the self as an aspect of women's special psychological, social and moral dilemmas" (Delamotte 113). However, I would like to envisage the figure of the ghost and its insubstantiality here not merely as a representation of woman's inner self but also as a highly visual representation of the outer self, hence collapsing the boundaries between the inner and outer self. As I will argue, Brontë's novel uses the spectral to examine and rewrite contemporary constructions of ideal femininity: the Gothic helps to shape Brontë's reflection on contemporary culture and aesthetics. This culture permeates the text through pictorial representations, as suggested above. The pictures which appear throughout the narrative hint at cultural norms, compelling the heroine to believe that her body must be wiped off, leaving but a spectral self— a "portrait of a governess, disconnected, poor, and plain." If, for David Punter, the written materials which haunt Gothic fiction often act as reminders of the law, trying to "will away" the body (Punter 3), in *Jane Eyre*, I will contend, pictures and paintings function as such written materials, the visual tracing the vanishing of the heroine's body as she compares herself to more attractive models of femininity and increasingly loses corporeality, ultimately becoming a voice which the blind hero can only hear.

The opening of the novel provides a very good illustration of this point. Jane is happy to stay indoors; she does not like long walks in the cold and "the coming home in the raw twilight, with nipped fingers and toes, and a heart saddened by the chidings of Bessie, the nurse, and humbled by the consciousness of [her] own physical inferiority to Eliza, John, and Georgiana Reed" (Brontë 20). The sentence merges references to Jane's body (her "nipped fingers and toes") and to her "heart"— her inner self. In so doing, it also places her sense of physical inferiority at the cross-roads between her inner self and her outer self. The Reeds then cluster around their mother and keep Jane "at a distance" (20). Jane cannot be part of the picture until she acquires "a more attractive and sprightly manner,— something lighter, franker, and more natural as it were" (20). If Mrs. Reed suggests that the "natural" body is attractive when "light"— hence when hardly fleshly and visible (which may seem paradoxical considering some of her children's striking substantiality), Jane instantly "slip[s]" into the breakfast-room, takes a book "stored with pictures," "mount[s]" into the window-seat and draws close the curtain to "shrin[e] [herself] in double retirement" (20). Revealingly, as Jane makes herself invisible she simultaneously constructs herself as a picture, as the term "mount" could intimate. The red curtain and the window before and behind her enhance even more the effect of dramatization by suggesting a stage. She is invisible yet framed; both concealed and revealed by the stage formed by the curtains and the window (24). If Jane could not be part of the original picture and displayed with her cousins in the drawing-room, therefore, her invisibility is turned back on itself behind the curtain. The heroine collapses boundaries between the inner self, "shrin[ed] in double retirement," and the outer self—the picture she has created.

It is this sort of ambivalence on which the novel increasingly hinges as the romantic plot develops. The heroine, though unattractive, is associated with images of ethereal, otherworldly and even spectral femininity which gradually rewrite her own invisibility in more theatrical terms, thereby dramatizing the inner self. Before dealing further with the novel, I would like to pause here in order to have a look at illustrations of the novel which particularly play upon theatricality: Paula Rego's lithographs of *Jane Eyre*. The artist, born in Portugal and settled in London since the 1950s, is rather subversive, "clearly deriv[ing] much pleasure from doing what is proscribed" (Rosenthal 10). As Ana Gabriela Macedo argues, her art "relates to woman's 'experience,'" highlighting "a real awareness of the need to rethink the politics of representation of women in the visual arts" (Macedo). Indeed, Rego frequently "subverts the family, the so-called traditional role of women" and is "a committed feminist who created visual images that are polemically far more effective than any essays or speeches of protest" (Rosenthal 10). It stands to reason that the feminist stance in *Jane Eyre* could not but appeal to Rego. What is particularly significant in her lithographs of *Jane Eyre*, executed from the end of 2001 through 2002, is her construction of femininity and her emphasis on theatricality:

> I came to Jane Eyre from Jean Rhys's *Wide Sargasso Sea*. *Wide Sargasso Sea* tells the story of Bertha (Rochester's wife) before she arrives in England and is imprisoned at Thornfield Hall. Bertha is mad. She is a victim. Bertha's childhood had been full of magic and violence in an exotic environment. Jane's childhood could not have been bleaker. She was tormented by her cousin constantly punished and humiliated at school. Both children had known terror. But Jane, though inwardly fierce, could contain her anger. Disciplined and determined, she used her good sense and intelligence. She knew that to be able to survive she would have to contain her passionate nature, and she did. She is an independent woman who earns her meagre living, but keeps her wits about her. These images are about both women and both women are played by the same model [166].

As she explains, though she sees Bertha and Jane as foils to one another, she confuses the two female characters through using the same model (Lila) and making her "play." The emphasis on role-play and representation stamps the layout of her works. The theatrical, as Macedo suggests, drawing on Mieke Bal's definition of "Visual Poetics" (Bal), "collapses words and images, and gives rise to a specific rhetoric, which is beyond the word-image dichotomy, since it comprises text, image and staging" (Macedo 180). As a result, the theatrical "entails insight into the politics of representation and is strongly bound up with issues of gender" (180). In Rego's paintings, the effect of theatricality often emerges through the conflation of multiple scenes that are situated apart from the main action. *Getting Ready for the Ball*, which revises Velàsquez's *Las Meninas*, introduces us to the world behind the scenes, as the women are getting dressed for the ball — like actresses. Rego's representation of the invisible turns the construction of femininity into a "visual drama" (12). As Michel Foucault argues in *The Order of Things: An Archeology of the Human Sciences*, *La Meninas* plays upon the tension between the visible and the invisible (Foucault). The most significant element is not directly visible; the painter, normally invisible, is revealed indirectly, reflected in the mirror hanging in the background. By mystifying the boundaries separating the inside from outside and turning the visible and the invisible upside down, Velàsquez's painting offers an insight into representation.

The hint at *Las Meninas* in Rego's *Getting Ready for the Ball*, which focuses on Miss Ingram, her mother and Rochester's guests, aims to reveal women as fictions, enamored of their own reflections and involved in self-representation. In Rego's painting, however, no one is looking at the beholder: the female characters are engrossed in their own appearance. Jane, on the other hand, is both watching the scene and leaning against the back of the dressing table, sketching the ladies. The relationship between women and representation is furthered in *Dancing for Mr Rochester* and *Pleasing Mr Rochester*. Both lithographs are highly theatrical too, though Jane is no longer portrayed as mastering representation. While Rochester is "done in a Hollywood swaggering style" or "posing, Rodin-like" (Rosenthal 171), Jane's obsequious posture and countenance in *Pleasing Mr Rochester* fashions her as a double of the dancing Adèle. Yet, details in the foreground, such as the voodoo doll on the floor, or in the background, such as Jane's picture of a body drowning, are ominous. They frame the two female characters and deconstruct the artificiality of the two women: the objectified women trying to please Rochester are turned into corpses, hinting at morbid corporeality. Likewise, the image of Jane, standing behind Rochester in *Dancing for Mr Rochester*, is counteracted by her shadowy and spectral self in the background which seems to be dancing, like Adèle, or vanishing — this time, through lack of corporeality.

Paula Rego's lithographs are interesting here because her highly theatrical representation of Brontë's female characters — or "visual rhetoric," in Macedo's terms (Macedo 76) — enhances the extent to which Brontë's novel hinges upon the issue of woman as an object of the gaze. Moreover, as her women try to turn themselves into objects of the gaze, they become spectral, are shadowy or are represented as corpses sinking in the sea and voodoo dolls lying on the floor. Thus, excess of visuality (or visibility) equates death, spectrality, and ultimately invisibility. The macabre frames Rego's representations of women subjected to masculine appraisal. It is in similar ways that Brontë seems to deconstruct ideal femininity. As I will demonstrate, Rego's lithographs illustrate Brontë's discourse of the self to a certain extent. The staging of the self in *Jane Eyre* works in tandem with an internalization of cultural standards of beauty leading the heroine to neurosis and to spectrality. The specter, of course, remains an ambiguous figure, capable of defying boundaries: it functions as a significant symbol of femininity, simultaneously signaling Jane's adherence to feminine conventions and subverting it. As already suggested, Jane Eyre's sense of her "physical inferiority" launches the narrative and she later wishes she could starve herself to death as a means of evading cultural standards of beauty, like Georgiana, for instance:

> Why could I never please?... Georgiana, who had a spoiled temper, a very acrid spite, a captious and insolent carriage, was universally indulged. Her beauty, her pink cheeks and golden curls, seemed to give delight to all who looked at her, and to purchase indemnity for every fault.... Resolve ... instigated some strange expedient to achieve escape from insupportable oppression — as running away, or, if that could not be effected, never eating or drinking more, and letting myself die [Brontë 27].

The artificial beauty of Georgiana is contrasted with Jane's (sometimes ravenous) appetite, and part of the heroine's education consists in teaching her to discipline her self by regulating and curbing her appetite and by remaining under constant supervision — whether under Mrs. Reed's eye, Mr. Brocklehurst's, Mr. Rochester's or her own reflections and portraits.

As Andrew Mangham argues, the second half of the nineteenth century was particularly marked by cultural pressures to look good. Though the term "dysmorphophobia" was coined in 1891 by the Italian psychologist Enrico Morselli (from the Greek "dysmorfia," meaning "ugliness"), the theme of obsession with one's appearance appeared from mid-century. It could be traced as early as in the writings of Jean Esquirol in the 1830s and was frequently found in mid–Victorian neurological models of consciousness (models based on fixed ideas or types of monomania) as in fictional narratives. Because, Mangham argues, the publication of Darwin's *Origin of Species* in 1859 launched a "growing obsession with human breeding" (Mangham 78), marriage — or, rather, marriageability — was more often than not linked to the issue of beauty. Mangham takes the examples of *Jane Eyre* and Dickens's *Bleak House* (1852–53), two mid-century novels in which the heroines' obsession with their physical appearance plays a central part in the plot. In *Jane Eyre*, Mangham shows, Jane often reveals how the idea of beauty is located in the heroine's mind, such as when Jane draws a mental portrait of Blanche Ingram, as evidence that "Jane's anxieties are the product of her own unhealthy feelings" (81). The pressures faced by Victorian women to look good shapes Jane Eyre's journey. The theme of beauty punctuates the novel, and Jane Eyre is aware of her failure to match cultural standards of beauty: "I sometimes wished to have rosy cheeks, a straight nose, and small cherry mouth; I desired to be tall, stately and finely developed in figure; I felt it a misfortune that I was so little, so pale, and had features so irregular and so marked" (Brontë 106). Her conversations keep revolving around appearances and beauty, as her conversations with Rochester exemplify or even when Bessie visits her at Thornfield and gives her news of her aunt's and cousins' physical changes (137). Jane is constantly anxious to "look as well as [she] [can], and to please as much as [her] want of beauty would permit" (106).

Additionally, Jane always compares herself to other models of femininity. She contrasts her appearance to Grace Poole's (161), Blanche Ingram's and even to St. John's ("The thing was as impossible as to mould my irregular features to his correct and classic pattern" [389]). The many portraits and pictures in the narrative underline as well how the heroine's sense of self is related to her physical appearance, thoroughly showing how contemporary culture informs Brontë's novel. Indeed, Kathleen Tillotson saw Jane Eyre as "a novel of the inner life, ... a private world.... A love-story, a Cinderella fable, a Bluebeard mystery" (Tillotson 257–8). But *Jane Eyre* is also fairly rooted in history, as Heather Glen has demonstrated. Heather Glen's exploration of the self in Charlotte Brontë's works is relevant to this discussion. For Glen, Charlotte Brontë's construction of "private experience" (Glen 1) appears in her engagement with the visual culture of early nineteenth-century England. *Jane Eyre* illustrates Brontë's awareness of fashion and, therefore, her access to contemporary magazines. Jane's depiction of Miss Temple, for instance, does not just offer the artist's vision of the character. Miss Temple's portrait is framed by references to fashion and ultimately presented as a "picture":

> Seen now, in broad daylight, she looked tall, fair, and shapely: brown eyes, with a benignant light in their irids, and a fine pencilling of long lashes round, relieved the whiteness of her large front; on each of her temples her hair, of a very dark brown, was clustered in round curls, according to the fashion of those times, when neither smooth bands nor long ringles were in vogue; her dress, also in the mode of the day, was of purple cloth, relieved by a sort of Spanish trimming of black velvet; a gold watch (watches were not so common then as now) shone at her girdle. Let the reader add, to complete the picture, refined features; a complexion, if pale, clear; and a stately air and carriage, and he will have, at least, as clearly as words can give it, a correct idea of the exterior of Miss Temple,— Maria Temple, as I afterwards saw the name written in a prayer-book entrusted to me to carry to church [Brontë 57–8].

Similarly, the "exterior" of other characters she encounters are often seen in relation to fashion. The girls at Lowood are "uniformly dressed in brown stuff frocks of quaint fashion" (54) with "coarse straw bonnet[s], with string of coloured calico, and a cloak of grey frieze" (58), contrasting with Mrs. Brocklehurst's "costly velvet shawl, trimmed with ermine" and her "false front of French curls" (74) or her daughters' fashionable gray beaver hats 'shaded with ostrich plumes' (74). The novel hinges upon contrasting various types of physical appearance in order to define the self through cultural standards of beauty. Of course, the more elaborate and fashionable the characters' clothes appear, the more Brontë suggests that "external show" cloaks "charnel relics." Yet, Jane's anxiety regarding her physical inferiority is frequently crystallized on clothes, such as when Brocklehurst spots her when she drops the slate she uses to conceal her face and places her upon a stool. What she sees then is "a spread of shot orange and purple silk pelisses, and a cloud of silvery plumage extend[ing] and wav[ing] below her" (75). When Miss Ingram arrives at Thornfield, Jane is hiding behind the curtain so as to see without being seen and describes the "[f]luttering veils and waving plumes" which fill the vehicles — Miss Ingram being described only through her purple riding-habit: "Her purple riding-habit almost swept the ground, her veil streamed long on the breeze; mingling with its transparent folds, and gleaming through them, shone rich raven ringlets" (169).

As Glen shows, Jane's fantasy world — her imaginary world of adventure, romance and fairy tales — derives from the world of fashion displayed in the best-selling "annuals," containing colorful engravings of society figures, which found their way to Haworth parsonage. As she argues, Charlotte Brontë made detailed notes on the illustrations of *Friendship's Offering* for 1829, for instance, and even copied engravings from two other annuals, *The Literary Souvenir* for 1830 and *Forget Me Not* for 1831 (Glen 108). Such cultural landmarks are very good illustrations of the way in which the inner self was increasingly visualized, defined in relation to or, rather, through the outer self. As the author of *Woman: As She Is and As She Should Be* lamented: "The intellectual is superseded by the *visible*" (107). Prominent in these annuals was the notion of "display" as exemplified by the engravings of society beauties. Consequently, Glen associates Jane's "bright visions" and tales peopled with Eastern sultans and slaves and seraglios with the engravings in the annuals. As a matter of fact, from the very beginning of the novel, Jane's imagination is fuelled by a merging of tales with the world of fashion: Bessie's old fairy tales and ballads or didactic stories are told around the ironing-table, while the nurse is handling Mrs. Reed's lace frills. At Thornfield, furthermore, Jane's fascination with drawing-room "display," her description of "high life" and the construction of Blanche's exoticism resonate with the emphasis on visual representation typically found in such annuals. Likewise, the verses in the songs which pepper the novel, from Bessie's ballads to Adèle's "canzonette" or Blanche's "tunes and airs" may also recall the world of annuals, as Glen suggests (109).

In her study, Glen positions such annuals poles apart from the references to evangelical advice books which may be found throughout the novel. However, I would like to argue that the tensions between the evangelical discipline advocated at Lowood and generally found in advice books and the fantasies of female beauty displayed in the glamorous annuals collapse in *Jane Eyre*: eventually, both types of literature deny the possibility of escape for women. If the annuals provided an outlet for women's imagination and even featured active women (as female contributors and editors) (112), their praise of female "beauty" constructed femininity as surface, thereby subordinating women to their own images. Worse, perhaps, by displaying cultural pressures to look good and glamorous, they could lead women to "neurotic obsession[s]," in Mangham's terms (82). This is why Jane Eyre's exercise in "self-control" (Brontë 165), when she draws the imagined portrait of Blanche and her own, is, in fact, an act of "aggressive enclosure rather than transformative power" (Glen 127).

The influence of visual standards of beauty throughout the novel brings to light the complexity of the relationship between inner and outer self at a period in which cultural pressures to look good permeated society. Though Mangham argues that Jane Eyre's and Esther Summerson's feelings are simply "unhealthy impressions" and that the heroines are not "driven to excessive forms of behaviour" (83), Brontë nonetheless emphasizes cultural ideals of feminine beauty and the urge to conform to such standards of beauty. Jane's feelings of "physical inferiority" result from her lack of conformity, which subjects her to punishments while beauties like Miss Georgiana "purchase indemnity for every fault" (Brontë 27). Ironically enough, Jane's lack of beauty often makes her too visible, and when she attempts to hide her face behind a slate at Lowood, the slate falls with a crash and draws every eye upon her. Miss Ingram, on the other hand, remains invisible: she is first simply visualized by Jane's miniature or narrated by Mrs. Fairfax's depiction, and when she arrives at Thornfield, Adèle complains that she has not had a glimpse of her face yet. As a cultural norm of female beauty, Miss Ingram is either defined through her clothing or through her "sloping shoulders" and "graceful neck," her dark eyes and black ringlets (175) — stereotypical body parts which, as Helena Michie has shown, efface the Victorian heroines' bodies more than unveiling them. This is why invisibility is what Jane constantly yearns for (244). Indeed, as Sander Gilman argues in her study of beauty and aesthetic surgery, "(In)visibility is the goal of all aesthetic procedures.... The 'normal' defines itself as invisible" (90).

Jane's longing for invisibility does not just appear in her standing or sitting in the shade and behind curtains. As already suggested, the heroine imagines she can escape her condition by "never eating or drinking more, and letting [herself] die" (Brontë 27). Jane often refuses to eat when her "physical inferiority" is at stake. She feels that "a drop or a crumb would have choked [her]" (77) after her display on the pedestal at Lowood. After comparing herself to Grace Poole (161), she stops eating as Mrs. Fairfax remarks, "You ate so little at dinner" (161). She then asks about Miss Ingram's appearance and Mrs. Fairfax notices again that she is not eating: "But you eat nothing: you have scarcely tasted since you began tea" (163). What Jane feeds on are tales — cultural fictions: "I had rejected the real and rabidly devoured the ideal" (164). Interestingly, Rochester, though depicted as an ogre, is constantly shown to starve Jane: though Jane "gather[s] flesh and strength" (151) at Thornfield, Rochester would feed her with manna on the moon (265), suggests that she eat her last meal with him on the eve before the wedding and allows her only ten minutes to eat some breakfast on the morning of the wedding. Later, her days of starvation after her departure from Thornfield are followed by St. John's regulation of her appetite, recalling her starvation at Lowood.

Brontë's linkage of her heroine's desire to conform to specific standards of beauty with her relationship with food typically recalls Victorian feminine practices. As Anna Krugovoy Silver has contended, cultural standards of beauty in the Victorian period were more often than not linked to "ideologies of food and fasting" (Silver 3). In *Jane Eyre*, the heroine's constant fasting and the repression of her appetite contribute to her education into womanhood and femininity, hinting at the cultural ideal of thinness which was to prevail throughout the second half of the nineteenth century. As Silver argues, Charlotte Brontë's novels often pivot around images of starved women. In *Shirley*, "while women stop consuming food, they are metaphorically consumed within romantic relationships" (20). In *Villette*, Lucy Snowe's regulation of her appetite is contrasted with images of fleshly and sexually promiscuous women (22). However, feminist analyses of women's starvation in Brontë's novels frequently offer conflicting interpretations of her heroines' regulations of appetite. Whether starvation acts as a rebellion, as Gubar and Gilbert posit, for instance, or highlights self-denial, as Silver argues, the ambivalence may bring to light Brontë's contradictory discourse. If subversive, Brontë's discourse yet endorses the feminine ideal of her time (Glen 86), and Jane Eyre undoubtedly belongs to "the crowd of tiny women who serve as the moral focus of so many Victorian novels" (Michie 27), her tiny body emblematizing normative femininity. The ethereal heroine's "otherworldliness" which Rochester praises, as Michie suggests, results from her stay at Lowood and her education in starvation (24). In fact, the evangelical mortification of the flesh that Jane experiences at Lowood is very similar to the type of perception of the self noticed in anorexic patients: "Metaphorically, ... the anorexic girl enacts the philosophy and theology that teach her that the body is somehow not her essential "self" — that she is in fact imprisoned within her body — and that this fundamentally evil body must be controlled and subjected" (Silver 9). As in evangelical discipline, which praises the mortification of the body and the denial of its materiality as a sign of spirituality, the Victorian "anorexic logic," in Leslie Heywood's terminology, praised woman's lack of corporeality as a sign of their "spiritual rather than their carnal nature" (11). However, as already suggested, Brontë negotiates the tensions surrounding the aesthetic feminine ideal through her revision of Gothic stereotypes. Indeed, Brontë uses the motif of the specter both to define the inner self and to map out her heroine's physical changes. The Gothic scenes in the novel are all related to mirrors and deal, therefore, with outer appearance. At Gateshead, Jane sees her own reflection as a "strange little figure ... with a white face and arms ... like one of the tiny phantoms, half fairy, half imp, Bessie's evening stories represented as coming out of lone, ferny dells in moors" (Brontë 26–7). At Thornfield, on the other hand, the reflection of Bertha Mason — too fleshly and carnal to be a "ghost" — functions as an ominous image of Jane's potential physical metamorphosis through marriage. Bertha's Gothic representation sheds light on Brontë's viewpoint on more visual types of femininity, like Adèle's mother and Miss Ingram (Brontë 258). Married for her money and symbolizing woman as a commodity, the giant mad woman illustrates how fleshly and substantial women are yet doomed to fall prey to male domination and be locked up — thereby paradoxically becoming invisible: Céline Varens, as a kept mistress, Miss Ingram, as "some Israelitish princess of the patriarchal days" (186), Bertha, "in the style of Blanche Ingram; tall, dark, and majestic" (301), locked up in the attic, or even Georgiana, who is no longer "the slim and fairy-like girl" but a "full-blown, very plump damsel" (228), all demonstrate that their erotic potential condemns them to male subjection. The fears related to marriage and rendered through Gothic tropes, as when Jane sees her own spectral appearance in the mirror on the morning of her wedding, thus shape the female body as the locus of anxieties. But, surprisingly enough, the motif of the ghost, which we have so far seen as an icon of the feminine ideal disciplining herself through fasting, develops into a more subversive image at the end of the novel.

If Jane appears more and more in spectral terms as the novel unravels, such as when St. John finds her or when Mary sees her at Ferndean (421), she nonetheless refuses to die, always wants to keep in good health and often speaks of "basic bodily experience" (Glen 139). She is "not cold like a corpse, nor vacant like air" (423) when she finds her blind lover. In this final scene, moreover, the dramatic irony once again rewrites Jane's invisibility in theatrical terms. If invisible to Rochester, she is yet substantial and appears through body parts which she teases Rochester with. As the scene turns the visible and the invisible inside out, it rewrites the image of woman as object or representation which has haunted the heroine throughout the novel. Jane revamps her disembodiment and turns it into a sign of control: fashioning a new version of the drawing-room display of beauties at Thornfield, she has effaced her body to prevent objectification and is yet presented to her lover in highly dramatic terms. Thus, Brontë reworks disembodiment as a feminist strategy and plays with the female body's "contradiction between ... absence and ... presence" (Mitchie 5), her heroine's recurrent ghost-like appearance both alluding to the aesthetics of thinness and providing the means of striking back — with a vengeance.

In one of Charlotte Brontë's manuscripts entitled "A Peep into a Picture Book," the character, Lord Charles Wellesley, turns the pages of a colorful annual and contends that he will "raise from the shadow of gossamer paper ... the spirit ... that animates its frontispiece." He believes he is answered by a "mighty phantom" (Alexander 86). As this example suggests, Brontë's reliance on annuals and the types of glamorous femininity they promoted meant more than blind belief in the standards of beauty displayed in the engravings. Similarly, Jane Eyre, as a "tiny little thing with a veil of gossamer on its head" (Brontë 265) is ultimately less confined by contemporary models of normative femininity and can turn the fine people into flitting figures "like shapes in a magic-lantern ... as if they were really mere shadows of human forms and not the actual substance" (199–200). As a conclusion, we could perhaps re-read Paula Rego's lithographs, and propose a new interpretation of her macabre representations of femininity: like Jane who, as an artist, turns women into mere flitting figures, Paula Rego's female characters find in art (as the portrait hanging on the wall typifies) and in black magic (as the voodoo doll suggests), the means of decomposing and disintegrating their own bodies, thereby eluding male grasping and subjection.

Works Cited

Alexander, Christine (ed.). *An Edition of the Early Writings of Charlotte Brontë*. Oxford: Basil Blackwell, 1991.

Bal, Mieke. *On Meaning-Making: Essays in Semiotics*. Sonoma: Polebridge Press, 1994.

Brontë, Charlotte. *Jane Eyre*. Ed. Beth Newman. Boston and New York: Bedford/St. Martin's, 1996. Preface to *Jane Eyre*, Dec. 21, 1847.

Delamotte, Eugenia C. *Perils of the Night: A Feminist Study of Nineteenth-Century Gothic*. Oxford: Oxford University Press, 1990.

Foucault, Michel. *Les Mots et les choses: Une archéologie des sciences humaines*. Paris: Gallimard, 1966.

Gilbert, Sandra M., and Susan Gubar. *The Madwoman in the Attic: The Woman Writer and the and the Nineteenth-Century Literary Imagination*. 1979. New Haven: Yale University Press, 1984.

Gilman, Sander L. *Creating Beauty to Cure the Soul: Race and Psychology in the Shaping of Aesthetic Surgery.* Durham: Duke University Press, 1998.

Glen, Heather. *Charlotte Brontë: The Imagination in History.* 2002. Oxford and New York: Oxford University Press, 2006.

Heywood, Leslie. *Dedication to Hunger.* Berkeley: University of California Press, 1996.

Macedo, Ana Gabriela. "Scandalous Bodies: Visual Poetics and the Politics of Representation." In *European Intertexts: Women's Writing in English in a European Context.* Ed. P. Stoneman, A.M. Sanchez-Arce and A. Leighton. Vol. 13. Oxford: Peter Lang, 2005.

Macedo, Ana Gabriela. "Through the Looking-Glass: Paula Rego's Visual Rhetoric, An 'aesthetics of danger.'" *Textual Practice* 15/1 (2001).

Mangham, Andrew. "How Do I Look? Dysmorphophobia and Obsession at the *Fin deSiècle.*" *Neurology and Literature, 1860–1920.* Ed. A. Stiles. Houndmills: Palgrave, 2005.

Michie, Helena. *The Flesh Made Word: Female Figures and Women's Bodies.* 1987. Oxford: Oxford University Press, 1989.

Punter, David. *Gothic Pathologies: The Text, The Body and The Law.* Houndmills: Macmillan, 1998.

Rosenthal, T. G. *Paula Rego: The Complete Graphic Work.* London: Thames and Hudson, 2003.

Silver, Anna Krugovoy. *Victorian Literature and the Anorexic Body.* Cambridge: Cambridge University Press, 2002.

Tillotson, Kathleen. *Novels of the Eighteen-Forties.* Oxford: Clarendon Press, 1954.

A Shock to the System,
A System to the Shocks:
The Horrors of the "Happy Ending" in The Woman in White

JUDITH SANDERS

What could be happier than the happy ending of Wilkie Collins's hoary old thriller *The Woman in White*? The true lovers are not only married but deep into the happily-ever-after, snug at last in the family castle with a healthy heir "crowing" a victory song. Their bravery, beauty, and loyalty have earned just rewards. Never did the course of true love run smooth, but love has found a way. The reader — having enjoyed a respite from plotless, inconclusive, mulishly unjust reality — can close the book content, clichés affirmed, preconceptions undisturbed....

Or maybe not. After all, the genre that this standard-issue hero and heroine inhabit, the sensation novel — that once wildly popular hybrid that grafted gothic horrors from exotic Italian palazzos onto the bourgeois English fireside — proceeds to its happy ending by shocks. In *The Woman in White* — one of the few exemplars whose power to electrify has demonstrated a long shelf-life — few pages turn without somebody being stalked, betrayed, abducted, imprisoned, drugged, assaulted, burned alive, drowned, or stabbed. Or worse. Here, the happy ending's fairy-tale fulfillment follows a gauntlet of such extreme tortures that a susceptible reader is left with an unsettling sensation — not just of ice dumped down the back, that thrill-of-the-chill Collins famously intended his intricately plotted surprise fests to evoke — but rather, of suspicion: that a double message, a covert story, has wormed in and sabotaged the soothingly familiar cover story.

The cost, after all, of this happy ending has been, well, the characters' character — their very identity. Feisty, sexy Marian is gelded into a nanny, nursemaid, and angel-in-the-houses; artsy Walter's been brutalized into the domineering macho man he'd just tried to roust, and sweet Laura — well, her identity had to be destroyed in order to save it. When Walter displays her disinterred for all to see, he has to prop her up like a lifeless doll (618–19). Their victory's been Pyrrhic, the marriage bed Procrustean. And what's been lopped off was any trait that stuck outside the tight rectangle of normal gender norms, as I'll anatomize later on.

That suspicion of subversive activity is shored up by the inconvenient truth that this hero and heroine — happy, handsome, good, and rich — are, frankly, as dull as the clichés out of which they are constructed. Capering about them is a distracting sideshow of freaks — a dwarf, a giant, a bearded lady, a zombie, a clairvoyant[1] — all dripping with the personality pizzazz that the hero and heroine lack. Here, to paraphrase apocryphal Luther, the devils get all the good tunes. Or, to paraphrase another rebel, the different drummers beat a catchier tattoo than the uniformed blokes in the parade band. Although the freaks are eventually retrofitted or fired, and the bad guys lose in the end, en route, they have stolen not just the heroine's identity, but the show.

Yet another element fertilizes our alleged reader's burgeoning suspicions: The tone fails to remain consistently sincere. Rather, it veers into irony — even downright camp; at times (as anyone who's read parts aloud can attest), it's a romp. Collins has wedged his tongue in his cheek; he's insincere about his hero's sincerity. His multi-lingual format swamps this earnest fellow's platitudes with far more amusing voices: Pesca's effusions; Mr. Fairlie's extravagantly limp-wristed mewlings; Fosco's enormities and sarcasms. Who can forget his "Postscript from a sincere friend"? — for my money, the best surprise in the Western canon — or his elaborate phony titles, his capitalizations of himself, and who can without strain dredge up more than a phrase or two from earnest Walter?

Likewise, cameos seeded through the text satirize that very marital respectability that Walter must earn through Herculean labors: Mrs. Catherick, contorted by a decades-long effort to sanitize away the imputation of an affair, bows like a bobble-head to the minister but holds stiff with everyone else; former suffragette and tamed shrew Mme Fosco, that parody of Sarah Stickney Ellis's self-abnegating *Wives of England*, has become a mind-controlled zombie operated by her husband; the spotlessly conventional Mrs. Vesey can barely fog a mirror. These walk-on zapped wives enhance this sensation novel's most enduring and — for our hypothetical reader, should she possess a *soupçon* of sympathy for outsiders, a secret relish of the subversive — possibly most pleasurable sensation: a *sotto voce* affirmation of a profound doubt as to whether that normative happy ending justifies its draconian means.

The novel's narrative structures reflect its mixed message: It seemingly complies with genre conventions while subversively interrupting and undermining them. As Gilbert and Gubar long ago pointed out, novels by Victorian women present both cover and covert stories;[2] this male-authored sensation novel does so as well. It soothes and almost anesthetizes with familiar tropes: a "governess story," the marriage plot, romance's sighs of thwarted lovers, social realist details of walks and teas. These refinements collide with another set of tropes that, while equally familiar, have diametrically opposite sources, in folk art fantasy and the blunt psychological fundamentalism of a rags-to-riches fairy tale. A poor orphan rescues the fair princess from the evil sorcerer's tower and then slays monsters and performs arduous labors to win her hand and the kingdom. The switchbacks between novel and fairy tale subdivide further with the famous forays into novelistic sub-genres, domestic realism and the gothic.

This very cross-cutting of realistic and fantastic literary modes makes for shocks. This novel punctuates its familiar tropes with sudden distortions and monstrous mismatches. The governess of this governess story is a man. The sunny domestic realism of Limmeridge darkens into the edgy, Udolpho-esque mystery of Blackwater Park, precipitated by a family-sanctioned marriage between two handsome, wealthy people which in Jane Austen would have made a happy ending. The boy-get-loses-gets-girl marriage plot interrupts itself for an abbreviated picaresque and then metamorphoses into a detective story. The medium becomes the message: The novel both deploys and disrupts literary conventions in service of its story about the deployment and disruption of gender conventions. And in so doing, it makes such disruptions into the very pleasure of the text, much as it clandestinely applauds aberration as more interesting than respectability. This sensation novel intriguingly destabilizes the familiar literary territory that it lures readers into exploring, so as to subtly reveal that uninterrupted convention itself— monotone, stifling, predictable, *boring*— is what it conceives of as so very shocking.

So why does the novel undercut its marriage plot? Because it's afraid of it — it conceives of marriage *as* a plot deadset against interesting but unconventional identity. The central event, the guiding metaphor, is identity theft — that crime, as Walter puts it (in perhaps his lone memorable phrase), that no court will prosecute. And the catalyst is that symbol-saturated encounter at the crossroads with a woman dressed in white like a bride. These two conflicting feelings — fear of being robbed of one's identity without recourse and yet being mesmerized by an alluring bride — underpin the elaborate construction, as I'll now diagram.

It is by now a commonplace of Collins criticism that his novels concern identity — specifically, anxiety, even anguish, over its impermanence, its vulnerability to theft, violence, dissolution. The tectonic social upheavals that generated the Victorians' compensatory rigid conventionality; the rapid technological and ideological shifts only tenuously counterbalanced by the stolidity of manners (and imperturbably weighty clothing and furnishings), broadly account for this literary preoccupation.

Of course such mass destabilizations played themselves out in individual lives. Collins's own precarious foothold in the shifting sands of nationality, class, and gender inevitably shaped the products of his imagination. While *The Woman in White* is obviously not literal autobiography, it runs on psychological fuel from the author's preoccupations and formative experiences. Relevant specifics follow, but because so much necessarily remains unknown, and to avoid a glib conflation of author and character, I propose construing the novel as the reflections of an ur-character whom I'll call *the narrative consciousness*.[3] This fictional mentality is composed of an inseparable mixture of authorial autobiography and broader cultural materials. This narrative consciousness dreams up the novel to explore its dilemmas; it sets up characters in a dramatic experiment to test how — and whether — its concerns about identity might be resolved.

The narrative consciousness rehearses the determination of identity through the stories of nearly all the characters, both major and minor. Walter, like the trench-coated hero of a *film noir*, cannot quite make out in the dim streetlight who anybody really is. The narrative consciousness imagines Pesca, Anne, Glyde, Fosco, et al., as well as extras Mrs. Catherick and Mrs. Rubelle, as masked mysteries whose real nature Walter must detect. The problem of identity — who is that person, really? — permeates the text, but the narrative consciousness does not solve the core problem as satisfactorily as its hero does that of his lady's loss.

What is that core identity problem? Whose identity is really at risk of being stolen through marriage without public, official redress? It is, I'll propose, that of the narrative consciousness itself. It runs the novel like a test case, an experiment, to explore the consequences for an unconventional man of channeling heterosexual desire into conventional marriage.

D. A. Miller, in his famous Foucauldian analysis, masterfully detects this novel's secret-policing of sexual norms. According to Miller, Walter, a feminized man, must masculinize himself. Laura must be incarcerated and cretinized to become a proper Victorian wife. Marian, a masculine woman, must be feminized, a violent process of silencing and claustration that begins with Fosco's rape-like intrusion into her diary. The adolescent association with the anarchic Brotherhood, alias homosexuality, must be ended. These covert operations work to sublimate all wayward desires into the patriarchal bond between father and son, solidified in the happy closing tableau in which Walter turns his "charmed gaze" to his "crowing" son, "the Heir of Limmeridge" (626–27). The policing of sexual norms works "to privatize homosocial desire within the middle class nuclear family, where it takes the 'normal' shape of an oedipal triangle." Miller incisively sums up the novel's sensational machinations as the "brutal prehistory" of the normative family which is shaped by these "defining injunctions: (1) shut up the woman ... and (2) turn from the man" (190). Miller bases his interpretation on what he has unforgettably christened the novel's "primal scene" (152): Walter's midnight encounter with the errant, unidentified woman in white. Miller claims that her touch contaminates Walter with a feminizing spirit that he then spends the novel exorcising.

I propose that the primal scene involves not the injection of feminine spirit into Walter but rather the revelation of a preexisting feared effeminacy that could inhibit fulfilling the heterosexual desire aroused by the bride-like figure. But that reading depends on considering this primal scene as a sequel to what might be called the pre-primal scene: Walter's rescue of drowning Pesca.

Miller and others have ignored not only this inaugural incident but Pesca's strange figure altogether,[4] perhaps diverted by his absence from the central plot or put off by the jingoism that determined his design. But it seems worth asking why the plot begins — and ends — with Walter's relationship with the dwarfish, excitable, ridiculous, and yet loyal, generous Pesca — and why their encounter precedes that with the woman in white herself.

The novel begins by identifying Walter with his Italian friend. Pesca dashes out of Walter's own home, where his mother and sister treat this foreigner like a member of the family — almost as if he and Walter were interchangeable. Both tutor in "great houses," signifying their marginal relationship to both normalcy and power. As the narrative consciousness dramatizes its private (though not unrepresentative) identity struggles, it aggregates in Pesca the qualities that it must soon dissociate from the ego figure: Pesca is foreign, weak, and emotional, and a penniless intellectual and revolutionary. He will never be properly English no matter how hard he tries, so he will never be impressively rich and virile. Not even Walter's genteel but impoverished spinster sister, who ought to be angling to hook any potential catch that her brother brings home, evinces anything but disdain for this odd-fish friend — and all we know of her is that her tastes are conventional. Pesca's adolescent association with the anarchist Brotherhood, as Miller observes, has homosexual, or at least homosocial, overtones. Pesca's overly-emotional attachment to Walter exhibits an improper overflow of such urges. He does not control himself, which makes him ridiculous. He is, in short, on every count, insufficiently a manly man. He serves as a warning: *Walter must not be like him*, nor must his future quest to become a real English man be as laughable. The narrative consciousness begins to cleanse its ego figure Walter of all that Pesca represents with a symbolic drowning and rebirth. "When I dived for him," Walter recalls, "the poor little man was lying quietly coiled up at the bottom, in the hollow of a shingle, looking by many degrees smaller than I had ever seen him look before..." (12). Pesca shrinks to a residual, a homunculus, as must the qualities he embodies.

The trappings of this baptismal renewal are not religious, but rather nationalistic — that is, constructed so as to use nationalism as a code for gender. As cultural historian Charles Sprawson notes, "Throughout the nineteenth century, the English were generally considered the best swimmers in the world. A Victorian treatise on swimming begins: 'There is no instance of any foreigner civilised or uncivilised, whose achievements in the water surpass those of the British'" (26). When immigrant Pesca tries to strengthen his English credentials by swimming, he nearly drowns. When Walter demonstrates his physical prowess through swimming, he begins solidifying his credentials as a real Brit, and therefore, a real man.

This pre-primal scene, drenched not only in water but symbolism, also inaugurates the pervasive fairy tale resonances, with their characteristic surface simplicity masking disturbing psychological undercurrents: As the nearly-drowned man's name suggests, the commoner Walter has rescued a magic fish who will grant his wishes for a princess and a kingdom; that is the soothingly familiar cover story (jarringly juxtaposed with the novelistic domestic realism of the preceding pages). Prefiguring his role as a White Knight rescuing a Lady in Distress, Walter gears up here by scooping up another powerless creature. But this scene inaugurates not only the cover story but the covert story as well. Beware what you wish for because it might come true: The magic fish offers a reward that will buy Walter much misery (here is the fairy tale's dark undercurrent), because the princess and the kingdom come at a very high price — as does the normative identity that their possession requires. Walter's reluctance to accept the magic fish's golden gift foreshadows the troubles that the conventional wish's fulfillment will bring, stirred up by the narrative consciousness' ambivalence.

Yet for all that Pesca might be ridiculous to men and undesirable to women, for all that his name suggests Italian "*peccati*" or sins, the narrative consciousness presents his affection and loyalty as admirable, his naive enthusiasm as endearing. Ultimately these very qualities, channeled into assisting a differentiated Walter — will make the final victory possible. The narrative consciousness seems a tad sorry to have to let this foreign character go under. Pesca, like the other major deviants, may be ostracized from the main story for not conforming to gender ideals, but he resurfaces; his resurgent appeal arises from to the narrative consciousness's ambivalence about the brutal socialization its ego figure must undergo.

Before I address the implications of this neglected pre-primal scene for the primal one, I must wrap up this discussion of Pesca by considering the other "Italian" embodying anarchic "foreign" traits. If undersized Pesca represents the life-threatening dangers of a man's being physically and emotionally weak, oversized Fosco limns the opposite boundary; together they mark the Scylla and Charybdis between which the ego figure must navigate. Fosco, whose name marks him as a creature of darkness, is diabolically clever rather than foolish like Pesca. He masters science, writing, medicine, and every other branch of knowledge, but in opposition to humble Pesca's almost fawning generosity, vain Fosco counterpoises self-congratulatory self-interest. Little Pesca fails at pretending to be a he-man, while huge, domineering Fosco purposefully pretends to be effeminate and child-like. Rather than strive to appear virile, as Pesca does with risible results, Fosco sheathes his iron fist in frilled velvet: He dandifies himself in embroidered shirts, coddles himself with pastry and sugar water, and pets white mice. Such effeminate and childish pleasures flimsily camouflage his diabolical masculine super-power. By controlling himself completely, he dominates for his own purposes the hot-tempered aristocrat Percy Glyde. He turns Englishness on itself in his mastery of his former-suffragette wife who, as he himself remarks, surpasses even Sarah Stickney Ellis's repressive ideal.[5] With criminal sangfroid, he silences and overpowers the outspoken and active Marian, even though he professes to admire her. Like Pesca, Fosco is a traitor to a Brotherhood not only in the sense of breaking homoerotic male bonds, as Miller emphasizes, but also to the Brotherhood as patriarchy in his outsized and nearly criminal abuses of male prerogatives: If *peccato*-riddled Pesca as a phallic fish is sinfully small, Fosco is a big dick, but too big.

The novel that opens with Pesca's drowning ends with Fosco's. He has been stabbed — punctured, deflated — for, anarchist that he is, having sabotaged marriage and the aristocracy. But some of his nefarious powers have by then been integrated, in moderated form, into Walter, the ego figure. He has wrested from Fosco control of rival Glyde, wife Laura/Anne's mobility, Marian's competing voice,[6] and indeed of the narrative itself. These parallel submersions imply that at last imbalances in masculinity have been drowned out.

The narrative consciousness does not entirely repudiate its Fosco-the-villain creation either, however — he is too entertaining. It seems to relish its outsized creation. But while it may find Fosco's nefarious power to master even powerful women to be attractive, it must distance this forbidden feeling from its ego figure — until it can be moderated into the socially acceptable form of a strong-minded husband caring for a childishly feeble-minded wife.

Flanked by cautionary figures of undersized and overblown masculinity, of too little power over women and too much, young Walter becomes this novel's envoy into a fantasy about what it would take to achieve a middle ground of normative adult manhood. In light of this interpretation, the primal scene (to return to it at last) takes on a meaning slightly different, as I've been hinting, from the one that Miller ascribes. Lyn Pykett summarizes Miller's argument as follows: "Using the nineteenth-century discourse which represents the male homosexual as having a woman's spirit caught within a male body, Miller reads the sensationalism of Hartright's meeting with Anne and Laura as figuring the threat of homosexuality as a dissolution of gender boundaries and contamination by 'feminine' nervousness" (12). But the narrative consciousness seems not so concerned with emptying its emissary of contaminating female spirit and converting him to Oedipality, as Miller asserts. Rather, having been heterosexually attracted, it tries not to recoil from turning itself into a conventionally manly man who can gratify his desires in a socially acceptable manner, i.e. marriage. The bride-like woman in white's touch does not infuse Walter with feminine spirit so much as sexually arouse him, expressing a deep connection between the two figures.

Like the errant madwoman, Walter, being socially powerless, is vulnerable to aristocratic control. He lives with his mother and sister, a family configuration that expresses his isolation from the networks of male power. He will have to be a self-made man since he cannot be a socially-assisted one. His position as a "mere drawing master," often so deprecatingly described, underscores the message. We learn immediately that he does not have enough money. An over-aged adolescent teetering too long on the cusp of adulthood, mythically departing the family home to meet his own destiny, he too pauses, isolated, directionless, and vulnerable, at a crossroads of his life to inquire which direction through the darkness leads to freedom and which to captivity. Anomalous and astray like the blank, helpless woman, as he forms his masculine identity (under the guise of discovering hers), he will navigate between the foreign, radical extremes that helpless Pesca and domineering Fosco represent. She touches him from behind, causing his "fingers [to] tighten ... round the handle of [his] stick" (23); this sexual image catches him in a passive and vulnerable position. And when he helps her evade her legal captors and then questions his action, he signals his own ambivalent relationship with the laws of gender convention; he is as yet unsure whether to align himself with or against them. He has not yet claimed the male prerogative of controlling the woman's movements face-to-face, which apparently he must learn to do or she will elude him. The novel, then, has opened with Pesca to warn of the necessity, before the heterosexual urges next awakened can be satisfied, of drowning an unmasculine ineffectuality. That pre-primal scene is a set-up; the subsequent encounter is fraught with expectations for male power and control that Walter must but cannot yet meet.

This focus on novel's agonized cost-benefit analysis of conforming to masculine norms gathers impetus from circumstances in Collins's life. Readers knowledgeable about it notice the striking gap between hero and creator. The character who most closely resembles its author is not the tall, conventional, romantic, strapping Walter, but the affectionately derided and nearly drowned-out foreigner, the unmanly and unmarriageable Pesca. This resemblance draws our attention to textual elements that we might otherwise leave unexamined.

From 1859, when Collins was thirty-five, a year before beginning *The*

Woman in White, he secretly cohabited with Mrs. Caroline Graves. She was reportedly a beautiful, personable, and self-dramatizing widow, a mother with lower-class origins and an opaque past. Collins allegedly first encountered her on a dark road at night. Although biographer Peters dismisses the famous story as apocryphal (192), the son of a participant reports that Collins and his friends while on a midnight ramble heard a scream and then saw a woman in a white gown flee a fenced yard. Collins abandoned his friends to follow her. Collins, who visited brothels in the course of such nighttime rambles with his buddy, Dickens, had always vociferously opposed marriage. He never did for his woman in white what Walter did for his — that is, he ever publicly established her identity and married her. (Perhaps this novel explains why.) But he lived with her for most of the rest of his life — alternating with another mistress, an uneducated country girl, with whom he eventually had three children. (His quasi-bigamist domestic arrangements rather resemble Walter's, for whom two women eventually fulfill wifely functions.)

Collins's unconventional domestic arrangements were in keeping with his unconventionality in other areas. In the patriotic age of empire, he was a devoted Italianophile; he was addicted to laudanum, which he had begun taking as medicine for gout; he was small, oddly-proportioned, nervous, and sedulously sedentary. And like his hero, he was an artist in an effeminate genre, operating on the periphery of masculine social power.

I hope this brief digression into biography justifies emphasizing the narrative consciousness' anxiety about conformity to gender norms, especially as aroused by the bride-like, white-gowned figure who haunts the hero at a crossroads in his life. Imagining its ego figure to have been sexually aroused by her touch, and feeling a kinship based on their comparable situations as outsiders, the narrative consciousness is tempted to contemplate marriage. But it fears that its Pesca-like unmanliness renders it unmarriageable. Further, the alluring lady in this bridal vision is not yet a conventional wife any more than Walter/Pesca is a conventional husband. So the narrative consciousness begins reconfiguring both lone, decontextualized wayfaring strangers as society types. It strives to translate the pure desire of the anonymous midnight encounter into socially-contextualized courtship and marriage. With unacceptable qualities split off into other characters, an imaginary testing of possibilities begins.

The novel switches from its dream-like, symbolically laden primal scenes into events more grounded in social realism as it imagines the conventional courtship. But the psychological concerns persist, generating the subversive images. The narrative consciousness contrasts its ego figure, the effeminately powerless Walter, to its image of a husband who would win conventional approval. So it constructs Percy Glyde, its nemesis, its competition for the vague muse's hand (and wealth — no one wants her voice or, in her curiously asexual liaisons, body), and proceeds to de-legitimize him savagely — and, by implication, all his kind.

Percy Glyde appears perfect: a suave, manly, wealthy aristocrat in the prime of life. He is apparently to the manner — and manor — born. He has glided into his position of power and entitlement on the basis of his purse. But Percy's purse is empty, and even a dog (Laura's greyhound) can sniff out his bastardy, although the representative dunce-like authorities — the father, the lawyer — cannot. Glyde (like everyone else) turns out to be not whom he seems: This paragon of British masculinity is barely British as he was raised abroad, barely a man in his asexuality, spineless in his servitude to a foreign power (Fosco), barely a member of society as he grew up in isolation. He proves to be bankrupt rather than rich, choleric rather than suave, brutal rather than mannerly, corrupt rather than conventional, and above all, not even legitimate. Percy Glyde is unmasked as a bastard in both senses, being both despicable and an imposter. Mr. Fairlie, the authoritarian father who endorsed Glyde's suit, turns out to have been a hypocrite: He himself fathered an illegitimate child (Anne, the captive, transparent Laura's wandering, cryptic double). His sexual history discredits his authority as matchmaker and by extension that of the gender-class conventions that he represents.

To dethrone such an entrenched but fraudulent rival as Glyde, the narrative consciousness will fight ferociously on behalf of its meritorious commoner. In one of the coincidences so characteristic of Victorian novels, in which accidents actualize destructive rage associated with, but not attributed to, an ego figure, Glyde incinerates himself in the very church that upholds the forged authority of all his kind. But ironically, as events masculinize Walter into a worthy husband, they infect him with some of the macho harshness that Glyde so revoltingly embodies. Glyde with crude brutality locks up both errant, prophetic Anne (who tellingly remains loyal to the mother's love rather than the father's law) and housebound, clueless Laura. Walter as her loving protector must do so as well. To establish the legitimate identity of wife, the narrative consciousness seems to imagine, one must deprive the woman of her mobility, her freedom of thought, her association with the night and sex and dreams, the artless sexiness offset by her virginal bridal robe (or white nightgown), and above all, her knowledge, however vague and intuitive, of the illegitimacy of any man's claim to all she possesses. The imagery hints at uncomfortable awareness of these paradoxes: There is no way to be a good husband or a free wife in this narrative consciousness's cynical view. All the crossroads lead to the madhouse.

This gallery of the narrative consciousness's images of masculinity would be incomplete without Mr. Frederick Fairlie, the literally and figuratively closeted, swishy aesthete. Like the other males arrayed around Walter, he's a cautionary figure. Through him, the narrative consciousness debunks the fantasy of locking oneself away — from women and everyone else — to dedicate oneself to Art, with only a compliant manservant ("He's an ass," Mr. Fairlie says of him, hinting at the principle use he makes of the hapless Louis) to satisfy one's desires. With this comical, even ridiculous figure, the narrative consciousness forecloses this secluded-wealthy-bachelor-esthete alternative to the role of conventional, heterosexual, socially engaged married man. The narrative consciousness portrays such a figure as not merely ridiculous, but immured in a narcissism so extreme that it actually endangers others' lives. He's an obstacle that must be gotten out of the way for "the will" to be fulfilled, and the narrative consciousness erases him with a few strokes at the moment propitious for its ego figure's ascension.

The novel's reworking of its female figures echoes that of its male figures. The troubled male consciousness's binaristic thinking, as it works through in imagination the theft of its own sense of legitimate identity in the sex-gender system, imagines an economy of distortions, of freaks whose mismatched parts must somehow be sorted into what Judith Butler calls culturally legible forms. The undersized Pesca and oversized Fosco, the chivalrous lover Walter and the evil husband Glyde, delineate the paradoxes of imbalanced masculine power. Likewise, the narrative consciousness introduces all the female figures as monsters and mysteries composed of contradictory or blanked-out parts.

The Woman first appears without social context — no name, no history, no reasons, no role — which opens a space for the pure erotic arousal that animates the imagery. This wandering, heartsick, doomed prophet of marital misery, will have to be buried (confined alongside the lost loving mother) before the conventional family can be established at the end. Back in social realism in the form of Limmeridge House's breakfast room, social norms and class divisions complicate heterosexual attraction. Here in broad daylight, attraction will be sublimated into chivalric romance; respectable love must have no body, no electrifying touch, no thrilled nerves. The sex/intimacy rift gapes wide.

The preparation for Walter's romantic attraction to disembodied Laura in this constrained locale comes in the form of his sexual revulsion at the embodied Marian. The narrative consciousness will famously introduce Laura as disembodied, an empty outline that the reader must fill in with his own associations (52–53), but first it reveals Marian in a kind of striptease (34–35). Building on the heterosexual excitation of the night before, the narrative consciousness perceives part after part of her shapely body in an ever more arousing display, only to have the climactic revelation squelch desire — as if when the last veil fell it revealed instead of a vulva, a penis, represented here metonymically by Marian's mustache.

The narrative consciousness' imagery reflects its uneasy convictions about the nature of a wifely woman, in which it is now intensely interested. The narrative consciousness imagines for Marian an incompatible body and mind. Her relaxed, uncorseted, attractive body is attached in a Frankenstein-ian mismatch to a head whose physical ugliness represents the sexual unat-tractiveness of what it contains: female intelligence, independence, frank speech, and agency — in short, power — to this insecure male viewer. Here, power cannot be feminine — that would be oxymoronic; power must wear a mustache. As attractive as Marian's physical and mental qualities are sepa-rately, they clash repulsively when stitched together; mustachioed power becomes monstrous atop feminine curves. Marian's secondary characteris-tics of definitive poverty and suggested lesbianism underscore an independ-ent-minded, sexily-embodied woman's unmarriageability. She too represents an intriguing but deviant possibility that the narrative consciousness must foreclose at the very outset of its marriage plot.

Yet spinster Marian's presence in the text as a foil to wifely Laura func-tions subversively: The active, thinking, boldly expressive, embodied woman proves far more engaging than the passive, vapid, cliché-spouting, disem-bodied angel. The text surreptitiously invites the reader to love its unmar-riageable creation. (According to Peters, Collins reported receiving letters from would-be suitors desiring to marry the real-life model for Marian Hal-combe.) It is difficult to tell whether the narrative consciousness rues this conundrum or simply records cultural assumptions as a character like Wal-ter would experience them; but it is hard to imagine that it could inspire the reader's love for Marian without sharing it, albeit with evident ambivalence.

The dubious honor of marriageability — given its consequences — falls to a blank: a character with social position but no personality or body. Constructed out of clichés, Laura is as spotlessly conventional a gender ideal as the narrative consciousness half-wishes its ego figure could be. But even Laura gets entangled in the plot's mysteries of missing identity. The conventions of literature and society have erased any trace of individual personality long before Glyde and Fosco conspire to steal her social position. Laura is the only major character who never verbalizes her side of the story. She takes no independent action. She says little that is memorable besides her petulant plea, "Oh, don't, don't, don't treat me like a child!" (478) — rather poignant as well as ironic, since such a dependent creature is by nature childlike. When Walter at last displays her to Limmeridge's tenants to reestablish her status among the living, he has, as I've mentioned, to lift her as if she were a lifeless puppet (619). Such is the condition, the imagery implies, of the allegedly desirable normative wife. Such is the prize, the lottery jackpot, of the happy ending.

Marian degenerates from a bantering, playful devil (as she, both tart and sweet, describes herself to Hartright over marmalade, being of similar savor, when they first meet) into a silent, dutiful angel in the house, selflessly and asexually serving as domestic and later as nanny. Her transformation begins immediately after the narrative consciousness sends her out on the roof in the dark to spy on the men, when it locks her up as if in punishment, sick and helpless. By going outside the house, she has gone out on a limb; by exercising power that threatens the men as they plot to control the women, she has ventured too far from the norm. So the narrative consciousness drags her back inside from the parapets where she had overheard the forbidden truth about male treachery and claps her in irons, in which, lined with velvet though they may be, she remains. Likewise, Laura, the prototypical white woman, the fill-in-the-blank muse who inspires Walter's masculinization through his brutal colonial adventures, for whose love he endures beatings, stalking, and all the other hardships of his quest to make her his wife, is rendered more dependent as Walter grows more powerful.

What is the narrative consciousness' attitude toward the images that it has created? Is it neutrally recording gender stereotypes — or is it endorsing or critiquing them? What is its opinion of the helpless heroine whom it presents as inspiringly lovely; of the association of female intelligence and agency with physical ugliness and unsettling sexiness; of the revulsion that the spectacle of an active, thinking woman seemed to induce in the conventional hero; and of her taming? What does it think of the aggregation of power, siphoned from the women, into its hero, who, unlike the arch-villain, uses it in socially acceptable forms? Some critics interpret the portraits as sympathetic to the woman's plight,[7] believing that the narrative consciousness was indicting the narrow sex-gender system for confining and silencing the woman as much as for hazing and toughening the man.

In the interpretation developed here, however, the women characters merely serve as thematic reflections of the primary male process. The narrative consciousness is not unsympathetic, but the women's suffering is simply not its principle concern. In contemplating the split between the passive and the active woman, between the embodied and the disembodied, the speaking and the silenced, the confined and the free, it may well be more concerned with the completeness of its own erotic satisfactions and its own ambivalence over the costs of male power than with the woman's subjective experience. Fundamentally its fervent imaginings work to legitimize not her identity in the gender system but its own.

By the last scene all the monstrous imbalances and mismatches are resolved; the narrative consciousness' ego figure is no longer wandering in a wilderness of frighteningly mismatched parts, unidentifiable conglomerates, and eerie blanks. Power has been conventionally distributed at last. Everybody onstage has an identifiable, conventional English gender role and secure class privileges. The imagery no longer derives from gothic horror or fairy tale's psychological primitivism. Everyone is securely settled in the comfortable, familiar domestic realism of hearth and family, here blessed with a particularly happy combination of middle-class values and aristocratic wealth.[8] The new, hard-won, reassuring clarity of identities is affirmed by the snippet of conversation allotted to the figures in this final family portrait:

> Marian ... held up the child, kicking and crowing in her arms. "Do you know who this is, Walter?" she asked, with bright tears of happiness gathering in her eyes.
>
> "Even *my* bewilderment has its limits," I replied. "I think I can still answer for knowing my own child."
>
> "Child!" she exclaimed. "Do you talk in that familiar manner of one of the landed gentry of England? Are you aware, when I present this illustrious baby to your notice, in whose presence you stand? Evidently not! Let me make two eminent personages known to one another: Mr. Walter Hartright — *the Heir of Limmeridge*" [626–27].

At last a riddle about an identity can be easily solved. No one need track down foreign villains, or brave the hazards of the barbarian wilderness, or escape from a madhouse, or incinerate usurpers, to prove whom this new

Walter Hartright legitimately is. And yet, even in this moment of certainty, there's a residue of ambiguity: Which Walter does Marian name as heir — the father or the son? This ambiguity implies that the hero, though his infant son is technically the heir, is himself reborn into a new identity. He has come into possession of all that he — a successful and powerful real man at last, a married British aristocrat and lord of lady, lad, and lands — could desire.

But by ending with forcing the father to recognize the name and superior rank of his son, the narrative consciousness almost seems to be muttering *sotto voce* that one does it for the children — one goes through all the identity loss inherent to getting married to legitimize *them* (something Collins never did for his — and they suffered for it). In that way, as in so many others, this narrative consciousness — animated by its Italianophile, misshapen, unwed bigamist genius author — has, through its imagined test case, confirmed its subterranean doubts.

This novel, then, has depicted the narrative consciousness's anxieties, aroused by heterosexual love and the possibility of marriage, about accommodating itself to gender conventions. These seemingly require that a husband must be indubitably British, rich, virile, and assertive, and a wife must be a voiceless, passive, captive, infantilized blank. Otherwise the man, like Pesca, is a ridiculous, powerless, and unmarriageable pariah, and the woman, like Anne, will be called mad. Both will hardly find language — one speaks Italian, the other purple poetry — for their unutterable warnings about the illegitimacy of the system's claims. In the narrative consciousness's fearful and angry view, marriage is nothing but robbery, a theft of identity as well as property, and normative gender identity develops though a course of shock therapy so extreme that it borders on the criminal. That is the real crime no real court will prosecute, so the trial must be staged in the fictional courtroom of this novel. The verdict of guilty-as-charged perhaps aims to legitimize a more realistic happily-ever-after, one not attained through shocks.

Notes

1. Pesca, Fosco, Marian, Mme. Fosco, Anne.
2. *The Madwoman in the Attic*, especially Chapter 2 after page 72.
3. Other critics, of course, propose similar reading strategies. For example, Wayne Booth in *The Rhetoric of Fiction* notes that the author "creates ... an implied version of 'himself'"; Booth bemoans the inadequacy of existing terms such as persona, mask, and narrator (70–75). Georges Poulet of the Geneva School posits the existence of the "cogito," an intellectual entity created out of the opinions expressed in the text; he empha-

sizes intellectual content rather than psychological processes. And Freud in "The Poet and Daydreaming" asserts broadly that all the characters in a fiction represent parts of the author.

4. Cannon Schmitt being a notable exception (298–300). He describes Pesca as follows: "Dwarfish, excitable, exaggerated in gestures and sentiment — in short, transparently and thoroughly un–English — Pesca is nonetheless bent on 'doing his utmost to turn himself into an Englishman'" (300) — an effort presented as futile and therefore ridiculous. For more on Schmitt's work, see note 8.

5. Ellis's (in)famous conduct manual, *The Women of England, Their Social Duties, and Domestic Habits* (1839), insists that women ought to selflessly serve male relatives so as to elevate the nation's moral character. Madame Fosco's story ironically contests that causality.

6. Miller observes that after Walter concludes, "Let Marian end our Story" (646), she does not actually say anything: "[W]hat follows is dead silence" (190).

7. See Barickman, MacDonald, and Stark, *Corrupt Relations: Dickens, Thackeray, Trollope, Collins, and the Victorian Sexual System* (1982).

8. Schmitt, in an analysis that complements Miller's, explores assumptions about the nationalist component of identity, with a nod to class. Schmitt concludes that this novel revises British nationalist ideology by incorporating atavistic aristocratic desires into the contemporary middle-class ideal.

Works Cited

Booth, Wayne. *The Rhetoric of Fiction*. Chicago: Chicago University Press, 1961.

Butler, Judith. *Gender Trouble: Feminism and the Subversion of Identity*. New York: Routledge, 1990.

Collins, Wilkie. *The Woman in White*. 1860. Ed. Matthew Sweet. London: Penguin, 1999.

Ellis, Sarah Stickney. *Women of England, Their Social Duties, and Domestic Habits*. 1839. In *Victorian Prose*. Ed. Rosemary J. Mundhenk and LuAnn McCracken Fletcher. New York: Columbia University Press, 1999.

Freud, Sigmund. "The Relation of the Poet to Day-Dreaming." 1908. *On Creativity and the Unconscious*. Ed. Benjamin Nelson. New York: Harper & Row, 1958.

Gilbert, Sandra, and Susan Gubar. *The Madwoman in the Attic: The Woman Writer and the Nineteenth-Century Imagination*. New Haven: Yale University Press, 1979.

Heller, Tamar. *Dead Secrets: Wilkie Collins and the Female Gothic*. New Haven: Yale University Press, 1992.

Miller, D. A. "*Cage aux folles*: Sensation and Gender in Wilkie Collins's The Woman in White." *The Novel and the Police*. Berkeley: University California Press, 1988. 146–191.

Page, Norman, ed. *Wilkie Collins: The Critical Heritage*. London: Routledge, 1974.

Peters, Catherine. *The King of Inventors: A Life of Wilkie Collins*. Princeton: Princeton University Press, 1991.

Pykett, Lyn, ed. *Wilkie Collins*. New York: St. Martin's, 1998.

Schmitt, Cannon. "Alien Nation: Gender, Genre, and English Nationality in Wilkie Collins's *The Woman in White*." *Genre* XXVI (1993): 283–310.

Sprawson, Charles. "Death of a Champion." Rev. of *The Crossing: The Glorious Tragedy of the First Man to Swim the English Channel*, by Kathy Watson. *New York Review of Books* 20 Sept. 2001: 26–7.

Hysterical Sensations:
Bodies in Action in Wilkie Collins's The Woman in White

Elizabeth Anderman

Wilkie Collins's *The Woman in White* is the story of a young art teacher, Walter Hartright, who falls in love with a woman above his station, the beautiful and innocent Laura Fairlie, and ultimately marries her. Hartright is only able to do so, however, after her mercenary and sadistic husband, Sir Percival Glyde, fakes Laura's death to get her money by putting the body of her double Ann Catherick (the mysterious woman in white of the title) in a grave bearing Laura's name and incarcerating Laura in a madhouse under Ann's name. Though the story has been fruitfully interpreted as a complex indictment of Victorian marriage laws[1] and practices of domestic abuse,[2] I am interested in exploring how the novel's use of multiple first person narratives affects the body of the reader. Though the reader formulates a coherent narrative for the novel, he[3] can only do so by suppressing the tension between association with and dissociation from the varying first person narratives. The cost of this sublimation is a kind of reading hysteria, which pits the intellectual pleasure of solving the novel's central mystery against the excesses of physicality, that earn this novel its preeminent rank among nineteenth century sensation novels.

In the mid-nineteenth century hysteria was considered the disease of a disordered female sexuality. English physicians attempted to cure their patients with a number of surgical practices, including clitorectomies, cervical removals, and hysterectomies, which all attempted to restore "propriety" to female sexuality (Moussaief-Masson). The sexualized and hysterical female body resisted dominant sexual codes in part because it was read as an active — hence masculine — body that needed to be returned to its normal gender roles. However, during the 1860s the French neurologist Jean Martin Charcot won international recognition for his research that showed hysteria could also be a male condition. His research, which included the photographing of hundreds of hysterical patients[4] in the various manifestations of their disease, opened the door for Freud who, in his essay on Dora, argued that hysteria is the physical manifestation of repressed traumatic sexual events. In other words hysteria is a condition where the body is reliving an experience that the mind has erased in favor of a more palatable narrative. It is my contention that the reader of *The Woman in White* experiences reading as a kind of conflict between these two discourses on hysteria. On the one hand the novel plays with questions of gender identity. The first person narratives allow the reader to experience the physical responses of men and women as if he were a kind of hybrid body able to enjoy all kinds of disorienting physical sensations. On the other hand, as the preamble of the novel insists, the purpose of reading this novel is to construct a narrative whole which contains all the disparate elements within the text. The reader then is forced to create a narrative which represses the physical excitement of reading, in favor of the rational. I propose that "hysterical" best defines the tension between these two simultaneous reading strategies the novel creates — somatic and psychic.

Meeting the Woman in White: The First Moment of Hysterical Reading

Hysteria surfaces in the opening narrative of *The Woman in White*, the first time Walter Hartright meets the woman in white: "Every drop of blood in my body was brought to a stop by the touch of a hand laid lightly and suddenly on my shoulder.... I was far too seriously startled by the suddenness with which this extraordinary apparition stood before me ... to ask what she wanted" (14). What I find particularly provocative is that the description of Hartright's encounter is remarkably like the description of a hysterical patient. He is so overcome with emotion that he literally freezes and becomes rigid and speechless. Charcot's photographs document hundreds of instances where hysterical women became cataleptic, one part of their body rigidly fixed (hand, eyebrow, mouth, leg) while the rest moves normally. Charcot tried to mechanically reproduce this cataleptic state through hypnotic suggestion and by having his patients enter a completely dark room in the hopes that the sudden illumination of the flash would startle his patients into a paralysis which the resultant photograph would document (Baer 41). The white hand coming out of the darkness is like that flash in the dark room — startling the patient, Hartright, into temporary paralysis.

The association between Hartright and a hysterical patient is further developed when Hartright finds himself walking the streets, completely disoriented, after Ann leaves him. "I found myself mechanically walking forward a few paces; now stopping again absently. At one moment, I found myself doubting the reality of my own adventure..." (20). The encounter with the woman in white puts Hartright outside himself; his body acting mechanically without his will being able to control it in any way. He is described like one of Charcot's patients, who after being hypnotically put in a hysterical state, acts out her disease like a kind of automata. Blanche Wittman was the most famous of these patients, the Parisian intellectual elite coming to see this hysterical "Lady Macbeth" who pretended to stab people in her hysterical state. As Felicia McCarren notes in her essay on hysteria, hypnosis, and dance, "Blanche in a state of somnambulism, had obediently performed the most blood-thirsty tasks, 'shooting,' 'stabbing,' and 'poisoning.' The notables withdrew from a room littered with fictive corpses" (McCarren 766). According to Charcot her condition was not a simple dream but a lived dream ("Ce n'est pas un simple rêve. C'est un rêve vecu" [Didi-Huberman 287]). Hartright's wandering accompanied by his own doubt of the reality of the adventure make the whole sequence seem dream-like, or like a kind of lived hysterical dream. The dream-like quality is so complete that it disorients Hartright to the point that he questions his own identity, asking "Was I Walter Hartright?" (17). Like a hysteric patient Walter's body and mind are completely at odds, creating a fundamental narrative instability, since the narrator does not even know if he is himself. Here the breakdown of Walter's narrative works directly toward Clare Kahane's argument that hysteria is represented in many nineteenth century texts through a breakdown in narrative voice: "Whether first-person or third-person, whether inside or outside the tale they narrate, the narrative voices of the texts ... can be characterized by their inability to sustain a neutral and consistent subject position, by their anxious subjection to ... the passions of the voice" (viii).

The unstable narrative voice is revealed and to a certain extent translated to the reader every time Hartright reads or encounters another first person narrative. His reading example demonstrates the hysteria of reading, particularly after the mystery of the woman in white has been introduced.

When Marian Halcombe reads aloud the letter which indicates who the woman in white might be, Hartright responds, "I started up from the ottoman, before Miss Halcombe could pronounce the next words. A thrill of the same feeling which ran through me when the touch was laid upon my shoulder on the lonely high-road chilled me again" (50). Here reading forces Hartright to experience a range of physical responses. He starts, feels a thrill, and is chilled. Reading creates an affective response, disguised as an intellectual one. His belief that he has solved a mystery forces his body to respond. Similarly, after he reads Ann Catherick's letter describing her foreboding dream about Laura's impending marriage, he questions his sanity. "I began to doubt whether my own faculties were not in danger of losing their balance. It seemed almost like a monomania to be tracing back everything strange that happened, everything unexpected that was said, always to the same hidden source and the same sinister influence" (68). Here the reader is in a precarious position. On the one had the pacing of the scene encourages the reader to feel Hartright's same excitement that he is being lead towards a solution. On the other the reader can recognize and deride the excess of Hartright's response. Either way however the reader participates in the novel's economy of affect, accepting or denying Hartright's affective response, based on the reader's personal physical sense of the appropriateness of Hartright's reaction. In other words, the only way the reader can gauge what is happening is by measuring, as Miller would have it, his "accelerated heart rate and respiration." The reader, like Hartright, gauges how to respond to what he reads through his physical response.

When the solicitor, Vincent Gilmore, takes over the narrative from Hartright, the reader has a brief moment of hope that rational adjudication of the facts will be possible, for Gilmore undermines Hartright's concerns and perspectives by reading the situation completely practically. His pragmatism temporarily put to rest the mysterious questions that the woman in white has created. Gilmore is comforted and reassured by his own legal sense and the protections he believes the law can afford. And yet, because of the reader's involvement with the first narrative and the resulting physical reaction of the reader's body when the hand comes out of the dark, the reader both questions if Gilmore is rational and simultaneously cannot quite take Gilmore seriously because he is so rational. Ultimately however, Gilmore's own sense of narrative authority is also undermined when Mr. Fairlie refuses his legal counsel, leaving Laura vulnerable to the worst kind of financial abuse from her husband. Gilmore warns against the dangers of abandoning the law by saying, "No daughter of mine should have been married to any man alive under such a settlement as I was compelled to make for Laura Fairlie" (140). The legal system fails and it is clear that nothing good will come of it. The reader then is in the problematic position of being a judge without recourse to legal systems or language. The only kind of adjudication possible is that of the senses — or affect.

When Marian Halcombe, half sister to Laura, takes over the narrative she is particularly troubled by her loss of reason and judgment. Because she was unable to see the intensity of the attachment between Laura and Walter, she feels unable to judge. Emotion, hidden in her sister's body, has disrupted Marian's impressive faculties. "The discovery that I have committed such an error in judgment as this, makes me hesitate about everything else. I hesitate about Sir Percival, in the face of the plainest proofs. I hesitate even in speaking to Laura" (141). Plain proofs no longer work for Marian. There is no judgment. There is only the embodied language of attraction which she cannot read. And yet, it is impossible not to relate to Marian. The text has set her up, much as the reader has been set up. She has heard both Hartright's discourse of emotions and Gilmore's of law and finds herself disoriented. Like Hartright in the presence of the woman in white she can no longer be sure of her own identity. It is as if the hysterical response has spread from Hartright, to Gilmore, to Marian. The hysteria spreads to the reader as he tries to contain the perspectives of these varying narrative voices. However, the reader like Marian hesitates, trapped between intellect and visceral response, not knowing whether to trust the body or the mind.

Miller and others have shown that Marian's androgyny is responsible for the visceral response the reader feels when Hartright sees her "masculine" face for the first time. Her body is somehow at odds with itself— neither one thing nor the other with any kind of clarity. Marian's body looks ideally feminine, while her face is remarkably masculine — a hermaphroditism that can be read as a kind of hysterical body. In his work on the history of madness, psychologist and art historian, Sander Gilman describes the tradition of the pictorial representation of madwomen as representing a tension between body and face. In the paintings, etchings, and photogravures of the mid–Victorian period, the madwoman's hair is untamed and she is partially undressed, usually in a generic hospital gown. When she is supposedly cured the representation changes and she is dressed in appropriate and conservative feminine attire. Her hair is done and her body is remarkably controlled. In fact it is her ability to *look* like a "normal" woman that marks her transition back to "sanity." The insistence that normality can only be established when gender codes are adhered, to points to madness as a time when those codes are transgressed in some way. Perhaps this is why representations of madwomen, particularly in the 1850s photographs of the English doctor Hugh Diamond, seem to masculinize the faces of the patients. Marian's hermaphroditism can therefore be read also as a representation of a kind of underlying madness. The fact that Marian is one of the most appealing characters in the novel, who best represents the kind of ideal reader that the preamble imagines, encourages the reader to relate to her. The madness therefore insidiously spreads from the woman in white, to Hartright, to Marian, and into the reader particularly as he is positioned in relation to the beginning facts much in the same way she is.

Charcot's photographs of hysterical women add a kind of overt sexuality to the representation of the madwoman. For example Augustine, one of the most photographed patients in the collection, is represented in a series of "extases" — where her hospital gown is provocatively loose, her hair is down, and her arms are stretched out in amorous supplication. Charcot attempted to use the distancing of photography to separate himself from the overt sexuality of Augustine's language which accompanied the photographs. He tried merely to look at her body in order to understand her disease. However, even today, her desire leaps from the frame. There is something wildly and erotically appealing about this woman who is being photographed in the throes of her disease. Perhaps it is the intensity of the desire which has nowhere to go but which seeks recognition that draws the viewer in. Perhaps it is because, as Susan Sontag describes it, each picture is a way of appropriating time and space — each picture is an assault on the other, as we attempt to make our meaning, our life most true, most visible. The photographs are a vibrant representation of one sexually charged moment where Augustine tries to represent her desire and inhabit it. The sexuality of the hysterical patient is important here, particularly since Marian's sexual appeal to the male reader is precisely because of her gender ambiguity. However, the hysteria of Marian's body is equally appealing, particularly to the female reader. Perhaps because hysteria was for so long considered a female disease, the representation of the hysterical body conjures up intense female desire. It makes the woman reader aware of her own desire; her pleasure in looking, through Walter's eyes, at Marian's perfect body; her excitement at discovering that this perfect body has a "masculine" face. Here female to female desire is mitigated by Marian's face and by her hysteria. The female reader can only distance herself from her own desire for the female body, protect herself from that threat, by recontextualizing it within the confines of hysterical discourse.

Desire and Destruction

It is my contention that the hysterical discourse allows the female reader's desire for and association with Marian to escalate until the dramatic scene where Count Fosco, the novel's corpulent villain, reads Marian's diary. Here, in the gap between Marian's narrative voice and Fosco's a kind of narrative rape occurs. On an intellectual level, the reader is shocked because Marian's most intimate thoughts are read by the man she is trying to outwit. The pacing of her diary has kept the reader frantically turning pages hoping that she will be able to rescue Laura from her increasingly dangerous situation, so when Fosco's oily and condescending language takes over the reader cannot help but feel defeated and violated. And yet, the reader keeps going — reads Fosco's narrative with anxious attention, determined to know what Fosco is going to do with the knowledge he has gained. In that move to continue, the reader begins to associate with Fosco, and may go so far as to feel pleasure in inhabiting the transgressive voice of the villain. But in that move the reader performs a dangerous act of repression, where the violence of the intrusion of Fosco's voice is overlooked in favor of a coherent narrative. The intellectual desire to get to the end sublimates the initial visceral response. Here the reader, not the characters, most obviously performs what Freud argues is central to hysteria, the repression of a traumatic sexual event.

The sexual transgression of Fosco's act of reading is particularly evident because of the way Marian's narrative focuses more and more intensely on her physical condition, in the paragraphs before Fosco enters. Her body becomes more and more important as she details its sensations in response to her fever. "I am afraid of this heat that parches my skin. I am afraid of the creeping and throbbing that I feel in my head..." (297). And, "I am shivering again — shivering, from head to foot, in the summer air" (298). Her body keeps her from writing and ultimately annihilates her intellectual activity. "My head — I am sadly afraid of my head. I can write but the lines all run together. I see the words. Laura — I can write Laura, and see I write it. Eight of nine — which was it?" (298). Her inability to write and the increasingly disjointed nature of her narrative forces the reader to focus on her body. The reader must hope, as Marian does, that she will be able to overcome her body and both seem to be involved in a battle against time, hoping that Marian will stay coherent long enough to thwart the villains. She fails as the final words to her incredibly coherent and intelligent narrative demonstrate how completely she has become the victim of her body. "So cold, so cold — oh that rain last night! — and the strokes of the clock, the strokes I can't count, keep striking in my head —" (298).

The reader relates to Marian's embodiment because the disjointed nature of the narrative and Marian's inability to control her own narrative voice are paced in such a way as to excite the senses of the reader. The reader rushes through the dashes and gaps hoping to discover that Marian has overcome her body. The lines run together as the reader tries to make sense of the repetitive language and circular images. So, like Marian the reader is breathless and agitated — embodied. Therefore when Fosco inserts himself into the pages of the diary, he enters a written space where both Marian and the reader are focused on their bodies, making his transgression overtly physical. He himself underlines the physical nature of his intrusion when he insists that his wife return the diary to Marian's desk. This eerily evokes how he took the diary from Marian's desk — placing his body at the scene — his hands within the pages of her book. Once he is done with the book, her written body, he can return it to his wife — an economy of exchange which seems to surreptitiously point to the sexual nature of his "writing." It also sets up a parallel between his wife and Marian's hands — as if his pleasure is measured in the quality of their hands. He also asserts the pleasurable nature of his violation: "The illness of our excellent Miss Halcombe has afforded me the opportunity of enjoying an unexpected intellectual pleasure" (298). Though he claims to have experienced an "intellectual" pleasure the complete vulnerability of Marian's body in the previous sentence evokes a much more carnal pleasure.

Here, Fosco evokes Charcot and his photographic reading practice. Though Charcot's photographs were taken within the context of supposedly benign scientific research, and though they were helpful in defining the ravages of hysteria as legitimate disease, they are hard to look at because they so intimately represent the pain of another human being. Looking at them feels like one is participating in some kind of visual assault on the unsuspecting body. Though Charcot believed his work could be completely intellectual (like Fosco's reading) because the photographs distanced him from the sexual content of some of his patient's attacks, the incredible physical-ity of the women in the photographs makes it impossible to look at them today without responding to their intensity of their sensations. Looking at unsuspecting bodies, bodies in pain, becomes a kind of sadistic scopophilia, where the viewer receives sexual pleasure merely by looking. The series on the patient Augustine, the "extases," are particularly erotic because one has the sense that all is not revealed. The series of images implies that she is mov-ing, performing some type of dance of the seven veils that will reveal her naked self, and yet all we can see is her rigid — posed form. Studying her pictures makes one want to reconstruct her movements, and reinvent what-ever emotions or arousal she was feeling. The time lapse between pictures acts like a textual gap, which invites interpretation.

Similarly the reader of *The Woman in White* must reconstruct Marian's body as her fever takes over in the final sequence and Fosco's physical intru-sion into her space, making it impossible for the reader not to imagine his body enjoying the "intellectual" pleasures of reading. Here the reader is in a precarious position. On the one hand she feels Fosco's intrusion as phys-ical violation because she has been so closely associated with Marian's body. On the other hand she is forced to associate with and participate in Fosco's violation as his narrative voice takes over. The gap between the two narra-tives marks the narrative rape which the reader is obliged to fill by partici-pating in both sides. She must be violator and violated at the same time — an untenable position for any one. This, I would argue, is the sexual trauma that the reader must repress in order to continue reading. The ensuing phys-ical manifestation of hysteria comes, when the reader closes the book and re-accepts a normal gender role. For if the reader has desired Marian because of her gender ambiguity and participated in her sexual violation because of another moment of multiple gender identities, then re-entering a rigidly coded world of sexual behavior represents the paralysis of this highly mobile and fluid textual gender.

Notes

1. See Marlene Tromp, *The Private Rod: Marital Violence, Sensation, and the Law in Victorian Britain* (Charlottesville: University Press of Virginia, 2000).

2. See Jenny Bourne Taylor, *In the Secret Theatre of Home: Wilkie Collins, Sensation Narrative, and Nineteenth-Century Psychology* (New York: Routledge, 1988) and Anthrea Trodd, *Domestic Crime in the Victorian Novel* (London: Macmillan, 1989).

3. Here I provisionally accept D.A. Miller's argument that the assumed reader of the sensation novel was male.

4. It is intriguing that though Charcot became famous for including men within hysteria most of his subsequent research focused almost exclusively on female patients. Thus the collection of photographs that detail his work include very few men. Instead there is female after female body in pain, contorted by her disease.

Works Cited

Baer, Ulrich. "Photography and Hysteria: Toward a Poetics of the Flash." *The Yale Journal of Criticism,* volume 7, no. 1. Massachusetts: Blackwell Publishers, 1994. 41–77.

Collins, Wilkie. *The Woman in White.* 1860. New York: Bantam Books, 1985.

Didi-Huberman, Georges. *Invention de L'Hysterie: Charcot et l'iconographie photographique de la Salpêtrière.* Paris: Macula, 1982.

Freud, Sigmund. *Dora: An Analysis of a Case of Hysteria.* 1905. Philip Rieff, ed. New York: Touchstone Books, 1997.

_____."The Uncanny." 1919. *The Standard Edition of the Complete Psychological Works of Sigmund Freud.* Vol. XVII. James Strachey, ed. London: Hogarth Press, 1953.

Gilman, Sander. "The Image of the Hysteric." *Hysteria Before Freud.* Berkeley: University of California Press, 1993.

_____.*Seeing the Insane.* New York: J. Wiley: Brunner/Mazel. 1982.

Kahane, Claire. *Passions of the Voice: Hysteria, Narrative, and the Figure of the Speaking Woman, 1850–1915.* Baltimore: Johns Hopkins University Press, 1995.

McCarren, Felicia. "The 'Symptomatic Act' Circa 1900: Hysteria, Hypnosis, Electricity, Dance." *Critical Inquiry* 21 (Summer 1995). Chicago: University of Chicago Press, 1995. 748–774.

Miller, D.A. "*Cage aux folles*: Sensation and Gender in Wilkie Collins's *The Woman in White.*" *The Novel and the Police.* Berkeley: University of California Press, 1988.

Moussaieff Masson, Jeffrey. *A Dark Science: Women, Sexuality and Psychiatry in the 19th Century.* New York: Farrar, Strauss, Giroux, 1986.

Pykett, Lyn. *The 'Improper' Feminine: The Women's Sensation Novel and the New Woman Writing.* London: Routledge, 1992.

Taylor, Jenny Bourne. *Embodied Selves: Anthology of Psychological Texts 1830–1890.* New York: Oxford University Press, 1998.

_____. *In the Secret Theatre of Home: Wilkie Collins, Sensation Narrative, and Nineteenth-Century Psychology.* New York: Routledge, 1988.

Trodd, Anthrea. *Domestic Crime in the Victorian Novel.* London: Macmillan, 1989.

Tromp, Marlene. *The Private Rod: Marital Violence, Sensation, and the Law in Victorian Britain.* Charlottesville: University Press of Virginia, 2000.

PART TWO

The Colonial Context of
Gothic and Sensation Fiction

Sensations Down Under*:
Australia's Seismic Charge in Great Expectations and Lady Audley's Secret

Julie M. Barst

The first fleet of convict ships from England arrived in Australia in 1788, beginning an eight-decade era of transportation to the land down under and symbolizing the creation of a striking dichotomy between the evils of colonization and the economic opportunities and benefits of empire building. Australia became a land tainted with dangerous criminals and the exploitation of land and people, yet also offered these criminals the hope for rehabilitation while simultaneously offering England a new economic outpost in the South Pacific. This contrast raises important questions about the overall image of Australia in literature during the nineteenth century. What forces led to such drastic differences, and how were these differences played out in the consciousness of England?

An analysis of representations of Britain's southernmost colony makes clear that this contradictory image was prevalent during the turbulent decade of the 1860s. This single decade was crucial in the transformation of Australia's image, as it saw the previously dark underworld of convicts and "savagery" finally combined with more positive portrayals of economic advancement and rehabilitation. This decade also saw the rapid rise to popularity of the sensation novel, and Australia's dual image was successfully converted into seismic charges for the sensation market, with two main goals in mind. I argue that the mystery and danger of the colony was advanced to fulfill the expectations of the sensation market, while the opportunistic image of Australia was advanced to justify and promote Great Britain's imperialism

*Originally published in Australasian Victorian Studies Journal

to its citizens. Through this dual literary representation, Australia became a colonial space for the analysis of ideological contradictions inherent to what Fredric Jameson refers to as England's "political unconscious" (167). An analysis of the works of Jameson and Freud enables a theoretical framework through which to read two examples of Australia's sensational representation.

The processes and effects of colonization are inherently complex and many-sided. Although the results of colonization were obviously brutal for the indigenous peoples of Australia, my focus here is the effects of imperialism upon the metropole of England, and the ways in which such effects influenced and were influenced by the sensation literature of the 1860s. The dark image of Australia involved both the harsh convict settlements known for chain gangs and floggings, as well as the "free" settlers who were mainly ex-convicts themselves. Until the 1850s, very few British citizens sought passage to this country of their own accord, since the prevailing opinion in England was that, as Patrick Brantlinger states, "Australia's first colonizers" were themselves 'white savages'" (110). Since the hopes for reformation and subsequent reintroduction to British society were slight, the British were happy to leave these criminals where it felt they belonged — on the far side of the world.

Freud's discussion of "the uncanny" can shed light on the workings of this process for the Victorians. He defines the uncanny as "in reality nothing new or alien, but something which is familiar and old-established in the mind and which has become alienated from it only through the process of repression" (47). Transported convicts were indeed "familiar" and "old-established" for the Victorians, who heard of crimes and captures in news reports, saw the hulks moored in harbors and knew that those aboard awaited passage to Australia, and were aware of the debates surrounding transportation. Still, the Victorians sought to repress all knowledge of those sent away, but were forced to acknowledge their existence when the convicts figuratively "returned" to the consciousness of society through literature. Craufurd Goodwin states that when gold was discovered in Victoria in 1851, this information "flowed from Australia to Britain quickly and in a variety of forms ... which ranged from sensationalist pamphlets" to more detailed publications, creating a "new El Dorado" in the minds of the British (405–6). Australia finally became as Catherine Hall states, "a place for white settlers in the English imagination" (33). New waves of emigrants poured into the colony seeking their fortunes in gold as well as in cattle and sheep farming, and the literature of England found a new location for many characters who could never realistically prosper in England.

So what ideological purpose did this combination of positive and negative representations of Australia serve for the British government and its people? In a time when the British Empire was expanding rapidly, serious concerns arose as to the validity and the handling of its claim to these "new" lands. Yet also visible were the opportunities for economic advancement on both the micro and macro levels: individuals who traveled there had excellent chances to earn money or to reform, while the country of England itself was benefiting tremendously from the riches of its farthest-flung colony. Because of this dual representation, Australia became what Fredric Jameson calls an "insoluble logical paradox" (167) for the citizens of England, and they sought a solution to these inherent contradictions. Jameson's concept of the "political unconscious" (167) can be applied to the ideological workings of literary representations for the Victorians. Because literature functions as a "symbolic enactment of the social within the formal and the aesthetic," literary representations of Australia allowed Britain to find "the imaginary resolution of a real contradiction" (77). By displacing their concerns about the expansion of empire onto fictional characters and events, people were able to view both the positive and negative impacts of imperialism through situations that were not real. Thus, Australia functioned as a zone in the British imagination that upheld the ideologies of imperialism, instead of an existing place where such horrors and opportunities occurred on a daily basis. "The aesthetic act is itself ideological," writes Jameson, "and the production of aesthetic or narrative form is to be seen as an ideological act in its own right, with the function of inventing imaginary or formal 'solutions' to unresolvable social contradictions" (79). The "political unconscious" of Britain during the 1860's was fed such imaginary solutions time and again in its literature, and the dominant ideology that imperialism works for the good of all was thereby upheld and maintained.

By analyzing two representative works from the sensation novels of the 1860s, *Great Expectations* and *Lady Audley's Secret*[1], one can begin to understand how these contradictory images of Australia functioned to produce sensation and "the uncanny," as well as how the dichotomy played out in the political unconscious of England. Charles Dickens's numerous portrayals of Australia managed to create a lasting image of the colony. One of his novels most instrumental in doing so was *Great Expectations*, published in 1861. Although Dickens is not commonly grouped with the core sensation authors of the 1860s, many critics, including Harvey Peter Sucksmith, feel that "Dickens may be correctly described as a 'sensation novelist'" (145). In fact, many critics have explicitly compared his techniques to those of Wilkie Collins (Lonoff, Hardy). *Great Expectations* involves many similar elements as the most popular sensation novels, including crime, suspense, danger, and mystery. It also nicely fits Kathleen Tillotson's definition of sensation fiction as "novels with a secret" (xv), here the secret being the true identity of Pip's benefactor. But the darker side of Australia is portrayed mainly through Magwitch, the escaped convict who terrifies Pip in the opening scene, threatening to kill him if he does not rob his sister's pantry and steal a file from Joe's forge to cut off his convict chains. Pip's forced association with Magwitch produces inestimable guilt for the young boy: "Under the weight of my wicked secret, I pondered whether the Church would be powerful enough to shield me from the vengeance of the terrible young man [Magwitch], if I divulged to that establishment" (23). He immediately begins trying to repress the memory of "his" convict. As Peter Brooks writes, "The fellowship with the convict ... will remain with Pip, but in a state of repression, as what he will later call 'that spell of my childhood' — an unavowable memory" (484). Because this association was stained with both the crimes of Magwitch and his own crimes of robbery and theft from his family, Pip desperately attempts to repress all memories pertaining to the convict.

In spite of these attempts at repression, circumstances keep reminding Pip of his association with Magwitch. Pip hears the guns of the hulk nearby signaling another convict escape, and both the leg iron and the file stolen from Joe resurface for different purposes. David Trotter writes, "From the outset, the taint of prison and crime clings to Pip [as] the re-emergence of the past in the future, about the return of the repressed" (xii). Pip's repressed "friend" constantly returns in other guises, a perfect example of Freud's "uncanny." Even though Magwitch cannot come back as himself until much later in the text, he returns in these other symbolic ways to remind Pip of his guilty youth, which bears out Freud's remark that "an uncanny effect is often and easily produced when the distinction between imagination and reality is effaced, as when ... a symbol takes over the full functions of the thing it symbolizes" (50). Pip's repression sought to displace his experiences with the convict into imaginary existence, yet the constant return of what Brooks calls the symbolic "convict-communion material" (487) never let him forget.

Much later in the text, Pip discovers that Magwitch is his true benefactor, which Brooks reads as a moment of psychic release when "the latent becomes manifest ... as a painful forcing through of layers of repression" (491–92). A large part of Pip's repulsion towards Magwitch centers on the fact that his convict had been transported to Australia under a life sentence and the dark images of Australia circulating around England leads Pip to feel ashamed at his further association with such a brutal, low-class, and harsh convict. Pip had believed that the money that made him a gentleman had come from the upper-class pocket of Miss Havisham, but instead it now appears to be tainted with convict blood, and his anger and shame makes him turn on Magwitch: "The abhorrence in which I held the man, the dread I had of him, the repugnance with which I shrank from him, could not have been exceeded if he had been some terrible beast" (*GE* 319–20). Magwitch tells of how he earned this money for Pip as a "sheep-farmer, stock-breeder, other trades besides, away in the new world ... many a thousand mile of stormy water off from this" (317) after earning his ticket-of-leave in Australia. Not only did Pip have to face the disappointment that Miss Havisham (and especially Estella) had nothing to do with his expectations, but he had also to face the reality that a convict toiling in Australia, the land of punishment, brutality, crime and savagery, had funded his rise to a gentleman.

Dickens chose to set Magwitch's prosperity in Australia for several reasons, all of which create sensational effects for the readers of the text. The constant allusions to and reappearance of Brooks' "convict-communion material" set up suspense for the readers, who wait and wonder when the convict will reappear in the story. In addition, by setting up readerly sympathy and identification with Pip, Dickens prepares us to experience the sensations of the uncanny just as Pip does. Therefore, the overall negative image of Australia is advanced in order to produce shocking and suspenseful energy for the reader through the effects of the uncanny, whereby *Great Expectations* finds success in what Henry Mansel, in his famous definition of sensation fiction, calls "preaching to the nerves" (482).

But Dickens also had other, more positive goals in mind with the portrayal of Australia in *Great Expectations*. After earning his ticket-of-leave, Magwitch is able to earn a small fortune, enough to fund Pip's rise to gentlemanly status, and he returns to England under the risk of death to see "his" gentleman. This prosperity for an ex-convict would not have been possible in England, since few employers were willing to risk their reputations and businesses to hire such dangerous men. Had he not been transported, Magwitch would probably have returned to his former ways of poaching and begging upon release, but instead he finds honest work in the colony and uses his money for acceptable purposes. Michael Hollington states that "in the great return scene it is Magwitch, for all the imprisonment in class-thinking that he shares with Pip, who cuts the more attractive figure ... his death has a stoic dignity" (30). Magwitch's transportation to Australia results in a much more dignified, conscious human being, one who seeks not only his own happiness, but that of others. "Dickens too seems to become aware ... that alongside the horrors of the colony were also potential opportunities — often far surpassing those on offer in Britain — that many convicts might enjoy, at least once they had earned their ticket-of-leave" (17–18). Therefore, Dickens was able to portray not only the dark side of Australia through convicts and repression, but also brings out the positive ideas and opportunities associated with the colony such as rehabilitation and economic advancement. The novel promotes empire-building to the British people through such characters.

Mary Elizabeth Braddon's novel *Lady Audley's Secret* functions as another highly representative example of Australia's contradictory image in the nineteenth century. Much like Dickens does with Magwitch, Braddon chooses to represent the dark side of Australia with a character who travels to the Antipodes, only this time he goes of his own accord. George Talboys chooses to leave his young wife and baby son to make a fortune during the gold rush, but he neglects to give his family advance warning. As he tells the governess Miss Morley on the return passage to England, "I left my little girl asleep, with her baby in her arms, and with nothing but a few blotted lines to tell her why her faithful husband had deserted her" (23). Miss Morley is horrified at this revelation and exclaims, "Deserted her?" (23). George may not have been a convict, but the fact that he deserted his wife and left for a colony in the new world, regardless of noble purpose, points to his unsavoriness as a husband and father and therefore to his low moral worth as a Victorian. The fact that he travels to Australia is vital to the country's image as a place for nothing but convicts and, as Toni Johnson-Woods terms them, other "English n'er do wells" (120). He may have been involved in the empire-building activities that would benefit the macro environment of his country, but on the micro level of his family and Victorian social values, George is nothing but a deserter. Jenny Bourne Taylor argues that "there is George himself, whose fantasy of colonial conquest is a thinly disguised displacement of his own inadequacies as a husband and father" (xxxiv). George had been unable to earn enough money for his family at home; therefore he deserted them to head for the land down under.

George Talboys also functions much like Magwitch in *Great Expectations*, because one of the main characters seeks to repress his existence, yet he eventually returns when least expected (and least desired). Lady Audley desperately desires to remain detached completely from her past because after George's desertion, she left her child and changed her identity in order to marry into a higher social standing. In the opening chapter, as her new husband Michael speaks to her, she "looked away — away into another world" (15). It is obvious from the beginning that Lady Audley's mind is not with her present husband, but wandering back to previous experiences in her life. She may have been worrying that her first husband George, far away in Australia, could actually return someday and expose the truth of her bigamy and false identity. In a similar fashion, Pip could never truly hide from Magwitch, the one person he desperately sought to repress. Yet outwardly, Lady Audley displays the sort of neurotic behavior that Freud associates with repression, such as her nervous excitability and her harsh language towards Roberty Audley, the man who continuously irritates Lady Audley in his obsessive attempt to discover the truth.

Although Robert may be the detective who discovers clues for the reader, many find themselves identifying with Lady Audley, wondering about her mysterious past and how it will tie into George's disappearance. When readers discover the events that take place, they again put themselves in the position of a character and experience the uncanny through her. This conforms to Freud's idea of something familiar "which has become alienated ... through the process of repression" (47). George was obviously something familiar to Lady Audley, since he was once her husband, yet upon his return from Australia he becomes part of "that class of the frightening" (20) because he has the power to expose her true identity. Australia functions as a space whereby repressed characters can hang in the balance, awaiting their opportunity for return, their chance to produce the uncanny and sensational in both those who repressed them and the readers themselves.

The negative images of Australia in this text functions in many of the same ways as *Great Expectations* to produce sensation in the readers' bodies. Right from the start, readers question how George Talboys, returning from Australia, fits into the snug picture of family and homelife, and when he disappears he becomes a central figure for suspense and mystery for the reader. Was he murdered? Did he return to Australia in grief over his wife's death? As Robert Audley fits together the pieces of this puzzle, readers become more and more frantic to discover the truth. George is repeatedly discussed in terms of Australia, as a few brief lines of conversation between Robert and Lady Audley clearly portray. When Robert raises the issue of George's disappearance, Lady Audley innocently inquires, "You mean — the Mr. Talboys who went to Australia?" George replies: "Yes, I mean the Mr. Talboys, who I was told set out for Liverpool with the idea of going to Australia" (143). Through constant repetition, George becomes directly associated with the colony of Australia, and everything dark and sensational about its image is ingrained in the minds of readers. He becomes geographically associated with the deserter and the convict, the man so far away that everyone but Robert Audley seems perfectly happy to forget about him, especially the one person who seeks to completely repress his entire existence. The fact that he was thrown down a well by Lady Audley now seems appropriate for George's fate; because he had figuratively become Australia, the farthest-flung colony on the other side of the world, it is only proper that he should visit another type of land down under, at the bottom of Lady Audley's well.

Yet he survives this fall, mainly because of skills he had learned in Australia. He was able to escape from the well because, as he later tells Robert and Clara, "I had my Australian experiences to help me in my peril, and I could climb like a cat" (434). His association with Australia is not completely centered around the dark and hostile environment of the land down under; George also portrays many of the positive images circulating around England about its colony in the Southern Hemisphere. When we first meet George, he is returning home aboard the *Argus* with "an elderly wool-stapler, returning to his native country with his wife and daughters, after having made a fortune in the colonies" (18). George himself had made his fortune in Australia, though it took him over three years of toiling in the gold fields to do so. He tells Miss Morley that before leaving for Australia, he was not able to earn enough money for his family, and therefore had decided to commit suicide by drowning himself. Yet upon overhearing some "talk of the Australian gold-diggings, and the great things that were to be done there" (24) he decided to seize this opportunity to finally earn a proper fortune. The image of Australia as a golden land of opportunity saved George Talboys from suicide — "This was better than the water at any rate" (25), and gave him hope for the economic future of his wife and son.

He did eventually earn enough money to return to his family, even though it meant three years of living in "the wilds of the new world" and being "in the centre of riot, drunkenness, and debauchery" (26). He himself experienced "rheumatism, fever, starvation" until he was "at the very gates of death," all dark images of the land down under, yet through this suffering he was finally able to discover "a gold deposit of some magnitude" which made him "the richest man in all the little colony" (26). Just like Magwitch, George worked hard for years before earning his fortune, and therefore upholds the idea that Australia was a land full of economic opportunities for the hearty and adventurous, for those who could not have found prosperity in England. As noted earlier, Lansbury states that "the fortune from Australia" could now be seen as a "credible" alternative to other means of enriching characters (116). George returns the fortune he earned in the Australian goldfields, and serves as an excellent example of why Britain should continue in its path of imperialism. For those willing to take risks, opportunities for economic advancement abounded in the colony. Johnson-Woods states: "When male fictional characters leave domestic confines ... they are escaping domesticity in order to experience adventure, the adventure of empire" (114). Braddon upheld the contradictory image of Australia because by portraying both viewpoints, she was able to satisfy the readers of sensation fiction while upholding the concept of British imperialism. As Johnson-Woods concludes, "Thus Australia is a land of contradictions for Braddon; on one hand it is filled with English n'er do wells, and, on the other, it provides them with an opportunity to do well" (120). Braddon is careful to portray both sides of this dichotomy, thereby producing sensational results for her readers through the uncanny, while simultaneously promoting the ideas of colonialism.

In the colony of Australia, both Dickens and Braddon, along with many other sensation authors such as Charles Reade, found a space for playing out the political contradictions of their time. Here the people of Britain could read about the dark side of Australia, finding the excitement and mystery of an unknown world, the danger of "savages," the repression of characters and desires, and everything else their nerves sought in sensation fiction. Yet at the same time, they could also see the colony as a land of reformation and opportunity for convicts, and an economically beneficial space for individuals, families, and the metropole of England. Through these literary representations, 1860s Britain could come to terms with the contradictions of empire-building in their imaginations, and as Jameson puts it, find an "imaginary resolution of a real contradiction" (77). Edward Said summarizes this point when he stresses that the "national and international context" of works from authors such as Dickens should not be lost in the analysis, because it is this context that connects fiction to its historical and geographical world.

Said insists that "because of their *worldliness,* because of their complex affiliations with their real setting, they are *more* interesting and *more* valuable as works of art" (526). Such outward-focused analysis, as Said so often performs, can provide inestimable benefits for the study of the culture and the political mindset of an entire nation. Although the political unconscious of 1860s England would also have encompassed their invisibilization of Australia's indigenous peoples, it is also important to analyze the effects of colonization upon the metropole of England itself. By studying literature through its historical and geographical lenses, these works of art indeed provide valuable and interesting insights into the political unconscious of England.

Notes

1. The following abbreviations will be used: *Great Expectations* (*GE*) and *Lady Audley's Secret* (*LAS*).

Works Cited

Bayly, C.A. "The British and indigenous peoples, 1700–1860: Power, Perception and Identity." *Empire and Others: British Encounters with Indigenous Peoples, 1600–1850.* Ed. Martin Daunton and Rick Halpern. Philadelphia: University of Pennsylvania Press, 1999.

Braddon, Mary Elizabeth. *Lady Audley's Secret.* Ed. Jenny Bourne Taylor. London: Penguin, 1998.

Brantlinger, Patrick. *Rule of Darkness: British Literature and Imperialism, 1830–1914.* Ithaca: Cornell University Press, 1988.

Brooks, Peter. "Repetition, Repression, and Return: The Plotting of *Great Expectations.*" *Great Expectations* by Charles Dickens. Ed. Janice Carlisle. Case Studies in Contemporary Criticism. Ed. Ross C. Murfun. New York: Bedford, 1996.

Dickens, Charles. *Great Expectations.* Ed. Charlotte Mitchell. London: Penguin, 1996.

Freud, Sigmund. "The Uncanny." *Studies in Parapsychology.* New York: Collier, 1963.

Goodall, Heather. "Authority Under Challenge: Pikampul Land and Queen Victoria's Law During the British Invasion of Australia." *Empire and Others: British Encounters with Indigenous Peoples, 1600–1850.* Ed. Martin Daunton and Rick Halpern. Philadelphia: University of Pennsylvania Press, 1999.

Goodwin, Craufurd D. "British Economists and Australian Gold." *The Journal of Economic History* 30.2 (1970): 405–26.

Hall, Catherine. *Civilising Subjects: Metropole and Colony in the English Imagination,* Cambridge: Polity, 2002.

Hardy, Barbara. "Dickens and the Passions." *Nineteenth-Century Fiction* 24.4 (1970): 449–66.

Hollington, Michael. "Dickens and Australia." *Cahiers Victoriens et Edouardiens* 33(1991): 15–33.

Hughes, Robert. *The Fatal Shore*. London: Harvill, 1987.

Jameson, Fredric. *The Political Unconscious: Narrative as a Socially Symbolic Act*. Ithaca: Cornell University Press, 1981.

Johnson-Woods, Toni. "Mary Elizabeth Braddon in Australia: Queen of the Colonies." *Beyond Sensation: Mary Elizabeth Braddon in Context*. Ed. Marlene Tromp. Albany: SUNY Press, 2000.

Lansbury, Coral. *Arcady in Australia: The Evocation of Australia in Nineteenth-Century English Literature*. Melbourne: Melbourne University Press, 1970.

Lonoff, Sue. "Charles Dickens and Wilkie Collins." *Nineteenth-Century Fiction* 35.2 (1980): 150–70.

Mansel, Henry. "Sensation Novels." *Quarterly Review* 113 (1863): 482–502.

Meyer, Susan. *Imperialism at Home: Race and Victorian Women's Fiction*. Ithaca: Cornell University Press, 1996.

Murfin, Ross C. "What is Psychoanalytic Criticism?" *Great Expectations* by Charles Dickens. Ed. Janice Carlisle. Case Studies in Contemporary Criticism. Ed. Ross C. Murfun. New York: Bedford, 1996.

Povinelli, Elizabeth A. "Sexual Savages/Sexual Sovereignty: Australian Colonial Texts and the Postcolonial Politics of Nationalism." *Diacritics* 24.2/3 (1994): 122–50.

Russell, Lynette. Introduction. *Colonial Frontiers: Indigenous-European Encounters in Settler Societies*. Ed. Lynette Russell. Manchester: Manchester University Press, 2001.

Said, Edward. "Dickens and Australia." *Great Expectations* by Charles Dickens. Ed. Janice Carlisle. Case Studies in Contemporary Criticism. Ed. Ross C. Murfun. New York: Bedford, 1996.

Shaw, A.G.L. *Convicts and the Colonies: A Study of the Penal Transportation from Great Britian and Ireland to Australia and other parts of the British Empire*. London: Faber & Faber, 1966.

Sucksmith, Harvey Peter. "The Secret of Immediacy: Dickens' Debt to the Tale of Terror in *Blackwood's*." *Nineteenth-Century Fiction* 26.2 (1971): 145–57.

Taylor, Jenny Bourne, with Russell Crofts. Introduction. *Lady Audley's Secret* by Mary Elizabeth Braddon. Ed. Jenny Bourne Taylor. London: Penguin, 1998.

Tillotson, Kathleen. "The Lighter Reading of the Eighteen-Sixties." Introduction. *The Woman in White* by Wilkie Collins. Boston: Houghton, 1969.

Trotter, David. Introduction. *Great Expectations* by Charles Dickens. Ed. Charlotte Mitchell. London: Penguin, 1996.

Reading Between the (Blood)lines of Victorian Vampires:
Mary Elizabeth Braddon's "Good Lady Ducayne"

SAVERIO TOMAIUOLO

Although they are considered an enduring species, vampires do not scare people anymore the way they traditionally did, probably because the contemporary world has surpassed their outmoded look — made up of sharpened teeth, dark dresses, pallid faces and foreign-sounding accents — with more terrifying realities. What is undisputable is their incredible capacity *to survive* and *to adapt*— in almost Darwinian terms — to a society which always needs menacing and vampirizing "others" haunting its institutions and its (presumably) advanced civilization. Thus, vampires' terrifying attributes have changed and evolved up to the twenty-first century "others" *par excellence*: vampire-like Muslin terrorists and Dracula-like Bin Ladens. In this sense, Nina Auerbach's definition of Bram Stoker's "children of the night" seems quite appropriate: "[an] alien nocturnal species, sleeping in coffins, living in shadows, drinking our lives in secrecy, vampires are easy to stereotype, but it is their *variety* that makes them survivors" (*Our Vampires* 1; emphasis mine). As a consequence, vampires cannot be considered unchanging creatures, but have undergone a slow evolution from scaring *myths*— which can be traced back to Greek legends and to Eastern Europe folklore — to mutating *tropes*, with the term to be intended in the double meaning of *rhetorical figure* (connected to the way vampires have been textually inscribed and described) and *ideological strategy*, referred to the modalities according to which they have become an expression of the "political unconscious" of society. But it was especially during the nineteenth century that this doubly-troped creature evolved in interesting ways. Among the most famous political uses of the vampire it is necessary to refer to Karl Marx's words included in chapter 10 of the *Capital* (1867), where he compares capitalism to a vampire: "Capital is dead labour, that, *vampire-like*, only lives by sucking living labour, and lives the more, the more labour it sucks.... The prolongation of the working-day beyond the limits of the material day, into the night, only acts as a palliative. It quenches only in a slight degree the *vampire thirst* for a living blood of labour" [233, 256].[1]

Mary Elizabeth Braddon's "Good Lady Ducayne" (1896)[2], one of the most intriguing Gothic tales written by the author of renowned sensation novels such as *Lady Audley's Secret, Aurora Floyd* and *Henry Dunbar*, recalls not only these "political" renderings of the vampire figure — since her tale describes a form of vampiric exploitation performed by a wealthy aristocrat over a poor girl — but suggests and stimulates many other parallel and alternative readings, connected to decayed female sexuality (and productivity) and to an anti–Semitic racial unconscious which was widespread during the years in which this short story was written and published. First of all, Braddon's own vampire tale was published one year before Bram Stoker's *Dracula* (in 1896), and it can be supposed that both writers discussed about vampires on many occasions, since Stoker repeatedly attended Braddon's residence in Richmond. "Good Lady Ducayne" is basically the story of the poor eighteen-year-old Bella Rolleston who lives in London with her mother (who has been deserted by her husband). After having applied to an employment agency, Bella receives an offer by a very old aristocrat named Adelaide Ducayne, who needs a strong and healthy companion to accompany her during her travels abroad. Bella accepts her offer and follows Lady Ducayne to Cap Ferrino, in the Italian Riviera, where she also meets Lotta and her brother Herbert Stafford, a young physician (or better, a practitioner) who studied in Edinburgh and Paris. After her friends leave Cap Ferrino, Bella — who stars missing her mother and her London home — begins to feel a strange creeping weakness and a lassitude upon her, casually overhearing two elderly Englishmen who discuss the mysterious death of Bella's predecessors at Ducayne's service. In the meantime, strange dreams start to recur and Bella finds what seems a mosquito bite on her arm, and in order to cure this wound she asks for the help of a mysterious Italian doctor named Parravicini, who is a close friend of Lady Ducayne. During a new trip to Bellagio, Bella and her travelling companions meet Lotta and Herbert again, who this time starts to be suspicious of Bella's strange wounds. Herbert confronts Ducayne and

Parravicini, accusing the doctor of having bled Bella through blood transfusions with the help of chloroform, a fact which explains the girl's strange dreams and her mosquito bites. Ducayne reveals that this has been done (as in the previous deadly cases) in order to prolong her life, admitting to be very old and to be born on the days in which Louis XVI was decapitated. Dissatisfied with Parravicini's services, the Lady sends him away, searching for new methods to survive aging. The story ends with "Good Lady Ducayne" discharging Bella and giving her a large check of 1,000 pounds to be invested in debenture stocks, thanks to which the girl will have enough money to afford to marry Herbert in England and to live comfortably for the rest of her life.

Braddon has probably derived the theme of the vampire-like desire to prolong unnaturally one's own life from the story of the sixteenth-century Hungarian countess Erzsebet Bathory (1560–1614) — better known as Elizabeth Bathory — who used to have baths in young and healthy servants' blood. In the case of "Good Lady Ducayne" Braddon adapts this gruesome tale to nineteenth-century cultural and scientific background. But, above all, her tale is connected with the nineteenth-century tradition of Gothic vampire stories, from the presence of the corrupted aristocrat who travels throughout Europe (derived from William Polidori's Lord Ruthven in *The Vampyre*, 1819) along with its female "variation" in Sheridan Le Fanu's *Carmilla* (1872), even though Braddon's short story avoids any reference to the complex homosexual attraction which characterizes the relationship between Laura and Carmilla. Last but not least, it is also necessary to bear in mind the enormous popular success of the "sensational" 8000 double-column pages saga of James Rymner's *Varney the Vampire*, subtitled *The Feast of Blood* (1847), which for the first time introduced the reference to male vampires' sexual seduction. Braddon mixes these (inter)textual influences with multiple references and allusions to all those new scientific and technological innovations which would be fundamental in *Dracula* as an example of what Kathleen L. Spencer perceptively calls the "Urban Gothic," which — in her own words — acknowledges "the eighteenth-century ancestry [of traditional Gothic fictions] while identifying the major modifications that have been made to adapt the fantastic to the needs of a new era" (201).

From a biographical point of view, "Good Lady Ducayne" could be seen as a reflection on ageing and death from a writer who had been experiencing many tragic losses in the years preceding the composition of the story — in 1885 three close friends died,[3] followed in March by Maxwell's illness and death — and who was realizing that her physical energies were decreasing (a fact which limited Braddon's travels abroad, even though she continued to visit Lake Como and the Italian Riviera, one of the places she liked most). Although "Good Lady Ducayne" is more than this, one of the main textual points remains the condition of Lady Ducayne as an old and sexually *unproductive* woman, juxtaposed with Bella as the expression of physical *productivity* and sexual *reproductivity*:

> Never had she seen anyone as old as the old lady sitting by the Person's fire: a little old figure, wrapped from chin to feet in an ermine mantle; a *withered, old face* under a plumed bonnet....
> "This is Miss Rolleston, Lady Ducayne."
> Claw-like fingers, flashing with jewels, lifted a double eye-glass to Lady Ducayne's shining black eyes, and through the glasses Bella saw those unnaturally bright eyes magnified to a gigantic size, and glaring at her awfully.
> "Miss Torpinter [the owner of the employment agency] has told me all about you," said the *old voice* that belonged to the eyes. "*Have you good health? Are you strong and active?, able to eat well, sleep well, walk well, able to enjoy all that there is good in life?*" [85; emphasis mine].

As readers know, Victorian ideas on reproduction and menstruation were varied, even though there were some shared opinions on women's general inferiority and weakness connected with their bodily cycles. While in 1873 Dr. Edward Clarke of Harvard College asserted in *Sex in Education* that menstruation was debilitating and marked out women's physical and "functional" difference from men — gaining Henry Maudley's approval in *The Fortnightly Review* (number XXI, 1874) — James MacGigor Allen had already listed in 1869 some clear points in Victorian medicine as far as the menstrual "question" was concerned:

> Although the duration of the menstrual period differs greatly according to race, temperament and health, it will be within the mark to state that women are unwell, from this cause, on the average two days in the month, or say one month in one year. At such times women are unfit for any great mental or physical labour. They suffer under a languor and depression which disqualify them for thought or action and render it extremely doubtful how far they can be considered responsible beings while the crisis lasts.... In intellectual labour, man has surpassed, does now, and will surpass woman, for the obvious reason that nature does not periodically interrupt his thought and application. [4]

Of course, it was not menstruation *per se* which interested (and puzzled) Victorian doctors most. Rather, it was its "control" which represented a determinant factor in the way female difference was managed and domesticated in cultural, sexual and even economical terms. In the words of Sally Shut-tleworth, "the Victorian concern with regulating the circulation of the female uterine economy only takes on its full historical meaning when read as part of the wider social and economic ideologies of circulation that underpinned the emergent social division of labour within industrial England" (48). Fur-thermore, the real alarm was represented by the suppression of menstrua-tions during the so-called "climacteric" stage of womanhood (the menopause), considered as a form of sexual and "economical" stagnation, to the point that some of the most original cures to allow the free circulation of blood included products such as Dr. Locock's female pills (1850), followed by the famous Widow Welch's pills. As a consequence, Ducaye's vampirism is justified not just by her desire to prolong her life and health but also to continue — through the physical regeneration guaranteed by blood transfusions — to enjoy the pleasures of wealth and money, in other words "capitalizing" the young girl's youth and health. Although in Ducayne's case blood spilling is not metaphorically associated with sexual intercourse — as in Sheridan Le Fanu's *Carmilla*, Stoker's *Dracula* or Arabella Kenealy's story "A Beautiful Vampire" (1896), which shares many elements with Braddon's tale — some theories of the period held that "woman's blood lust came from her need to replace lost menstrual blood" (Showalter 180).[5] On his turn, Herbert Spencer in one of his essays made a significant connection between the "circulation" of blood and the "circulation" of commodities in market economy, suggest-ing an implicit association between economic stagnation and female unpro-ductivity. For him, in fact, there was a homologous relation between "the blood in a living body and the consumable and circulating commodities in the body politic" (294). As far as Victorian literature is concerned, the most famous example of unproductive female sexuality associated with an arrested economic flow is obviously represented by Dickens's Miss Havisham, which could be considered a sort of paradigmatic figure: dressed in her worn wed-ding suit, surrounded by dusty reminders of her unconsumed wedding day and living in the ironically-sounding Satis House — where her dreams of love will be never "satiated" — she establishes a complex relationship with Estella (the young and sexually "(re)productive" heroine of *Great Expecta-tions*) made up both of sympathy and of a vampiric affection which antici-pates Lady Ducayne and Bella's. Like Miss Havisham, Lady Ducayne represents another "aging female body [who] figures a dysfunctional market economy" (Welsh 75).[6]

These cultural (and economic) reflections are of course strongly connected with political ones — in particular with Marx's association between capitalistic economy and vampirism — since the exploiter is a rich and wealthy woman and the exploited is a poor London girl who willingly offers herself (literally, her healthy body) to have a job. Moreover, it must be emphasised that in an increasingly bourgeois society such as the Victorian was — with Samuel Smile's *Self Help* (1859) as its cultural and ideological manifesto and with Sir Francis Galton's *Hereditary Genius* (1869) as a (para)scientific attack against old feudal nobility and inherited welfare — there was a widely shared negative view of old nobility and of its privileges (who Lady Ducayne and Vlad Tepes so evidently embody). This cultural and "political" background is complicated by the fact that — in capitalistic economies — there is a sort of mutual acceptance of one's roles and limits between the characters involved in the narration: Lady Ducayne knows that she has the economic power but that without the girls' blood/labour she cannot survive, while Bella — despite her physical repulsion for the Lady (and for Parravicini) — follows her wherever she goes in order to earn money:

> Yes, they were uncanny, certainly, the pair of them — she so like an aristocratic with her withered old age; [Parravicini] of no particular age, with a face that was more like a waxen mask than any human countenance Bella had ever seen. What did it matter? Old age is venerable, and worthy of all reverence; and *Lady Ducayne had been very kind to her* [93; emphasis mine].

In Julia Kristeva's terminology, Bella and Lady Ducayne establish an "abject" relationship based both on repulsion and attraction, since this vampire like bond involves the two women in a specular way: Ducayne despises Bella's social condition and ingenuousness but is attracted by her youth and health, while Bella is confused (and sometimes disgusted) by the Lady's strange behaviour and physical appearance, but needs her money. At the end of the story this abject exchange of each other's services — Lady Ducayne's money and Bella's young blood — will be interrupted by Dr. Herbert Stafford, a representative of those new professional classes who during the Victorian age embodied an alternative both to decayed aristocracy and aggressive capitalism (Ducayne), as well as to those poor working classes who accepted to be exploited only to have the opportunity to work (Bella).[8] It is thus significant that in Braddon's story the Gothic "mode of excess"[7] — based upon the presence of transgressive events and literary codes which are alternative to ordinary everyday existence and "realistic" literature — is put alongside economic discourses connected with Bella's low social condition, as for instance in another scene (describing Lady Ducayne's carriage) which recalls

Carmilla's mother arrival at the General's castle in Stiria and anticipates a notorious scene in *Dracula*:

> It was a dull October afternoon, and there was a *greyness* in the air which might turn to fog before night. The Walworth Road shops gleamed brightly through that *grey* atmosphere, and though to a young lady reared in Mayfair or Belgravia such shop-windows would have been unworthy of a glance, they were a snare and a temptation for Bella. *There were so many things she longed for, and would never be able to buy....*
>
> The Person's office was at the further end, and Bella looked down that long, *grey*, vista almost despairingly, more tired than usual with the trudge from Walworth. As she looked, a carriage passed her, an old-fashioned, yellow chariot..., drawn by a pair of high *grey* horses, with the stateliest of coachmen driving them, and a tall footman sitting by her side [84; emphasis mine].

This passage shows a lexical and isotopical predominance of "greyness" which points to the condition of *in-betweeness* which is characteristic of the creatures inhabiting *fin de siècle* Gothic tales, which usually conceal references to socio-political and economic questions behind their supernatural surface, related in this case to Bella's low social condition ("There were so many things she longed for, and would never be able to buy").

"Good Lady Ducayne" was significantly published when the ideas on degeneration — connected with the Imperial fears of invasion which will largely inform *Dracula* — were widespread, with Lady Ducayne representing the cultural, sexual and even racial "other" who tries to penetrate, corrupt and infect the healthy Englishness embodied by Bella and defended by Herbert. In fact, the year in which Braddon's tale was published saw the first English translation of Max Nordau's *Degeneration* (1892) and the first French translation of Cesare Lombroso's *L'uomo delinquente* (1876), two texts that both Braddon and Stoker had certainly in mind in the characterization of their "alien" vampires. A famous passage from Nordau's text — in which the author reflects on and condemns the phenomenon of the literary, cultural and even "physical" degeneration of late nineteenth-century Europe — explicitly refers to the intellectual inferiority of Eastern peoples, accused of being inveterate consumers of opium and hashish:

> We have recognized the effects of diseases in these *fin-de-siècle* literary and artistic tendencies and fashions, as well as in the susceptibility of the public with regard to them, and we have succeeded in maintaining that these diseases are degeneracy and hysteria....
>
> That the poisoning of civilized peoples continues and increases at a very rapid rate is widely attested by statistics.... The increase in the consumption

of opium and hashish is still greater, but we need not concern ourselves about that, since the chief sufferers from them are *Eastern peoples, who play no part in the intellectual development of the white races....*

The enormous increase of hysteria in our days is partly due to the same causes as degeneracy, besides which there is one cause much more general still than the growth of large towns — a cause which perhaps of itself would not be sufficient to bring about degeneracy.... This cause is the fatigue of the present generation [525–27].

Along with these influences, the ideas related to racial inferiority included in works such as Robert Knox's *The Races of Men* (1850) cannot be overlooked, since they all contributed to create the image of an invading monstrous creature constantly menacing the stability of the most important Victorian institutions: the state, the Empire and the family, the "norm" against which the other is constructed. Here is an extract from Knox's much debated essay:

But who are the dark races of ancient and modern times? It would not be easy to answer this question. Were the Copts a dark race? Are the Jews a dark race? The Gypsies? The Chinese, &c.? Dark are to a certain extent; so are all the Mongol tribes — the American Indian and Esquimaux — the inhabitants of nearly all Africa — of the East — of Australia [478].

Vampires seem to exemplify and embody a widespread fear of invasion and contagion during a moment in which England was experiencing both its triumph as Empire — with Queen Victoria crowned Empress of India in 1876 — and was facing and confronting with the problems related to the control over the various colonies. But while Stoker's Dracula clearly comes from an Eastern mysterious and "dark" country as Transylvania, Adelaide Ducayne's racial origin is not easy to discern. The only thing readers know is that she is *not* English. As a further sign of corruption, Lady Ducayne enjoys reading French morally-corrupting novels, considered as another "alien" cultural product which, according to many Victorian critics was infecting (along with sensational novels) English "healthy" literary tradition. Reviewing Wilkie Collins's *The Woman in White* (1861) on *The Reader* on January 3, 1863, an anonymous critic describes in fact the Victorian novelists' interest in adultery, crimes and moral corruption as a "plant of foreign growth" (qtd. in Rance 31) imported from France.

To try and solve the mystery of Ducayne's origin it could be useful at this point to reflect on two readings which occupied Braddon's late nineteen-nineties, when she was writing "Good Lady Ducayne": Henry James's *The Portrait of a Lady* (1882), which — along with its Italian setting — illustrates a form of "vampirism" through the character of Osmond, and Arthur P. Stanley's *Jewish Church* (1865, in 3 volumes), which demonstrates Braddon's interest in the Jewish question. Considered by many a "degenerate" and "criminal" population, as well as — by Robert Knox — one of the "dark races" of mankind, Jews have experienced a long tradition of discrimination and persecution which can be traced back to Medieval times, where they were described as monstrous and devilish creatures, since they were considered the main persecutors of Christ during his trial. In many libels they were charged with drinking blood (just like vampires), eating children and even cooking the Passover *matzah*— a kind of bread — with Christian blood. Jews were thus constantly associated with a secretive and lethally parasitic kind of behaviour: the difference in their dietary laws, religious rituals and language led in fact to the belief that these attitudes involved the perversion of Christian sacraments. Moreover, during the late years of the nineteenth-century Britain was inflamed by a strong anti–Jewish campaign partially related to a massive wave of immigrants coming from Russia since 1884, where they had been persecuted. The climax of this anti–Semitic attitude, which corresponded to the desire to protect the English "stock" from any form of blood pollution and from any moral (and economic) invasion, was represented by the institution of the Royal Commission on Alien Immigration in 1903 (followed by the Immigration Act in 1905), which was the last step of a long debate concerning racial questions. In a speech held to the Royal Commission in 1903, Arnold White expressed a commonly-shared alarmist position as far as the Jewish immigration from the East was concerned, saying that these races were "feeding off" and "poisoning" the blood of Londoners, implicitly using the metaphor of the vampire.[9] Along with other dark races, the Jews were thus one of the many "vampirizing" aliens trying to "pollute" English institutions, which contributed to inspire the themes and the characterizations of those literary productions — including Stoker's *Dracula*, Rider Haggard's *She*, Captain Marryat's writings and Conrad's *Heart of Darkness*— which Patrick Brantlinger includes in the literary genre of the "Imperial Gothic."

As a consequence, in defining (both physically and culturally) Lady Ducayne's traits as vampire Braddon drew inspiration from a "racial unconscious" which emerged during the last decades of the nineteenth-century, and which focused on Jews and Eastern Europeans as the main source of an alien invasion. In fact, apart from the foreign-sounding name of the Lady (probably of French origin), many of her physical traits recall those traditionally and stereotypically attributed to Jews, in particular the sharp facial features and the peculiar shape of the nose:

> [Her] face was so wasted by age that it seemed only a pair of eyes and a *pointed chin. The nose was peaked*, too, but between *the sharply pointed chin* and great, shining eyes, the *small aquiline nose* was hardly visible [85; emphasis mine].

Even Ducayne's condition as "wandering" vampire in search of new methods to try and fight against the doom of ageing and extinction seems a parodic revision of the myth of the wandering Jew and, generally speaking, of the destiny of the Jewish population, always in search of a definitive place to settle down and find its peace. But, of course, Braddon's is not the only vampire which is associated with Jews in late–Victorian literature, since even Bram Stoker's *Dracula*—according to Andrew Smith—"articulates a contemporary anti–Semitic view in the association between the Count, eastern Europe and disease, which tapped into a popular anxiety of an 'alien invasion' of Jews" (35). By just looking at Dracula's physical traits, the association with a "dark," "degenerate" but also "enduring" race (such as the Jewish was considered at the time) is explicit:

> His face was a strong — very strong — aquiline, with high bridge of the thin nose and peculiarly arched nostrils; with lofty doomed forehead, and hair growing scantly round the temples, almost meeting over the nose, and with bushy hair that seemed to curl in its own profusion. The mouth, so far as I could see it under the heavy moustache, was fixed and rather cruel-looking, with peculiarly sharp white teeth; those protruded over the lips, whose remarkable ruddiness showed astonishing vitality in a man of his years. For the rest, his ears were pale and at the tops extremely pointed; the chin was broad and strong, and the cheeks firm though thin. The general effect was of an extraordinary pallor [Stoker 48].

Furthermore, is it thanks to the well-paid services of an unscrupulous Jew named Hildesheim, "with a nose like a sheep, and a fez" (390), that Dracula will be able to leave London with his coffin on board the *Czarina Catherine*. Thus, it is highly probable that, given the intertextual similarities between "Good Lady Ducayne" and *Dracula*— the mysterious carriage, the alien intruder, the common physical traits, the aristocratic origin, even the capacity to deal with modern technologies and new scientific discoveries — Braddon more or less "unconsciously" built Lady Ducayne's cultural and physical traits upon what was at the time considered among the "darkest races" of humankind. Provocatively, Kathleen L. Spencer compares medieval witch-hunting with many persecuting attitudes which characterized the last decades of the nineteenth century, and which were evidently related to the most debated gender and cultural issues of the times, including the Jews among the dangerous groups to be "seized":

> Though the late Victorians did not explicitly attribute evil to whites, they manifested the same fears of pollution from the outsiders, the same suspicion of deviants as traitors, and the same exaggerated estimation of what was at stake — in short, the same social dynamics as more traditional witchcraft societies.... The battle produced numerous cries of "seize the witch!" directed both at groups (Jews, Germans, Slavs, Orientals, birth control advocates, promiscuous women, decadent French authors [especially Zola], homosexuals) and at individuals — most spectacularly, though by no means solely, Oscar Wilde [207–8].

From a narrative point of view, Braddon's story dramatizes the clash between the conventions and strategies of realistic fiction and the peculiarly Gothic violations of those same conventions. If, on the one hand, realism aims at giving an organic form and meaning to the events that are narrated, on the other hand the Gothic codes signal the decomposition of traditional literary genres (and their reassuring assertions) through the presence of multiple voices and perspectives on the events which help complicating and deforming the perception of reality. This is the case, for instance, of *fin-de-siècle* Gothic fictions such as Robert Louis Stevenson's *The Strange Case of Dr. Jekyll and Mr Hyde* (1886) and *Dracula*, where there is a deliberate inclusion of documents, diaries, letters, reports and, generally speaking, conflicting (or at least confusing) narrations. Also in the case of Braddon's "Good Lady Ducayne," there is a meaningful coexistence of third-person omniscient narration and of many letters written by Bella, as if to offer readers two faces of the same story: an objectively realistic one and a subjectively impressionistic one, where the intrusion of the Gothic codes is more easily retraceable. As a general rule, it is here necessary to point to the fact that Gothic narrations and stories *do not* represent a total rejection of realism, but rather tend to "vampirize" — particularly in late–Victorian literary productions — its formal conventions and semantic references to contemporary events (in this case, medical and scientific innovations), using them to give more credit to its deforming perspective. For Rosemary Jackson the Gothic and the fantastic exist in fact "as the inside, or underside, of realism, opposing the novel's closed, monological forms with open, dialogical structures, as if the novel had given rise to its own opposite, its unrecognizable reflection" (25).

Apart from Ducayne's mysterious carriage, from the Lady's disquieting physical traits and vampirizing attitudes, and from the casual (and ironic) reference to the mosquitoes which presumably cause Bella's wounds — "What a vampire!" exclaims Parravicini while curing the girl (95) — Bella's dreams represent one of the most explicit Gothic elements of the tale, since her hallucinations seem to plunge into the recesses of the girl's most unspeakable experiences:

> The dream troubled her a little, not because it was a ghastly or frightening dream, but on account of sensations which she had never felt before in sleep — a whirring of wheels that went round in her brain, a great noise like a whirlwind, but rhythmical like the ticking of a gigantic clock; and then in the midst of this uproar as of winds and waves she seemed to sink into a gulf of unconsciousness, out of sleep into far deeper sleep — total extinction. And then, after that blank interval, there had come the sound of voices, and then again the whirr of wheels, louder and louder — and again the blank — and then she knew no more till morning, when she awoke, feeling languid and oppressed [94–95].
>
> She was homesick, and she had dreams — or, rather, an occasional recurrence of that one bad dream with all its strange sensations. It was more like an hallucination than dreaming — the whirring of wheels; the sinking into an abyss; the struggling back into consciousness [99–100].

Here Braddon has evidently taken inspiration from Le Fanu's *Carmilla*, even though Laura's dreams — during which she is "vampirized" — include allusions to (homo)sexual intercourse and *post-coitum* exhaustion which are absent in "Good Lady Ducayne."

As far as Ducayne's "peculiar" form of vampirism is concerned, readers discover that it is actually performed with the help of Parravicini and consists of blood transfusions. From a narrative point of view, Braddon succeeds in gradually de-Gothicizing her own story through Herbert Stafford's cultural and narrative "realistic" perspective, which he illustrates in the course of his unmasking of Parravicini and Lady Ducayne's crimes:

> I could take upon myself to demonstrate — by most convincing evidence, to a jury of medical men — that Dr. Parravicini has been bleeding Miss Rolleston, after putting her under chloroform, at intervals, ever since she has been in your service. The deterioration in the girl's health speaks for itself; the lancet marks upon the girl's arms are unmistakable; and her description of a series of sensations, which she calls a dream, points unmistakably to the administration of chloroform while she was sleeping [106].

The use of chloroform and the practice of transfusion was a contemporary theme of discussion Braddon deliberately chose to include in order to give "realistic" credit to her Gothic tale. Chloroform was in fact introduced by Sir James Young Simpson, professor of midwifery at Edinburgh

University (the same university where Herbert studied) who had begun to use chloroform instead of ether — because of its unpleasant side effects — since 1847. The medical choice of chloroform was characterized by an intense debate connected, first, with the state of near-oblivion it induced in patients (a halfway condition between wakefulness and death) and, most especially, with the crucial role played by medicine (and chloroform-use) during child-birth in re-negotiating what was held to be woman's "naturally painful" reproductive function (and limited place in the social sphere).[10] But Simpson's success arrived in 1853, when Queen Victoria herself decided to be anaesthetized with chloroform during the birth of her ninth child: from that moment on this procedure stated to be widely accepted, with Simpson awarded a baronetcy in 1866. As for blood transfusions, James Bluddell (a British obstetrician) performed the first successful one in the treatment of a postpartum hemorrhage in 1818. Using the patient's husband as a donor, Blundell extracted a small amount of blood from the husband's arm and, using a syringe, successfully transfused his wife. Between 1825 and 1830 he performed ten documented transfusions, five of which proved beneficial for his patients, while devising various "instruments" to better perform transfusions. But the most famous Victorian doctor connected with blood transfusions was Joseph Lister, who introduced the use of antiseptics to control infections during blood transfusions, a choice which helped reducing the number of infections caused by lack of hygiene. Not until 1870, however, did the antiseptic idea firmly catch; in 1877 Lister demonstrated that surgery — and blood transfusions — through the use of antiseptics reduced the mortality rate by fifty percent. While Braddon in "Good Lady Ducayne" makes only implicit references to blood transfusion without actually illustrating what happened under Parravicini's supervision — using a narrative ellipsis which is probably more disturbing and disquieting than any accurate description — Stoker's novel illustrates on the contrary the practice of transfusion in detail, showing both his debt to Braddon's tale and to the reports of the Irish doctor Robert McDonnel, who published the description a famous blood donation in the *Dublin Quarterly Journal of Medical Science* in 1870. The (four) transfusions described in *Dracula* have a strong sexual connotation — where blood represents metonymically sperm — which is absent from "Good Lady Ducayne," since they enhance a male homosocial bond through an act imitating a rape performed by each of the men involved in the vampire-hunting over the victimized (and vampirized) Lucy Westenra:

"Young miss is bad. She wants blood, and blood she must have or die. My friend John [Steward] and I [Van Helsing] have consulted; and we are about to perform what we call a blood transfusion — to transfer from full veins of one to the empty veins which pine for him. John was to give his blood, as he is the more young and strong than me" — here Arthur took my hand and wrung it hard in silence....

We all went up to Lucy's room. Arthur by direction remained outside. Lucy turned her head and looked at us, but said nothing. She was not asleep, but she was simply too weak to make any effort. Her eyes spoke to us, that was all. Van Helsing took some things from his bag and laid them on a little table out of sight. Then he mixed a narcotic, and coming over to the bed, said cheerily: —

"Now, little miss, here is your medicine. Drink it off, like a good girl....

Van Helsing, turning to me, said —

"He is so young and strong and of blood so pure that we need not defibrinate it."

Then with swiftness, but with absolute method, Van Helsing performed the operation. As the transfusion went on something like life seemed to come back to poor Lucy's cheeks, and through Arthur's growing pallor the joy of his face seemed absolutely to shine [Stoker 157–59].

But the most problematic and disquieting element in Braddon's tale remains the vampire-like use of Victorian modern technologies and scientific discoveries by "degenerate" creature such as Lady Ducayne who, in her final dialogue with Herbert, reveals and asserts her dangerous Gothic modernity. Just like Dracula — who takes advantage from Victorian technological innovations such as telegraphs and phonographs — Lady Ducayne's attitude can be approached as "nineteenth century up-to date with a vengeance" (Stoker 67):

"You are young, and medicine is a progressive science, the newspapers tell me. Where have you studied?"

"In Edinburgh — and in Paris."

"Two old schools. And do you know all the new-fangled theories, the modern discoveries — that remind me of the medieval witchcraft, of Albert Magnus, and George Ripley; you have studied hypnotism — electricity?."

"And the transfusion of blood," said Stafford, very slowly, looking at Parravicini.

"Have you made any discovery that teaches me to prolong human life — any elixir — any mode of treatment? I want my life prolonged, young man. That man there [i. e. Parravicini] has been my physician for thirty years. He does all he can to keep me alive — after his lights. He studies all the new theories of all the scientists — but he is old; he gets older every day — his brain-power is going — he is bigoted — prejudiced — he can't receive new ideas — can't grapple with new systems" [105].

The conclusion of "Good Lady Ducayne" is a conciliatory one, with a repented Lady Ducayne donating a large sum of money to Bella. But Braddon's happy endings — as for instance in *Lady Audley's Secret* and *Aurora Floyd* — are usually marked by an ironic undertone which pervades them. At this point, it could be useful to approach the epilogue in "Good Lady Ducayne" as a parodic rewriting of Dickens's *Great Expectations* (a novel with which Braddon's tale shares many elements): the implications of Ducayne's economic donation recall in fact Magwitch's, since both are "aliens" — the latter coming from an Australian penal colony — whose money are the product of criminal acts which will paradoxically help two young people (respectively, Pip and Bella) to gain economic stability, to the point that the 1,000 pounds check Ducayne gives Miss Rolleston — after suggesting her to "[go] and marry [her] doctor" (109) — seems to be still stained with the blood of the other girls who helped the lady to survive for so long, contributing to the "unnatural" prolongation of her wealthy life as aristocratic and capitalistic vampire.

As Braddon's tale demonstrates, vampirism is not only what fictional characters experience as (potential) victims, but a "floating" paradigm which could also have uncanny and unexpected outcomes. In this sense, it could be useful here to refer to a small episode occurred during the writing of this article, which demonstrates that vampire can still haunt readers (and critics) in unpredictable ways. During my research, I casually came across one of the most famous paintings devoted to the vampire figure: Edward Munch's *The Vampire* (1895). I was sure about the title of the picture but, after a brief look at one of Munch's biographies (by Heller), I realized that that was a famous example of critical misunderstanding of the painter's message and intentions. The original title was in fact *Love and Pain*, although a critic named Stanislaw Przybyszewski mistakenly interpreted the picture as being vampiric in theme and content. As a consequence, Munch's painting was known as *The Vampire* from that moment on. Through this case I was, in a way, facing the condition — and sometimes even the nightmare — of the critical reader as strange and liminal creature, always on the verge of *vampirizing* the meanings laying between the lines (and the bloodlines) of literary texts.

Notes

1. The comparison between capitalism and vampires is given further relevance and analyzed by Franco Moretti (83–108). Ken Gelder asserts that "the representation of the capital or the capitalist as a vampire was, then, common both to Marx and to popular fiction in the mid-nineteenth century. It would not be an exaggeration to say that this representation mobilised vampire fiction at this time, to produce a striking figure *defined* by excess and unrestrained appetite — whose strength increased, the more victims he consumed" (22). Of course, Karl Marx was not the only political thinker to use the vampire as metaphor. According to Engels, religious beliefs "serve only to weaken the proletariat and to keep them obedient and faithful to the capitalist vampires" (270). Later on, Engels defines the middle classes as vampires who "first suck the wretched workers' day so that afterwards they can ... throw a few miserable crumbs of charity at their feet" (313).

2. "Good Lady Ducayne" was published in *The Strand Magazine*, vol. XI, February 1896 (185–199) and in the *Sheffield's Weekly Telegraph* in two parts, on 21 and 28 March 1896.

3. The three friends were Madame Delpierre (an intimate of the Braddon family since the fifties), Miss Elizabeth Philip, a frequent guest at Richmond, and Mrs. Browne.

4. This speech will be published in the *Anthropological Review* VII (1869): CXCVIII–CXCIX.

5. As far as Arabella Kenealy's "A Beautiful Vampire" (another variation of the Countess Bathory-theme, published in *Ludgate Magazine* in 1896) is concerned, "Whereas Kenealy's menopausal vampire is principally a figure of sexual and racial anxieties, Braddon's operates on a more social and economic level. Lady Deverish steals beauty and sexual energy from those around her in order to remain beautiful and sexually attractive herself. In contrast, Lady Ducayne merely wishes to prolong her life and retain her wealth and privileges" (Swenson 30). For a recent analysis of Kenealy's short story and its allusions to (contradictory) anti-feminist politics, see Heilmann and Sanders. For the authors "what is particularly interesting about this text is the ambivalent and unstable violence of (menopausal) femininity as an emblem of both vampirism and debility" (295). Here I wish to thank Prof. Ann Heilmann for her help and support in finding (and generously offering me) materials related to Kenealy's tale.

6. With reference to Dickens' novel, Nina Auerbach in *Woman and the Demon* explores the double status of "old maids" in Victorian literature and culture, perceived both as unoffensive pathetic figures, "plaintive variant of the angel of the house" (111) and as dangerous creatures: "[the] vision of a new race of old maids assuming power over the future seeps into some of our most beloved and familiar works of Victorian fiction.... In Dickens' *Great Expectations*, Miss Havisham's withering power over her ward Estella's nature and destiny is more irresistible still: this demon mother has the power to lay waste the younger generation, remaking the future in her own deformed image" (114).

7. For a definition of the Gothic as "mode of excess," see Botting. According to Kelly Hurley the "*fin-de-siècle* Gothic consistently blurs the boundaries between natural and supernatural phenomena, hesitating between scientific and occultist accountings of inexplicable events. The realm of genre explored is the grey area at the borderline between known and unknown, or extra-rational phenomena, with the supernatural defined not as the occult per se, but as the product of mysterious natural forces the scientist has not yet been able to explain" (16–17).

8. "Lady Ducayne's late-century capitalism-as-vampirism is brought to a halt, almost anticlimactically, by an exemplary English *professional*: Dr. Herbert Stafford," since

Braddon's short story "details an anti-capitalist rhetoric, especially prevalent in mid–Victorian middle-class culture, in which professionalism asserts its merits less by reference to its technological capabilities than to its putative monopoly over gentlemanliness" (Goodlad 217, 220).

9. "Edwardian legislation was characterized both literally and metaphorically by the dream of national insurance; a desire to tighten the supervision and welfare of the national stock, to exclude and eliminate degenerate 'foreign bodies.' Indeed the Royal Commission on Alien Immigration in 1903 and the ensuing Act of 1905 should not be seen as a mere anomaly, nor, exclusively, as part of some timeless, centuries-old phenomenon of anti–Semitism, but in relation to those wider contemporary attempts to construct a racial-imperial identity, excluding all 'bad blood' and 'pathological elements,' literally expelling anarchists, criminals, prostitutes, the diseased, and the hopelessly poor — all those declared 'undesirable aliens'" (Pick 215–16).

10. For a detailed analysis of nineteenth-century questions concerning the use of chloroform, see Stratmann. As for the debate on childbearing and chloroform (headed by Sir James Simpson from 1846 to 1856 on the pages of *The Lancet*) see Poovey.

Works Cited

Auerbach, Nina. *Our Vampires, Ourselves.* Chicago and London: University of Chicago Press, 1995.

_____. *Woman and the Demon. The Life of a Victorian Myth.* Cambridge: Harvard University Press, 1982.

Biberman, Matthew. *Masculinity, Anti-Semitism and Early Modern English Literature. From the Satanic to the Effeminate Jew.* London: Ashgate, 2005.

Botting, Fred. *Gothic.* London and New York: Routledge, 1996.

Braddon, Mary Elizabeth. "Good Lady Ducayne." *At Chrighton Abbey and Other Horror Stories.* Holikong, PA: Wildside Press, 2002.

Brantlinger, Peter. *Rule of Darkness: British Literature and Imperialism, 1830–1914.* Ithaca: Cornell University Press, 1988.

Carnell, Jennifer. *The Literary Lives of Mary Elizabeth Braddon. A Study of Her Life and Work.* Hastings: The Sensation Press, 2000.

Engels, Friedrich. *On the Condition of the Working Classes in England.* Trans. W. O. Henderson and W. H. Chaloner. Stanford: Stanford University Press, 1958.

Gelder, Ken. *Reading the Vampire.* London and New York: Routledge, 1994.

Goodlad, Lauren M. E. "'Go and Marry Your Doctor': Fetishism and 'Redundance' at the *Fin de Siècle* and the Vampires of 'Good Lady Ducayne.'" *Beyond Sensation. Mary Elizabeth Braddon in Context.* Ed. Marlene Tromp, Pamela K. Gilbert, and Aeron Haynie. Albany: State University of New York Press, 2000.

Heilmann, Ann, and Valerie Sanders. "The Rebel, the Lady and the 'Anti': Femininity, Anti-Feminism, and the Victorian Woman Writer." *Women's Studies International Forum* 29 (2006): 289–300.

Heller, Reinhold. *Edward Munch: His Life and Work.* London: Murray, 1984.

Hurley, Kelly. *The Gothic Body: Sexuality, Materialism and Degeneration at the Fin de siècle.* Cambridge: Cambridge University Press, 1996.

Jackson, Rosemary. *Fantasy: The Literature of Subversion.* London and New York: Methuen, 1981.

Jordanova, Ludmilla. *Sexual Visions: Images of Gender and Science in Medicine between the Eighteenth and the Twentieth Centuries*. New York, London, Toronto, Sydney, Tokyo: Harvester Wheatsheaf, 1989.

Knox, Robert. "The Races of Men." *Literature and Science in the Nineteenth Century: An Anthology*. Ed. Laura Otis. Oxford and New York: Oxford University Press, 2002.

Kristeva, Julia. *Pouvoirs de l'horreur. Essai sur l'abjection*. Paris: Editions de Seuil, 1980.

Le Fanu, J. Sheridan. *Carmilla. In a Glass Darkly*. Ed. Robert Tracy. Oxford and New York: Oxford University Press, 1999.

Marx, Karl. *Capital*. Vol. 1. Trans. Samuel Moore and Edward Aveling. New York: International Publishers, 1987.

Moretti, Franco. "Dialectic of Fear." *Signs Taken for Wonders: Essays in the Sociology of Literary Forms*. Trans. Susan Fletcher, David Forgacs, and David Miller. London: Verso, 1983.

Nordau, Max. "Degeneration." *Literature and Science in the Nineteenth Century: An Anthology*. Ed. Laura Otis. Oxford and New York: Oxford University Press, 2002.

Pick, Daniel. *Faces of Denegeration: A European Disorder, c.1848–c.1918*. Cambridge: Cambridge University Press, 1996.

Poovey, Mary. "'Scenes of Indelicate Character': The Medical 'Treatment' of Victorian Women." *Representations* 14 (Spring 1986): 137–168.

Rance, Nicholas. *Wilkie Collins and Other Sensation Novelists: Walking the Moral Hospital*. London and Basingstoke: Macmillan, 1991.

Schmitt, Cannon. *Alien Nation: Nineteenth-Century Gothic Fictions and English Nationality*. Philadelphia: University of Pennsylvania Press, 1997.

Showalter, Elaine. *Sexual Anarchy: Gender and Culture at the "Fin de Siècle."* London: Virago, 1992.

Shuttleworth, Sally. "Female Circulation: Medical Discourse and Popular Advertising in the Mid-Victorian Era." *Body/Politics: Women and the Discourses of Science*. Ed. Mary Jacobus, Evelyn Fox Keller, and Shally Shuttleworth. New York and London: Routledge, 1990.

Smith, Andrew. *Victorian Demons. Medicine, Masculinity, and the Gothic at the "Fin-de-siècle."* Manchester and New York: Manchester University Press, 2004.

Spencer, Herbert. "The Social Organism." *Essays: Scientific, Political, and Speculative*. Vol. 1. London: Williams and Norgate, 1891.

Spencer, Kathleen L. "Purity and Danger: *Dracula*, the Urban Gothic and the Late Victorian Degeneracy Crisis." *ELH* 59, 1 (Spring 1992): 197–225.

Stoker, Bram. *Dracula*. Ed. Glennis Byron. Peterborough, Ontario: Broadview Press, 2000.

Stratmann, Linda. *Chloroform: The Quest for Oblivion*. London: Alan Sutton, 2003.

Swenson, Kristine. "The Menopausal Vampire: Arabella Kenealy and the Boundaries of True Womanhood." *Women's Writing* 10, 1 (2003): 27–46.

Weeks, Jeffrey. *Sexuality and Its Discontents: Meanings, Myths, and Modern Sexualities*. London: Routledge and Kegan Paul, 1985.

Welsh, Susan. "Bodies of Capital: *Great Expectations* and the Climacteric Economy." *Victorian Studies* 37 (1993): 73–97.

Wolff, Robert Lee. *Sensational Victorian. The Life & Fiction of Mary Elizabeth Braddon*. New York and London: Garland, 1979.

The Vamp and the Good English Mother:
Female Roles in Le Fanu's Carmilla *and Stoker's* Dracula

MARILYN BROCK

In J. Sheridan Le Fanu's *Carmilla* (1872) and Bram Stoker's *Dracula* (1897), the most famous vampire tales of the nineteenth century, conventional definitions of domestic ideology are pitted against influences of the Other. The British fear of miscegenation is shown through depictions of demonic characters with racially associated characteristics deracinating victims through sexually aggressive acts. The fear of the Other is illustrated as most potent in relation to the Other's sexuality, as the uncertainty of the imperial project in the late Victorian era was reflected in a sense of decline in patriarchal potency around the world and at home. Dracula and Carmilla are characters who represent a fear of the Other's more vital sexuality overtaking the English colonizers, a fear which is representative of the conflation of the sexually aggressive female and the racial other, both victims of the British patriarchal regime. The female victims in both tales are characterized as potential "good English mothers," which is the most critical component of the stabilized definition of the Victorian home; therefore, these women symbolize the site at which the British feel most vulnerable. The location of sexual exchange is between the racial Other and the young English female at menarche, which connects theories of reverse-colonization and vampire narratives in relation to female bonding, sexuality, and reproduction, as clearly demonstrated by *Dracula*'s two principal female characters, Mina and Lucy, and Laura and Carmilla from Le Fanu's tale.

At the time of *Carmilla*'s publication, the gothic had been a fixture in western literature for about one hundred years and had produced more than a few vampire tales, but none had captured the horror associated with the late Victorian's definition of what Lyn Pykett calls "the improper feminine" like *Carmilla* (9). Ideological definitions of proper feminine behavior are documented in Nina Auerbach's *The Woman and the Demon* and are clearly in relation to the female's role in the home as wife and mother (185). In *Carmilla*, Laura initially demonstrates Auerbach's feminine category of the angel, who is to become the devout young bride and mother-to-be. The Victorian notion of the angel was, of course, an important part of an ideology that supported a society dominated by the middle class. The containment of bourgeois female sexuality and reproduction was met through the restrictions of marriage. Women were described as prone to hysteria without the commitment to this marital role. In *The History of Sexuality*, Foucault writes regarding the nineteenth century, "The hysterization of women, which involved a thorough medicalization of their bodies and their sex, was carried out in the name of the responsibility they owed to the health of their children" (140–41). The good English mother, as she'll be called for the purposes of this essay, is a derivative of the angel, an ideological creation that was reinforced by Victorian Society's "medical gaze" as Foucault calls it in *Birth of the Clinic* (146). The medical gaze, which diagnoses of hysteria developed from, manifested through the assumption that female sexuality needs to be monitored or it would burst out uncontrollably, harming benevolent societal structures. Marriage was to control female sexuality within a legal bond by preventing sexual disease and deviance, and was to ensure the reproduction of a healthy English race.

These goals were translated into a cultural paradigm of female mythological dualities, such as domestic angels and villainesses who did not conform. In *Carmilla*, this paradigm is characterized in the depiction of Laura, who is initially represented as an angel in the house, and then is slowly drained of her socially productive potential by Carmilla, her strange houseguest. Carmilla is a vampire and therefore, categorically a demon. In the narrative, Laura's English father invites Carmilla into their home when her carriage breaks down in front of their Styrian castle. Carmilla and Laura, both in late girlhood, become close friends. There is a scene early in the story where Laura describes a childhood dream.

> I saw a solemn, but very pretty face looking at me from the side of the bed. It was that of a young lady who was kneeling, with her hands under the coverlet ... she caressed me with her hands, and lay down beside me on the bed,

and drew me towards her, smiling; I felt immediately soothed, and fell asleep again. I was wakened by a sensation as if two needles ran into my breast very deep at the same moment, and I cried loudly [244].

When the two girls meet, Laura recognizes Carmilla from the dream. This scene depicts Carmilla's sexual prowess, as she is able to soothe Laura into sleep while caressing her, which allows her to vamp Laura. The combination of sexual imagery and terror illustrates the threat that Carmilla's sexuality poses to Laura. Through such use of the supernatural, Le Fanu gothicizes lesbianism; Carmilla is able to vamp a potential good English mother because Laura is mesmerized by her aggressive sexuality. The description of the sensation of needles in Laura's breast illustrates the menacing kind of threat inherent in Carmilla's sexuality, which the medical gaze thought to contain. Once Carmilla enters Laura's household as a young woman, her nocturnal visits to Laura become regular. Laura becomes increasingly sleepy, cannot tolerate food, and at the time she writes her story years later that she has never married or been able to resume a normal life. Carmilla's visits permanently corrupt and debilitate Laura, even after Carmilla's subsequent execution by the masculine figures in Laura's life. Carmilla's aggressive female sexuality is therefore associated with a slow death as well as violation by the end of the narrative. Additionally, since Laura never has children, the violation serves as an act of sterilization. Carmilla's bite, described as needles, associates her vampirism with a type penetration which does not reproduce, displacing the patriarchal role of the British male. Le Fanu's depiction of Laura as a Victorian angel is not just a sentimental act on his part; it puts Laura's corruption within the context of England's growing national concern with their imperialist interests in the world, associating themes in *Carmilla* with the fear of reverse-colonization.

The Indian rebellion of 1857 was the first obvious manifestation of the growing unrest in England's colonies and an event which caused panic in England's political consciousness. The bourgeois idealization of the angel in the house was integral to the domestic ideology that stabilized British national identity, and when interests abroad were threatened, insecurities developed in the national psyche of the metropole. This identity crisis caused England's gaze to turn inward, and a political self-doubt began surfacing in many forms of literature. In *Fictions of Loss at the Fin de Siècle*, Stephan Arata defines this as the "fear of reverse-colonization," which he sees as "a fearful reversal ... the colonizer finds himself in the position of the colonized, the exploiter is exploited, the victimizer is victimized" (108). In *Carmilla* and *Dracula*, this fear manifests through aggressive sexuality and miscegenation, where vampires identified with non–British racial characteristics exchange blood with young British women, which is symptomatic of an envy of the racial Other's potency, concerns about England's decaying imperialist fecundity, and guilt about colonial involvement. Foucault asserts, in *The History of Sexuality*, that blood is the classic symbol for sovereignty and national ownership, so it is a logical representative progression that a fear of reverse-colonization might be demonstrated by invasive Others draining England's life blood. As he states, "The new procedures of power that were devised during the classical period and employed in the nineteenth century were what caused our societies to go from a symbolics of blood to an analytics of sexuality" (148). Foucault continues to demonstrate this "transition from sanguinity to sexuality":

> Beginning in the second half of the nineteenth century, the thematics of blood was sometimes called on to lend its entire historical weight toward revitalizing the type of political power that was exercised through devices of sexuality. Racism took shape at this point ... and a whole politics of settlement, family, marriage ... received their color and justification from the mythical concern with protecting the purity of the blood and ensuring the triumph of race [149].

Le Fanu describes Carmilla with many non–English racial characteristics to associate her with the racial Other, illustrating England's fear of reverse-colonization. For example, Carmilla is discovered to be of a foreign, ancient family. She has dark hair and expresses perplexing responses to English traditions, such as her strange reaction to a funeral procession, "her face underwent a change that alarmed and even terrified me ... it darkened, and became *horribly livid* ... she *trembled all over* with a continued shudder as irrepressible as rage ... a *low convulsive cry* of suffering broke from her, and gradually the hysteria subsided" (264). This description contains sexual and racial references that distinguish Carmilla as Other, particularly when confronted with an English ritual. Tamar Heller explains, "As Carmilla's face darkens, she becomes what figures like the black woman in the carriage symbolize in nineteenth-century racist and sexist iconography: the woman as an angry, demonic, sexually animalistic Other" (Heller 84). Her face darkens — an allusion to race, which Carmilla also demonstrates when she first enters Laura's home, the defining structure of the stable domestic realm, which causes Carmilla's racial Otherness to become manifest. A related description in the passage contains a reference to Carmilla's teeth, "her teeth and hands were clenched, and she frowned and compressed her lips," which recalls the description of the dark woman who rides in the carriage with Carmilla when she first arrives, described as wearing a turban and smiling ghoulishly from inside the vehicle. This is one of the moments in the text that most explicitly depicts the racial Other as savage and grotesque, revealing Le Fanu's reactionary perspective. He describes this character as "a hideous black woman ... nodding and grinning derisively towards the ladies, with gleaming eyes and large white eyeballs, her teeth set as if in fury" (254). Le Fanu associates the woman with bestial qualities, by emphasizing her teeth and her foreignness. Carmilla's reaction to the funeral therefore associates her with the savage racial Other and its corresponding otherworldly appetite, such as in instances of cannibalism or vampirism. This appetite is also an important metaphor to the medical gaze and illustrates the fear of reverse-colonization in response to Victorian discourses on the body. In Le Fanu's world, the racial Other comes to infect the English race in the most dangerous form, that of a beautiful, young, sexually aggressive vampire.

Carmilla is particularly frightening because she is a grotesque example of what Lyn Pykett calls the "improper feminine," and is therefore antithetical to the definition of the kind of women needed for Britain's empirical domination. Though Laura's mother is of foreign blood, her father is English and she is represented as associated with British ideologies. The foreign blood of her mother may cause her to be more vulnerable to Carmilla's advances, suggesting the fear of reverse-colonization is a response to the English living among the colonized and losing their potency in the process. The proximity of the colonizer to the colonized manifests a cultural exchange that can in fact reshape British culture, threatening current systems of rule. What is depicted as particularly frightening is the image of the colonized infiltrating British society by appropriating their customs and subsequently miscegenating. The characters of Dracula and Carmilla both pose as respectable visitors in order to infiltrate English blood. Dracula studies English customs and laws prior to sailing to England in order to blend into the community. Stoker's novel, like *Carmilla*, illustrates that the fear of reverse-colonization becomes most terrifying when the racial Other infects the future wives and mothers of British society under the guise of the colonizer.

Count Dracula is able to enter England, though he clearly represents the ultimate racial Other, as Jonathon Harker narrates: "His face was a strong — very strong — aquiline, with high bridge of thin nose and peculiarly arched nostrils ... his eyebrows were very massive, almost meeting over the nose ... the backs of his hands ... were rather course ... there were hairs in the center of the palm" (15). These physical descriptions have obvious racial associations. H.L. Malchow's *Gothic Images of Race in Nineteenth Century Britain* observes how a long nose was an indicator of Jewishness, and the bushy eyebrows and hairy hands could be denoted as Italian, demonstrating Stoker's intention for Dracula's race to represent a combination of non–English racial categories. His initial home, Transylvania, is located in Eastern Europe, a historically bloody site reminiscent of many rises and collapses of empires. In the late nineteenth century, with the increasing perception of colonial unrest, fear was circulating that the British empire had reached its height, and a collapse, as seen in eastern European, Roman and Jewish history, seemed to be a growing possibility. Dracula's racial associations symbolize the fear that a stronger race would conquer the British Empire, especially by infiltrating their blood — essentially deracinating the English entirely.

Like Carmilla, Dracula finds categorical angels — young women at the beginning of menarche, groomed for marriage and motherhood — and attempts to corrupt them. His intention is to infect them with vampire blood in order to produce more vampires. The crew of light, *Dracula's* patriarchal group of men intent on stopping the vampire, attempt to reverse what Dracula has done to Lucy by transfusing their blood with hers, which has been infected by Dracula. This effort proves ineffective and demonstrates the Western male characters' impotence in comparison to Dracula — their very life blood is useless to stop him — further illustrating the fear of the Other's return. The Western European men are at risk of losing their dominance when Dracula moves in to infect their future wives. Furthermore, the Count's arrival is prompted by Jonathon's initial business trip to Transylvania, mimicking the process of the colonized pursuing the colonizer into his homeland after the act of colonization. In addition to Dracula, Jonathon's Transylvanian host who manifests the capabilities to deracinate England, Jonathon also meets three "weird sisters" in the castle, which appear to be the count's concubines (31). The castle houses a racially threatening male along with sexually aggressive females, as shown in the scene where the sisters look to penetrate Jonathon with their teeth. The conflation of the threat of the racial Other and the sexually aggressive female depicts the fear of reverse-colonization as manifest through unclean sexual acts as a threat to British reproduction and survival. The sexually aggressive concubines depict a reversal of categorical gender sexual roles, as Barbara Belford explains, "Vampire wives/daughters usurp the male prerogative of initiating sex" (7).

Harker responds passively to their sexual threat, mirroring the typical female pose in sex, which continues the categorical gender reversal and renders him impotent for the rest of the narrative. Moreover, when the female vampires are about the penetrate Jonathan, Dracula steps in, crying, "This man belongs to me!" (33). Belford explains, "The fear remains that Dracula will seduce, penetrate (with his phallic-shaped canine teeth), and drain another male" (9). This demonstrates the fear of the Other as foreign but also a deadly fear of homosexuality as a threat to British reproduction, as is depicted in Carmilla. Aggressive sexuality of the colonized, in the form of the racial Other and the female, threatens to usurp the potency of the English male by miscegenation or displacing reproduction altogether through homosexuality. Jonathon survives in order to return to England, but his impotency continues. His marriage to Mina, which constitutes the central love story in *Dracula*, occurs while his is lying in his sickbed, a virtual invalid after his encounter with Dracula's women. Thereafter, Harker continues to be an impotent husband, has brain fever, and sleeps soundly while Dracula, after having traveled to England, enters their bedroom to attack Mina. This passage, perhaps the most frightening of the novel, describes Dracula infecting Mina:

> On the bed beside the window lay Jonathon Harker, his face flushed, and breathing heavily as though in a stupor. Kneeling on the near edge of the bed facing outwards was the white-clad figure of his wife. By her side was a tall, thin man, clad in black. His face is turned away from us, but the instant we saw we all recognized the count — in every way, even to the scar on his forehead. With his left hand he held both Mrs. Harker's hands, keeping them away with her arms at full tension; his right hand gripped her by the back of the neck, forcing her face down on his bosom. Her white nightdress was smeared with blood, and a thin stream trickled down the man's bare breast which was shown by his torn-open shirtdress [242].

Dracula infects Mina in close proximity to her sleeping husband, who lies undisturbed. Stoker's language describing the attack illustrates the image of Mina becoming completely overtaken by Dracula's body. He has already drained her blood and she is forced to drink his blood from his breast, a perversion of the image of a mother nursing her child, and again, demonstrating the fear of reverse-colonization through violent sexuality. Dracula's sexual assault on Mina serves to destabilize British ideological domestic roles as the future good English mother is forced to suckle at the breast of the foreign male. Like Carmilla's attack on Laura, Dracula's infection serves to hypnotize Mina for the remainder of the narrative.

Another Threat

When Mina and Lucy are introduced in *Dracula*, both women are on the brink of marriage. Mina is engaged to Jonathon and Lucy has received three proposals; "Just fancy! Three proposals in one day!" Lucy writes in a letter to Mina, gloating over her feminine prowess (48). The proposals are symbolic of her power in the domestic realm. However, her power is rapidly drained when Jonathon returns from Transylvania and is followed by Dracula, whose infiltration debases Victorian domestic ideology by rendering both sexes impotent. Lucy's loss of influence is shown when is stripped of her ability to marry just as Jonathon is rendered incompetent in his marital role to Mina.

In another early scene, where Lucy and Mina are drinking tea, Stoker illustrates an additional threat to Victorian domestic ideology at the *fin de siècle*, the emerging concept of the New Woman, which is important to this notion of female influence. As she drinks with Lucy, Mina ridicules the New Woman, saying that such a modern female would be astounded by their appetite for tea. This scene illustrates these characters' relationship with the media's concept of the New Woman, often the subjects of parodic jokes. Rather than having an overwhelming priority for childbearing, the New Woman was depicted as intelligent, if rather bookish, and was illustrated as riding a bicycle rather than sidesaddle on a thoroughbred. Parodic images of the New Women depicted her as to be so intellectual that she was separated from her body and its natural function to procreate, as Lyn Pykett suggests (140). Associated with this discourse was the idea that the New Woman was prone to anorexia nervosa, because she fed her intellect rather than her body, as Heller states: "The thematics of appetite in '*Carmilla*' ... link to medical discourses about the related female maladies of hysteria, anorexia, and chlorosis-encode this fear of the devouring, sexually voracious woman lurking beneath the docile surface of the devoured woman, her apparent victim" (79). Beneath the suppression of the New Woman's bodily urges waited an intense and monstrous hunger, caused by the denial of naturalized bodily processes, such as reproduction. In *Dracula*, the concept of the New Woman is placed within a vampire narrative, which adds an important dimension to the threats associated with British fecundity. If the New Woman starves her body from its natural functions, then she becomes increasingly receptive to Dracula's "unclean" nourishment and becoming a vampire herself. Due to the development of this unearthly appetite, the New Woman could become sterile, as defined by Victorian scientific theory that there was a finite amount of energy in a woman's body, and if she were to read too much, she would starve her womb (Pykett 140). Mina's remark alienates she and Lucy from the New Woman, suggesting that she and Lucy are fit to be good English mothers; they are feeding their appetites and laughing at the New Woman. However, though the British media was busy depicting the New Woman as the threat, evident through the use of parody, Stoker proves that it is the racial Other that can transform Britain's own angels into vessels for England's destruction. Stoker's novel illustrates that is it the return of the colonized that is the real danger to England's future when it is Dracula who successfully infects Mina and Lucy, not the feminists.

Carmilla pre-dates the concept of the New Woman, but like Stoker, Le Fanu depicts an additional threat to English motherhood, that of the female homoerotic bond (Heller 79). Dracula's race and sexuality are radically ambiguous as he bisexually vamps Britain's children; he desires Jonathon in Transylvania as well as Mina and Lucy in England. Carmilla, however, is only attracted to females. Le Fanu's description of Carmilla's reaction to the funeral procession, in addition to the racial connotations, contains sexual language such as "shudder," "breathless," and "trembled all over," which allude to the experience of orgasm (264). Victorian domestic ideology prohibited female expression of sexual emotion and accompanying physical sensations outside of marriage and the realm of reproduction. The Othering of Laura's sexuality with racial categorization demonstrates Le Fanu's demonization of the homoerotic female indicated in Laura's dream. The terror of the homoerotic bond defines a fear of reverse-colonization by women, not unrelated to anxieties associated with the threat of the New Woman, which displaces the dominating and reproductive role of the male. As Heller explains, "Female homoeroticism excludes men and eludes male control, to figure female sexuality as lesbianism underscores the threat that women's desire poses to male authority" (79). When Laura and Carmilla develop their friendship, there are no male suitors in the story, and Laura wonders if Carmilla is a "boyish" lover (262). This description associates Carmilla's sexuality with male aggressiveness. Furthermore, aggressive female sexuality is demonstrated by many descriptions of Carmilla's thick, black hair. In much sensation fiction, such as M.E. Braddon's *Aurora Floyd,* thick hair is representative of aggressive sexuality. Moreover, Dante Rossetti's paintings of the sexualized woman, such as those of his model Jane Morris, were depictions of a woman with strong features and yards of thick hair.

Le Fanu associates the bond between the girls with something bestial when Laura describes Carmilla's bedside presence as appearing like a "sooty black animal" (264). This associates her Othered sexuality with animal imagery. Laura additionally describes Carmilla as a "monstrous cat" (264). Stoker continues this association of aggressive sexuality and animals when Dracula orders the wolves to attack at will and has the ability to transform himself into one himself. More images of wolfish sexuality are described by Jonathon when he is approached by the three sisters in Dracula's castle, one of whom "actually licked her lips like an animal, till I could see in the moonlight the moisture shining on the scarlet lips and on the red tongue as it lapped the white teeth" (32). Later in Jonathon's narrative, he refers to the wolves with "their red jaws, with champing teeth." This recalls Carmilla's vampire act on Laura in the form of a wolf, which involves the champing of bloody teeth. Also, on the same page, Jonathan again describes "the three terrible women licking their lips" further demonstrating the monstrous specter of aggressive female sexuality (32). The reoccurring references to wolfish teeth and bloody mouths recall the illustration of a monstrous female sexual appetite, represented by the *vagina dentata*.

In *Carmilla*, there is an attempt by the patriarchal authorities to sever the bond between Laura and Carmilla. When Laura becomes ill, male doctors are brought in, and her father attempts to take charge. The attempt is unsuccessful, though the men solve the mystery of Carmilla's identity, find her coffin, decapitate her and mutilate the corpse. Regardless, Laura never recovers, never marries, and dies after her note to the doctor some years later. Even after having been mutilated, Carmilla's essence continues its reverse-colonization, much like Dracula's influence which continues to hypnotize Mina after his attack. *Carmilla*, like *Dracula*, delivers a narrative of a failed attempt at British patriarchal dominance over threats of aggressive sexual deracination by those colonized.

Stoker describes another attempt to reassert patriarchal authority into the story by virtue of Lucy's violent death. After she is caught by the Van Helsing group, the undead Lucy is described using terrifying sexual imagery: "she seemed like a nightmare of Lucy as she laid there ... the bloodstained, voluptuous mouth" (183) and "her face became wreathed with a voluptuous smile" (182). She reaches out her arms, in order to suck her fiancé Arthur's blood, and he nearly comes to her because he is mesmerized by her terrible sexuality. Van Helsing stops Arthur and tells him that he must drive a stake through Lucy's heart. Arthur, after some hesitation, takes the huge stake and drives it through her very aggressively. Obviously, the huge stake is representative of the phallus, as Arthur's act attempts to reinstate male reproductive power into Lucy's infected body. The text's description reads like a violent sexual act.

> The body shook and quivered and twisted in wild contortions; the sharp white teeth champed together till the lips were cut, and the mouth was smeared with a crimson foam. But Arthur never faltered. He looked the figure of Thor as his untrembling arm rose and fell, driving deeper and deeper the mercy-bearing stake, whilst the blood from the pierced heart welled and spurted up around it [185].

Arthur fulfills a kind of perverse matrimonial mandate to control Lucy's reproductive acts from producing vampires rather than English heirs. The violent mutilation of the bodies of both Lucy and Carmilla demonstrates the perceived threat of aggressive female sexuality; Dracula, on the other hand, suffers a rather anti-climatic death. When the Crew of Light finds Dracula in Transylvania, they seize him and they stab him in the heart and neck. The extreme violence of the destruction of the infected women, such as Lucy and Carmilla, stands in marked contrast to the relatively "easy" death of Dracula himself. In "Kiss Me with Those Red Lips: Gender and Inversion in *Dracula*," Christopher Craft describes this difference as a result of a fear of homosexual penetration of the male. A graphic scene of stabbing Dracula would allude to the violent sexual act performed on Lucy by her fiancé. However, the description of the deaths of Lucy and Carmilla seem almost as if their authors had to punish these characters for their own existences, which reveals a sense of patriarchal guilt over the creation of these female characters. In both narratives, the concept of the racial other is inextricably linked with female sexuality by nature of the vampire's acts, therefore, the violent deaths of the women show that the threat of the female Other is a far greater threat than the male Other and needs to be made an example of, which is consistent with Victorian views about the need for the containment of female sexuality.

Victorian discourses on the body purported that female sexual appetite was most apt to become uncontrollable during menarche, therefore increasing a good English mother's susceptibility to vampirism. The female victims in *Carmilla* and *Dracula* appear to be most vulnerable when they have reached menarche, which makes them suitable vessels for sexual reverse-colonization. The fear of reverse-colonization and its relationship to late Victorian domestic ideology is demonstrated in *Dracula* and *Carmilla* when foreign, sexually aggressive Others serve as threats to British patriarchal potency and the future of the English race is jeopardized. Stoker and Le Fanu depict young, bourgeois women, on the threshold of marriage, as converted into vampires by national outsiders and thereafter unable to reproduce good English children. The return of the colonized is demonstrated through a conflation of the female and the racial Other with the capabilities to defeat and deracinate the British empire by nature of their aggressive sexuality. Only through the repeated, symbolically phallic attempts to reinstate patriarchal authority are these threats mediated. Stoker and Le Fanu's seminal tales of horror construct the vampire as the deliverer of the female and racial Other's sexual dominance.

Works Cited

Arata, Stephen D. *Fictions of Loss at the Fin de Siècle*. London: Cambridge University Press, 1996.

Armstrong, Nancy. *Desire in Domestic Fiction*. Oxford: Oxford University Press, 1987.

Auerbach, Nina. *The Woman and the Demon*. Cambridge: Harvard University Press, 1982.

Belford, Barbara. *Bram Stoker: A Biography of the Author of Dracula*. London: Phoenix Giant, 1996.

Craft, Christopher. "'Kiss Me With Those Red Lips': Gender and Inversion in Bram Stoker's *Dracula*." *Dracula*. Bram Stoker. Ed. Auerbach and Skal. New York: W. W. Norton and Company, 1997.

Foucault, Michel. *The Birth of the Clinic: An Archaeology of Medical Perception*. New York: Vintage, 1994.

_____. *The History of Sexuality: Part One*. New York: Vintage, 1990.

Gilman, Pamela K. *Disease, Desire, and the Body in Victorian Women's Popular Novels*. London: Cambridge University Press, 1997.

Heller, Tamar. *Dead Secrets*. New Haven: Yale University Press, 1992.

_____. "The Vampire in the House: Hysteria, Female Sexuality, and Female Knowledge in Le Fanu's *Carmilla*." *The New Nineteenth Century: Feminist Readings of Underread Victorian Fiction*. Ed. Harman and Meyer. New York: Garland, 1996.

Le Fanu, J. Sheridan. *In A Glass Darkly*. Stroud, Gloucestershire: Alan Sutton, 1993.

Malchow, H.L. *Gothic Images of Race in Nineteenth Century Britain*. Stanford: Stanford University Press, 1996.

Moretti, Franco. "A Capital Dracula." *Dracula*. Bram Stoker. Ed. Auerbach and Skal. New York: W.W. Norton and Company, 1997.

Pykett, Lyn. *The Improper Feminine*. London: Routledge, 1992.

Roth, Phyllis. "Suddenly Sexual Women in *Dracula*." *Dracula*. Bram Stoker. Ed. Auerbach and Skal. New York: W.W. Norton and Company, 1997.

Senf, Carol. *Science and Social Science in Bram Stoker's Fiction*. London: Greenwood Press, 2002.

Stoker, Bram. *Dracula*. New York: Dover, 2000.

Liminality and Power
in Bram Stoker's
Jewel of Seven Stars

KATE HOLTERHOFF

French folklorist Arnold Van Gennep (1873–1957) coined the phrase *liminaire* (liminality) as a means of describing the second of three steps inherent to cultural rituals, particularly rites of passage. Bram Stoker's *The Jewel of Seven Stars* (1903) provides a rich text with which to analyze liminality because, though the narrative concerns affluent Londoners in early twentieth century Britain, its plot revolves around anthropological notions of an Egyptian resurrection ritual. Because cultural significations within the narrative are twofold, a hierarchy of preference and marginality is evident. Using instructions provided by the hieroglyphics of Queen Tera's tomb, Abel Trelawny prepares to enact an ancient Egyptian rite intended to resurrect her mummy. What cultural anthropologist Victor W. Turner terms as "*rites de passage* are found in all societies but tend to reach their maximal expression in small-scale, relatively stable and cyclical societies, where change is bound up in meteorological rhythms and recurrences rather than technological innovations" (Turner 4; emphasis in original). This definition indicates that, though rituals occur in all human societies, they are not endemic to post–Industrial Revolution Western cultures. Because native ceremonies were rare in late Victorian England, importing exotic rituals would doubtless have been of interest to both ethnological dilettante and doctor alike. A ritual's liminal stage is significant as it marks the crossing of a threshold from one state to another; according to Van Gennep, rites of passage include these three stages:

> separation, transition, and incorporation. In the first stage, the "initiand" of neophyte is isolated from the rest of the community through the rite that

separates sacred from secular time and space; during the transition, which van Gennep calls "margin" or "limen" (meaning "threshold" in Latin), the initiated goes through an ambivalent social phase or limbo. During the final stage of incorporation or "reaggregation," the initiated returns to a new and relatively stable position in society at large [Spariosu 33].

Turner goes further in explicating the role of "liminal personae," asserting they are "at once *no longer* classified *and not* yet classified" (Turner 6; emphasis in original). By "no longer classified" he means the neophytes are "structurally dead," and "not yet classified" meaning, paradoxically, both living and dead expressed using "symbols modeled on processes of gestation and parturition" (Turner 6–7). The conception of initiates in a rite of passage spending an amount of time in a liminal state before being permitted to pass the threshold into community "reaggregation" applies on a number of levels to the narrative in *Jewel*. First, what does Tera's supernaturally long stay in the liminal state signify about gender politics, especially in relation to Margaret Trelawny? Second, how does *Jewel* function to explain late Victorian European understandings of science, pseudoscience, and magic? Third, how does marginalization apply to Western Imperialism and the psychology of the exotic?

Based upon scholarship into the contents of Stoker's library and the identities of his acquaintances it is clear that Stoker conducted much research into popular, nineteenth century, Western conceptions of Egyptology when writing *Jewel*. The steps of the ritual are whimsical, including the acquisition of a number of objects including seven lamps, a Magic Coffer, a ruby, cedar oil, and, of course, Tera's perfectly preserved, ivory skinned, seven-fingered, seven-toed cadaver. The mummy of Tera is significant as an artifact dated "between the twenty-ninth and twenty-fifth centuries before Christ," [2] yet it possesses contemporary agency via her astral body, feline familiar, and Margaret (Stoker 111). The soul of Tera has existed in limbo for five centuries, waiting to be resurrected in a world where she can attain the promise of patience and love, words engraved in hieroglyphs on the massive scarab-shaped ruby after which the book is titled. These words signify a "'hekau,' or word of power, ... all-important in certain rituals," with "love" ruling over the Upper World and "patience" ruling the Lower (Stoker 148). *Jewel* is brought to a Shakespearean comic ending in the 1912 rewrite, in which the Great Experiment of resurrecting Tera is unfulfilled and, after being happily married, the young protagonists Malcolm Ross and Margaret muse upon the notion that "love and patience are all that make for happiness in this world; or in the world of the past or of the future; of the living or the dead. [Tera] dreamed her dream; and that is all that any of us can ask" (Stoker 214)! This sugary conclusion to what was originally interpreted as a gothic horror condemning the hubris of man in *Jewel's* 1903 version, wraps up the narrative with a sweeping generalization contiguous to the Wife of Bath's eternal question: "What thing is it that women most desire" (Chaucer 905). Of course an answer of "sovereignty" is far from the message any Victorian man would wish to convey to either reader or wife, though power relations between the female characters Tera and Margaret and males Trelawny and Ross are interesting indeed (Chaucer 1038)[3]. Rather, the message of love and patience as a transcendent dream allude to the romantic desires of Tera, which Margaret empathically conveys to the men engaged in conducting the Great Experiment:

> I can see [Tera] in her loneliness and in the silence of her mighty pride, dreaming her own dream of things far different from those around her. Of some other land, far, far away under the canopy of the silent night, lit by the cool, beautiful light of the stars. A land under that Northern star, whence blew the sweet winds that cooled the feverish desert air. A land of wholesome greenery, far, far away. Where were no scheming and malignant priesthood; whose ideas were to lead to power through gloomy temples and more gloomy caverns of the dead, through an endless ritual of death! A land where love was not base, but a divine possession of the soul! Where there might be some one kindred spirit which could speak to hers through mortal lips like her own; whose being could merge with hers in a sweet communion of soul to soul, even as their breaths could mingle in the ambient air! [Stoker 153].

Margaret expresses a remarkable construction of Tera's desires which concurrently envisions the Queen as wholly feminine in her warm and demonstrative sensibilities while rejecting the "gloomy" pursuits of pagan priests. This knowledge is attained via the psychic link between Tera and Margaret formed in the womb as the latter was "born of a dead mother during the time that her father and his friend were in a trance in the tomb at Aswân" (Stoker 177). They look identical "in both feature and colour" according to Trelawny's interpretation of "pictures of Queen Tera," and, additionally, Margaret possesses a jagged scar precisely located where the mummy of Tera had her arm removed (Stoker 118). However, Trelawny forges a very different vision of Tera based on evidence accrued from the hieroglyphs of her tomb. According to her father's research, Tera "had power over Sleep and Will. This was real magic — 'black' magic.... She had been an apt pupil; and had gone further than her teachers. Her power and her resources had given her great opportunities, of which she had availed herself to the full" (Stoker 111). The manner in which Trelawny acquires his information is scholarly, requiring esoteric and linguistic knowledge making it less surprising that both characterizations of Tera are entirely different.

Gender Politics

Yet the question remains: Who is the real Tera — cold, commanding sorceress or misunderstood, romantic girl? The two conceptions seem at times in Ross's narration to be exceedingly disparate, negating any room for overlap. Yet critic Andrew Smith explains unreliability in the narrator is expected due to "Ross's fantasies about Margaret which control the narrative" (82). It would seem that both interpretations of Tera's voice and history rely on interpretation by a secondary source since we never get to "hear" Tera speak in first person. The mediumistic nature of our relationship with Tera indicates that Stoker wished to construct her as an ideal, making her paradoxically terrifying. Sexually, the ivory flesh of Tera signifies perfection reminiscent of Poe's necrophilic "love that was more than love" for Annabel Lee (9). In one of the more carnal scenes in *Jewel* the men unwrap Tera's mummy supposedly in the service of the Great Experiment, discovering her flesh to be "full and round, as in a living person; and the skin was as smooth as satin. The color seemed extraordinary. It was like ivory, new ivory" (Stoker 203). Although Trelawney assures Margaret that Dr. Winchester and Corbeck are professionals whom "custom has made ... think nothing of sex," Ross is horrified by the spectacle, declaring the unwrapping to illustrate the "sordid side of death" (Stoker 199, 201). Once the Queen lies naked upon the table "all the romance and sentiment of fancy had disappeared" leaving Ross to feel "miserable, and ashamed" (Stoker 201). This indignity likewise horrifies the sympathetic Margaret who perceives Tera as a vulnerable woman for whom "sex is not a matter of years," but an indelible condition (Stoker 199). Trelawney paternalistically pacifies his daughter through implicating her intelligence: "They didn't have women's rights or lady doctors in ancient Egypt" (Stoker 199). Therefore, although Tera is being resurrected in a time period that is dabbling in women's rights via higher education, access to the work place, and suffrage, because the Queen is from an era and continent without these liberal mores, she is not entitled to contemporary rights. The exoticism of Tera supersedes her rights as a woman, as she is eternally African, with all the baggage of "European myths about Africans as strange, disordered, evil, superstitious and dangerous" (Ogede 129). This assertion rips apart the essence of the Queen's mission to attain the hekaus "love" and "patience." Although "she had intended her resurrection to be after a long time and in a more northern land," the promise of tolerance for the "longing soul, of that sweet and lovely Queen, so different from her surroundings, so high above her time" foreseen by Margaret and evidenced in the wedding robe she "slept" in for centuries, can never be fulfilled (Stoker 112, 153). Therefore, the liminality of Tera is double; she is physically a corpse while simultaneously undead in her astral body, and Tera is both a woman and an exotic curiosity capable of conveying knowledge, but not subject to the strictures and freedoms of white British citizenship[4].

The empathic relationship between Tera and Margaret becomes increasingly convoluted as the narrative progresses. To the extent that it is possible the two actually merge into one: "there was no Margaret at all; but just an animated image, used by the Double of a woman of forty centuries ago to its own ends" (Stoker 178). The double identity of Miss Trelawny and Tera poses problems for the male protagonists in *Jewel*. Whereas Mr. Trelawny accepts this state willingly, stating that "if in addition there be the spirit of that great and wondrous Queen, then [Margaret] would be no less dear to me, but doubly dear" (Stoker 185). Because Trelawney accepts "that the spirit of her mother is within her," he is willing to add another esteemed identity to the seemingly limitless vessel of Margaret's soul. Unlike the split personality in Robert Louis Stevenson's *The Strange Case of Dr Jekyll and Mr Hyde* (1886), the replacement of souls in *Invasion of the Body Snatchers* (1956), possession by a demon in *The Exorcist* (1973), or even the three-headed knight in *Monty Python and the Holy Grail* (1975), the layering of identities within Margaret is perceived as an acceptable, even desirable end. However, distorted mores may be attributes of Margaret's father since Ross depicts "Mr. Trelawny [as] a peculiar man," and her betrothed remains far more wary of this merger (Stoker 134). In hopes of possibly saving Margaret's identity from occupation by the murdering Tera, he attempts unsuccessfully to convince the Trelawnys to halt the Great Experiment. As the plot progresses Ross' agency is discontinued as he finds himself less and less able to pinpoint who exactly Margaret is at any given moment, seeing at once "a caged lion" and "wonted sweetness" (Stoker 186, 195). Smith explains that this unusual male gaze demonstrates that "Ross's feelings of love represent an inability to properly objectify Margaret," thereby enacting the Female Gothic (85)[5]. However, as the connection between Miss Trelawny and the mummy grows stronger, Ross's affections fluctuate. After realizing that "Margaret was changing," evidenced by a "negative condition as though her mind — her very being — was not present," Ross experiences difficulties maintaining their bond, explaining "hour by hour we drifted apart" (Stoker 176). The fluctuating personality of Margaret suggests a truly liminal state as she is neither wholly herself nor a "speaking parrot," being simultaneously both and neither (Stoker 176).

Indeed Margaret's identity constitutes a particularly germane subject by which to interpret liminality. The content of Margaret's soul is a dynamic plot element throughout *Jewel*, as she functions in three distinct roles: first, as "the old Margaret whom [Ross] had loved at the first glance"; second, as Tera herself who is revealed by primal behavior, as in one instance she falls "into a positive fury of passion. Her eyes blazed, and her mouth took a hard, cruel tension"; and third, as the combination of Tera and Margaret, able to garner the praise of listeners for possessing a "wealth of affection, such a splendour of spiritual insight, such a scholarly imagination" (Stoker 176, 173, 154). And yet Margaret is continuously floating between these three states. Because she never wholly embraces one above the others Margaret resides somewhere betwixt and between.

Science and Magic

Science arises as an important element in the resurrection of Tera. She is represented as "the concrete embodiment of the past ... a creature of magic rather than science," and yet scientific means are used by those engaged in the Great Experiment to explain the wonders termed magic by Ancient Egyptians (Senf 85). The fictions of Bram Stoker occupy a curious space between science and the occult. Much has been written on this relationship, as Stoker's literary career was largely unexceptional in this regard, coinciding with the development of Victorian science fiction[6]. In *Dracula* this curious binary is highlighted by Van Helsing's assertion "there are things done today in electrical science which would have been deemed unholy by the very man who discovered electricity, who would themselves not so long before been burned as wizards. There are always mysteries in life" (Stoker 201). While electricity had been deemed relatively benign and natural by the early twentieth century, Stoker represents a positivistic era when knowledge regarding the bounds and definition of power, transcended genre. While Harry Houdini toured Europe performing fantastic feats of illusion, the number of adherents to spiritualism remained substantial, and French neurologist Charcot probed the persuasive capabilities of hypnotism, the line between science, showmanship, religion, and magic blurred impenetrably. The conflation of science and magic is recurrent in Stoker's oeuvre, leading Carol Senf to state that "despite his apparent enthusiasm for science, he might even be accused of confusing science, pseudoscience, and technology" (4). Though the lines Stoker draws between these fields remains unclear, that he utilizes contemporary scientific discoveries recurrently as plot elements is undeniable and thereby serviceable to our inquiry of threshold crossings.

At the turn of the twentieth century the pace of science was quickening exponentially. The inception of the Industrial Revolution was now over a century in the past, and science looked as though it could close all society's gaps, since economics, health, recreation, mobility, communication, and energy were in the process of revolution. Though exciting, "progress" was anxiety producing among many urban Europeans[7]. Overall Stoker was optimistic about the new era of science. However, the horrific elements of his novels tap into notions that "the fin de siècle revival of the Gothic was intricately connected with the anxieties produced by the various new scientific discourses" (Byron 50). *Jewel* documents much of the good in science, witnessed in Trelawny's utilization of "turbines moved by the flowing and ebbing tide, after the manner of the turbines at Niagara" to generate power, as well as his humanistic optimism: "I am willing to run any risk. For science, and history, and philosophy may benefit; and we may turn one old page of a wisdom unknown in this prosaic age" (Stoker 190, 140). However, in the 1903 edition of *Jewel*, man's hubris ultimately causes the demise of all those engaged in the Great Experiment.[8] Interestingly, this makes *Jewel* singular among Stoker's novels in that it "is consistently more ambivalent about the mysterious powers that are generally labeled Gothic and less optimistic about the power of modern science" (Senf 75). Whereas in *Dracula* science is "working to identify, control, and eliminate the transgressive and the monstrous," in *Jewel* "science works to release it" (Byron 57).

Both Glennis Byron and David Glover note, it is not until the protagonists categorize Dracula under the blanket term of criminal that his agency is greatly diminished: "As soon as Dracula is so categorised, then ... his actions can be predicted," intercepted, and obstructed (Byron 55). The ability to order the Powers that Be into sterile and systematic compartments removes much of the horror from gothic themes, neutralizing an existential anxiety of the unknown. Often what lies at the margins of Western knowledge defies compartmentalization and upsets civilized norms. Increased encounters with the new, monstrous, and liminal were ensured by Britain's colonial holdings, making imperial concerns of particular import to the English psyche.

Western Imperialism

The power of liminality lies in its ability to upset the materialist notion of categorization which so concerned Western naturalists and anthropologists of the nineteenth and early twentieth century. Another Victorian novel, Joseph Conrad's *Lord Jim*, epitomizes this attitude, especially the Bavarian colonial trader and "naturalist of some distinction" Stein (146). During Marlowe's brief visit to his old friend Stein, the latter communicates that the bronze winged butterfly upon which he muses is particularly rare: "Only one specimen like this they have in your London, and then — no more" (Conrad 147)[9]. However, instead of sending it to the grand British Museum, renowned for its vast collection of exotic curiosities, Stein asserts that "to my small native town this my collection I shall bequeath. Something of me. The best" (Conrad 147). Apparently Stein is little concerned with immortalizing his reputation in urban centers where lepidopterists would eagerly pour over the spectacle of this, and assuredly other rare specimens[10]. Stein is concerned with accomplishing something else altogether in sending home his butterfly collection. Although he is economically successful in the East Indies, the trauma of acclimating to non–Western life has affected his understanding of divine purpose. While musing over his specimen, Stein tells Marlowe:

> "Man is amazing, but he is not a masterpiece," ... "Perhaps the artist was a little mad. Eh? What do you think? Sometimes it seems to me that man is come where he is not wanted, where there is no place for him; for if not, why should he want all the place? Why should he run about here and there making a great noise about himself, talking about the stars, disturbing the blades of grass?" [Conrad 150].

This expostulation thinly veils the ecologically tinged guilt felt by Stein regarding European imperialist tendencies. In the process of capturing, labeling, and discovering new species, fear of non–Western imports to Europe is partially assuaged, yet by the act of categorizing species, man is all the time "disturbing" the natural order. The implication is that this desire can be traced to a psychological imbalance programmed by the playful Creator imbuing humanity with an incurable restlessness. By returning the most beautiful and exotic fauna he has collected to his native Bavaria, Stein hopes to remind his fellow man to remember the quiet wonders, tread lightly, and question the motivations of mankind. Of course, colonial imports are rarely as benign or beautiful as butterflies under glass.

Exotic importation, while economically beneficial and often titillating, was accompanied by unease in Europe. A number of Arthur Conan Doyle's Sherlock Holmes mysteries touch on this colonial intolerance. "The Speckled Band" (1892) is considered the most "Poesque" of Doyle's mysteries, while also being the author's personal favorite (Hodgson 173). The gothic elements of "The Speckled Band" make its positioning in the detective fiction genre tenuous[11], but its importance to late nineteenth century gothic discourse is incontrovertible. The villain, Dr. Grimesby Roylott, is an extreme example of a British man unwilling and possibly unable to extract his identity from the British Empire's colonial holdings. After living in India for a number of years, Roylott returns to Stoke Moran, his family estate in Surrey, with numerous foreign items and mannerisms: acquisitions perceived at best as bemusing but monstrous at worst. The befriending of gypsies, wearing of Turkish slippers, and keeping of exotic pets including a baboon, cheetah and, of course, the fictitious milk drinking, whistle-trained "swamp adder" that Holmes instantly recognizes to be "the deadliest snake in India" would doubtlessly be construed as incomprehensible by mainstream, middle-class, British society (Doyle 171). The adder arises as the filicidal weapon used by Roylott, making this specific importation a tangible and deadly threat amongst the ordinarily benign European flora and fauna. Though he is exceedingly crafty in his mode of execution, "Roylott, with his links to the Orient ... is associated with 'eastern irrationality'" (Hennessy & Mohan 389). Holmes, the representative of Western normalcy and reason, must forestall the "Eastern training" Roylott internalized overseas and brought back to Europe (Doyle 172).

Like the dangerous acquisitions of Roylott, the artifacts collected by Trelawny are far from harmless. As a wealthy Egyptologist, Trelawny's collection of ancient Egyptian paraphernalia is substantial. He has even employed a man, Eugene Corbeck, to find specific items to enable execution of the Great Experiment. Corbeck explains to Miss Trelawny that a number of her father's "treasures — and he has some rare ones, ... he has procured through me, either by my exploration or by purchase — or — or — otherwise" (Stoker 69). This description alludes to the suspect manner in which Trelawny's collection was augmented. Of course, Corbeck's assertion seamlessly foreshadows the unpleasant repercussions of meddling in hazardous exotic affairs: that which is unlawfully acquired is disentitled from civilized notions of science, decency, and order. Though in the 1912 revision of *Jewel* the Great Experiment concludes with a less tragic ending, the perpetual colonization of Margaret's soul with Queen Tera's parasitic/divine presence cannot be written off as a possible interpretation of this supposedly comically happy ending[12].

The narrative of *Jewel* is dynamic with all protagonists attaining a new state and identity after the Great Experiment. Whether we consider the horror of death and loss experienced by all mortals via Tera's terrible resurrection in the 1903 version, or the marriage rite performed on Ross and Margaret while Trelawney assumedly laments the failure of his project in the 1912 rewrite, a threshold has successfully been crossed and lessons learned. Although Stoker's fictional resurrection ritual in *Jewel* does not literally epitomize the three steps identified in Van Gennep's rites of passage, using the liminal stage as a metaphoric instrument allows for profound analysis of power and disenfranchisement in early twentieth century European conceptions of both those "like us" and the milieu of colonial, gender, and scientific others.

Notes

1. Carol Senf asserts in "Reservations about Science, Popular Egyptology, and the Power of the Natural World in *The Jewel of Seven Stars*" (2002) that Stoker's personal acquaintance with Sir Richard Burton and Sir William Wilde may have peaked Stoker's interest in Egyptology (76). In addition, records from the July 7, 1913, Sotheby's auction at which Stoker's library was sold, and recorded in William Hughes's already canonical work of Stoker criticism *Beyond Dracula: Bram Stoker's Fiction and its Cultural Context* (2000), indicate that Stoker had so many books on Egyptology he "might be considered an amateur Egyptologist" (Senf 77).

2. This possibly flippant allusion to Christ made by Treawny gains increased significance as Tera is resurrected via supernatural powers after an extended period existing in limbo just as Christ was dead for 3 days before his resurrection from the grave, and subsequent ascension to heaven. Joseph Campbell describes "the passage of the threshold [as] a form of self annihilation," where the resurrected individual is somehow changed after their experience (91). It is peculiar then to note that Tera intends to be resurrected twice. According to Trelawny's research:

> She had won secrets from nature in strange ways; and had even gone to the length of going down into the tomb herself, having been swathed and coffined and left as

dead for a whole month. The priests had tried to make out that the real Princess Tera had died in the experiment, and that another girl had been substituted; but she had conclusively proved their error [Stoker 111].

It would seem that the function of resurrection is not metaphysical or spiritual, as is the function of Campbell's essential Hero's Journey, but a more material, scientific experiment capable of duplication. This is especially harrowing when considered in light of Trelawny's assertion that "after all, the Bible is not a myth," which might indicate that Jesus' resurrection is a scientifically demonstrable fact, God's supernatural abilities exist beyond science, or both (Stoker 142).

3. Andrew Smith states in "Love, Freud, and the Female Gothic Bram Stoker's *The Jewel of Seven Stars*" (2004) that *Jewel* must be understood in light of the Female Gothic affirming, "ultimately Jewel represents a horror of women's empowerment" (88). Ellen Moers defines the Female Gothic as a literary form "characterised by concerns about motherhood and associated images of birth trauma," though later critics included "specific structural features, including images of absent mothers and 'lost' daughters ... related to the form's anti-patriarchal politics" (Smith 80).

4. Women, regardless of race, were excluded from comprehensive social involvement even late into the nineteenth century. See Dorothy Stetson's *A Woman's Issue: The Politics of Family Law Reform in England* (1982) for analysis of the Married Women's Property Act (1882).

5. A psychoanalytic interpretation of Ross and Margaret's relationship is utilized by Smith to show that as a lawyer, and therefore bearer of the "prosaic side of authority and order," Ross wishes to extract Margaret from being stifled by domesticity and patriarchal control in a romantic bid to win her affections (Smith 82). This heroic fantasy illustrates Ross' conflation of love and will as he learns Margaret is far from helpless. Smith notes the "creeping influence of Tera over Margaret represents a move from a Female Gothic plot concerning the search for a missing mother and an escape from a tyrannical father figure ... to one in which Margaret, and more importantly love, become reconfigured as suspicious" (Smith 83).

6. See Judith Wilt's extended investigation of this burgeoning genre in "The Imperial Mouth: Imperialism, the Gothic and Science Fiction" (1981).

7. See Friedrich Nietzsche's investigation of European nihilism in *The Will to Power* (1889).

8. Of course, excepting Ross whose survival allows this terrifying but didactic story to be told.

9. Chandler interprets Stein's butterfly and beetle specimens as allusions to Jim and his plight. Marlow explicitly describes Jim as a specimen, though "Nothing so perfect" as a butterfly (Conrad 152). Because Jim is eternally "one of us," Chandler concludes "the analogical link between the two specimens, Jim and the rare butterfly, is thus introduced by way of a key difference already established between the two species:" sorting men into those who are "like us" and those unlike (Chandler 846). This reading makes intriguing links between categorization as a means of anxiety control and the Darwinian bonds connecting man and animal.

10. Marlowe somewhat ironically concedes "entomology was [Stein's] special study. His collection of *Buprestidae* and *Longicorns*— beetles all — horrible miniature monsters, looking malevolent in death and immobility, and his cabinet of butterflies, beautiful and hovering under the glass of cases on lifeless wings, had spread his fame far over the earth" notifying the reader that through his offering of insect cadavers Stein's place in history is already assured (Conrad 146).

11. See John A Hodgson's "The Recoil of 'The Speckled Band' Detective Story and Detective Discourse" (1992) for a more in-depth study of genre amalgamation in the Sherlock Holmes mysteries.

12. Another interpretation of Stoker's decision to move away from a tragedy is offered by Smith who posits "the first ending suggests Stoker's inability properly to control the rebellious aspects of the Female Gothic, whereas the second, as in Dracula, implies the possibility of exerting social control through marriage" (87). This reading works in conjunction with earlier discussion regarding the notion of the female as *tabula rasa*, a vessel with cognitive "room to spare" for population by the divine, or, more commonly masculine agency.

Works Cited

Byron, Glennis. "Bram Stoker's Gothic and the Resources of Science." *Critical Survey* 19. 2 (2007): 48–62.

Campbell, Joseph. *The Hero with a Thousand Faces*. Princeton: Princeton University Press, 1973.

Chandler, James. "On the Face of the Case: Conrad, Lord Jim, and the Sentimental Novel." *Critical Inquiry* 33.4 (Summer 2007): 864–837.

Chaucer, Geoffrey. *The Wife of Bath's Prologue and Tale from the Canterbury Tales*. Ed. James Winny. Cambridge: Cambridge University Press, 1965.

Conrad, Joseph. *Lord Jim*. New York: Oxford, 2002.

Doyle, Arthur Conan. "The Speckled Band." *Sherlock Holmes: The Major Stories with Contemporary Critical Essays*. Ed. John A. Hodgson. New York: Bedford, 1994. 152–173.

Hennessy, Rosemary, and Rajeswari Mohan. "'The Speckled Band': The Construction of Woman in a Popular Text of Empire." *Sherlock Holmes: The Major Stories with Contemporary Critical Essays*. Ed. John A. Hodgson. New York: Bedford, 1994. 389–401.

Ogede, Ode S. "Phantoms Mistaken for a Human Face: Race and Construction of the African Woman's Identity in Joseph Conrad's *Heart of Darkness*." *The Foreign Women in British Literature*. Ed. Marilyn Button and Toni Reed. Westport, CT: Greenwood, 1999. 127–138.

Poe, Edgar Allan. "Annabel Lee." *The Norton Anthology of American Literature: 1820–1865*. 6th ed. Ed. Nina Baum. Vol. B. New York: Norton, 2003. 1524.

Senf, Carol A. "Reservations about Science, Popular Egyptology, and the Power of the Natural World in *The Jewel of Seven Stars*." *Science and Social Science in Bram Stoker's Fiction*. Westport, CT: Greenwood, 2002. 73–95.

Smith, Andrew. "Love, Freud, and the Female Gothic Bram Stoker's *The Jewel of Seven Stars*." *Gothic Studies* 6.1 (May 2004): 80–89.

Spariosu, Mihai I. "Liminality, Literary Discourse and Alternative Worlds." *The Wreath of Wild Olive*. New York: SUNY, 1997. 31–72.

Stoker, Bram. *Dracula*. Ed. John Paul Riquelme. Boston: Bedford, 2002.

_____. *The Jewel of Seven Stars*. New York: Oxford, 1996.

Turner, Victor W. "Betwixt and Between: The Liminal Period in Rites de Passage." *Symposium on New Approaches to the Study of Religion by the American Ethnological Society*. Pittsburgh: University of Pittsburgh, 1964. 4–20.

Wilt, Judith. "The Imperial Mouth: Imperialism, the Gothic and Science Fiction." *Journal of Popular Culture* 14.4 (1981): 618–628.

PART THREE

Fallen Woman, Fallen Man in the Victorian Novel

Ruth:
An Analysis of the Victorian Signifieds

· MARIA GRANIC-WHITE

Elizabeth Gaskell's novel *Ruth* (1853) represents a creative response to the social and religious life in mid-nineteenth century England. Characteristically Victorian, the novel illustrates a world in which artificially constructed values change their signifieds. Reflecting the Victorians' dichotomous view of the world strongly influenced by the Manichean philosophy, the text proposes that both good and evil are active and quintessential elements in the creation, fall, and redemption of man. The binary oppositions in Gaskell's novel reveal the values of the Victorian society, challenging the reader to rethink or reread the relations among them; they also suggest that the Victorian society itself is a construct, based on clear signifiers whose signifieds appear as evasive. At first appearing to privilege one of the terms of the binary, the text dismantles the Victorians' views and proves that both terms are privileged, supplementing each other as parts of a whole. Blurring the boundaries between the two terms of the binaries, and more so, illustrating that there is male in female, an angel in a fallen woman, sinlessness in sinfulness, and so on, Gaskell's text challenges the Victorians' paradigms and dramatizes the possibility of the fallen woman to become sanctified by society upon her death.

Studying the binary oppositions, one can examine the proto-sensational elements of the text, whose narrator's seemingly insouciant attitude goes against the grain of the Victorian mindset. Among the scandalous elements of the novel are the story of Ruth's seduction, the Dissenting minister's lie, and Ruth's "sanctification" toward the end of the narrative. Although other novels of the same era depict fallen women (such as Aunt Esther in Gaskell's *Mary Barton* or Alice Marwood in Charles Dickens's *Dombey and Son*), Gaskell's *Ruth* is the first to include the fallen woman as the protagonist, and thus to question the definition of sin itself by making heroic an innocent, poorly educated, gullible, young girl. Like Charles Dickens, George Eliot, Wilkie Collins, George Gissing, George Moore, and Thomas Hardy, Gaskell questions the absolute nature of the two groups of women — the pure and the fallen — exposes the complex problems of the Victorian society's dichotomous worldview, and dismantles them in order to reconstitute them.

A close reading of the novel reveals, as Elizabeth Langland argues, that "Gaskell represents reality as a construction" (120), and encourages the reader to play with signification, to utilize the Derridean terms ("Structure, Sign, and Play" 886). Having established the putative centers, the novel decenters them as the narrative thread evolves. Thus, both the structure of the text and the decentering of the Victorian transcendental signified permit "interplay of signification *ad infinitum*" (Derrida, "Structure, Sign, and Play" 879). Analyzing the signifieds in Gaskell's novel, various critics emphasize that gender is a construct in *Ruth*. Langland focuses on class barrier that makes its presence felt in doomed romances of couples such as Ruth Hilton and Henry Bellingham, and on the intersection of class and gender ideologies. Hilary Schor and Deborah Anna Logan emphasize the Victorian gender ideology and the condition of the woman as a construct. George Watt follows Ruth progress from victim to tragic heroine to contend that the newness of the text stands in its portrayal of a sinner as heroic, an important attribute of sensation novels. Robyn Warhol addresses the author's intrusion in the text to pinpoint ideas of the feminine respectability and authority, while Joanne Thompson contrasts the feminine sympathy with the sternness and rigidity of male virtue. Finally, Andrew Dowling examines the meaning of manliness in Victorian literary texts, considering masculinity to be a complex construction rather than a natural given.

The male/female binary as well as of the other aspects of the Victorian society, such as faith, Christianity, sinfulness, redemption, and so on, unveils the Victorian society depicted by the text as a construct. Establishing male as the privileged term in the binary, the novel dislocates it to replace it with female. Given that "Gaskell seldom commits herself to gender stereotypes" (Thompson 24), the unprivileged term in the binary takes the place of the privileged one and becomes a supplement. Thus, Gaskell's novel reverses hierarchies and proposes its own definitions of masculine and feminine values, which do not correspond to those of the Victorian culture. According to Susan Morgan, gender definitions are the products of human imagination and, therefore, can be reimagined:

Thinking about gender critically requires that we become constantly attentive to three continuing but still historical truths: our culture's hostility to what it calls feminine, indeed, its use of the label feminine to function precisely as a catch-all for qualities and values it would devalue; the pressure to cloak coercion in inevitability ... by identifying culture with nature, feminine and masculine with actual women and men [13].

Gaskell's text does exactly this: by bringing to surface the unconscious schisms that produce gender ideologies, it attempts not just to "examine these bifurcations, but to effect changes in them" (Johnson 1).

Ruth, the protagonist of the novel, acquires equivocal characteristics. Her female demeanor, symbolized by her rides in the cart, which expose her passivity, discloses her inability to influence the adult world, her tractable nature, and her vulnerability (Watt 23). In different instances in the novel, she does not act but instead is acted upon as the passenger driven by her guardian to the workshop, by Bellingham to Wales, and by the Bensons to Eccleston. Possessing little individual agency, Ruth does not seem to think for herself: Thurstan and Faith Benson make decisions for her, creating her new identity, which appeals to both Mr. Farquhar and Mr. Bradshaw. Mr. Farquhar considers the apparently quiet and gentle Ruth a better choice over Jemima, whose frank, spirited, and passionate nature abates her external beauty and implicitly reduces her chances of marriage. The text explicitly aligns beauty with femininity implying the sexual division and privileging masculinity, expressed by (paternally) looking over the female. The female's condition, therefore, is of being looked at (Hartley 20), of being objectified and studied. Referring to the passiveness of women, Schor maintains that the dilemma in Gaskell's novel is that a culture which breeds women as objects will breed them altogether diminutive and not bright (163). However, Gaskell challenges this Victorian idea by having not only Ruth's beauty attract the reader's attention, but also her ethics of care and her analytical power.

Ruth's natural beauty presents her as an object of interest: "'She is a very lovely creature,' said one gentleman, rising from the breakfast table to catch a glimpse of her, as she entered from her morning ramble" (Gaskell 70). Not only men, but also women find Ruth attractive: "But even Sally could not help secretly admiring Ruth. If her early brilliancy of color was gone, a clear ivory skin, as smooth as satin, told of complete and perfect health, and was as lovely, if not so striking in effect, as the banished lilies and roses" (Gaskell 208). The epithet "banished" alludes to Ruth's status as exiled, expelled, or put out of one's thoughts, which implies that Ruth is to be perceived as an outsider by the other characters and the reader as well, as a fallen woman. However, the context in which the epithet appears, the simile, confers it a positive connotation: flowers are harmless, defenseless organisms, which exist outside the moral realm. Likewise, as an orphan, deprived of her parents' wisdom and affection, Ruth is a harmless person, whose beauty makes her extremely vulnerable.

Out of her own need for someone's care, Ruth develops a commendable desire to care for and to devote herself to other people. Abandoned by Bellingham, desperate, Ruth wanders away from the inn where she received Mrs. Bellingham's cold and accusing letter together with a fifty-pound banknote. When the deformed man (Mr. Benson) who tries to comfort her falls down the rocks, Ruth helps him and accompanies him to the inn (Gaskell 97–99). Later in the novel, while tending to Bellingham, the selfish man who caused her misery, Ruth realizes that the people in her community will never hear her voice because their ears are not attuned to hearing women; the unprivileged term in the male/female binary has no voice in the Victorian mind. Rather than complying with the Victorian rules, however, the text portrays Ruth as a character who chooses to make herself heard by the community through her deeds, which nobody can efface. Like all the nonphonemic signifiers, Ruth's deeds involve "a spatial reference in [their] very 'phenomenon,' in the phenomenological (nonworldly) sphere of experience in which [they are] given" (Derrida, *Speech and Phenomena* 76). Through her acts, Ruth becomes what Langland calls "a different kind of angel," engaging in philanthropic acts in the form of house-to-house visits (296), and acts with generosity towards the others and especially towards Bellingham. Although Ruth may have a natural impulse to care for the others, the fact that she sustains her care to her own detriment shows her moral commitment to the ideal of caring: the fallen woman acts morally and becomes the others' guardian angel. Through the acts of its protagonist, the novel raises difficult questions for the Victorians to answer, such as: Can the fallen woman be/become virtuous? Should the image of the woman be reinvented? Can/Should a pariah such as Ruth become reintegrated into society? What makes the terms in the binary oppositions gain a supplemental relation is the fact that Ruth's actions demonstrate her ethics of care, her work and expenditure of energy while acting on behalf of her community's interests.

Rather than merely providing a service for Bellingham, Ruth cares for him, expressing thus her devotion to him. She offers care in the way in which

Diemuth Bubeck defines it: "Caring for is the meeting of needs of one person by another person, where face-to-face interaction between the carer and cared for is a crucial element of the overall activity and where the need is of such a nature that it cannot be possibly met by the person in need [himself]" (129). In her face-to-face interaction with Bellingham in his room at the Queen's Hotel, Ruth exhausts herself, endangering her life. Hence, the narrator claims that "it was but too evident that Ruth 'home must go, and take her wages'" (Gaskell 447). These words offer several possible interpretations. The unusual word order, place preceding the verb, calls the reader's attention to the word "home," to its connotations — family, love, safety, etc. The same word can also suggest the authoritarian, patriarchal voice of the narrator functioning here similarly to the chorus in the Greek tragedies, alluding to an ominous future for Ruth. "To go home" could either suggest that Ruth has to die or that she has to leave away from Bellingham and seek the protection which a home can give her; at the same time, the "wages" Ruth should take could either denote punishment or reward. The biblical vocabulary employed by the text evokes the phrase "the wages of sin is death" (Romans 6:23), and thus it entails that the text may condemn Ruth for her past. However, Ruth is providing care as a nurse, and she needs to be remunerated for her hard work. Viewed through the latter interpretation, Ruth's behavior on the deathbed, more exactly, her joyous singing and especially the light she sees immediately before her death, intimates that Ruth receives payment for her hard work. In this context, light can symbolize the guarantee of heaven for Ruth's afterlife. Thus, care represents more than work for Ruth: it becomes a value which all those who attend her funeral seem to acknowledge, and more so, it becomes a virtue rewarded. Despite having established Ruth's status as a fallen woman, the text presents Ruth as morally admirable.

The social making of the heroine echoes the tendency of the plot to remind the reader of its making, of its constructed character. In "The Victorian Place of Enunciation," Warhol considers the author's intervention as a figure which the speaker creates, employing the idiom of the minister in order to add authority to a text that advocates feminine respectability (190). The personal pronoun "you," having the reader as a referent, unveils the narrator's attempt to suggest to the reader that the omniscient voice has a deeper insight into societal problems than society itself, "One who had known them at the date of Ruth's becoming a governess in Mr. Bradshaw's family, and had been absent until the time of which I am now going to tell you, would have noted some changes" (Gaskell 201). Yet, postmodern theories suggest that the "you" of the novel does not refer to individual subjects, but instead it is only the product of *différance,* "an economic concept designating the production of differing/deferring" (Derrida, *Of Grammatology* 23), among the signifiers in the text.

At times, Ruth's signified is that of male, her identity depending upon the renegotiation of the traditional concepts and experiences of authority. Early in the novel, when Bellingham does not attend church at St. Nicholas one Sunday, Ruth reflects on herself, a male-like characteristic in the Victorian view, and realizes that she is "self-conscious all the time" (Gaskell 39). Also, at the Bradshaws' house, where she works as a governess, upon seeing Bellingham (now called Donne) Ruth ruminates on her sentiments for him and analyses herself as a woman and as a mother (Gaskell 273–74). The naïve and weak Ruth acts like a strong and determined woman, endowed with the faculty of reflection with which she tries to save herself and her son from the traps set by the hostile society. Although her meditation does not gain a deep tone, it conveys her striking realism, which does not allow her to perceive evil or sin in society as a fatality (in Schopenhauerian vision). However, she proves to be too strong-willed, to the point of self-annihilation. At Benson's house, Ruth metaphorically kills the non-existent husband taking control over her life, and accepts her new name, Mrs. Denbigh, reinventing herself and symbolically reinventing her reality. The heroine overpowers Bellingham when she refuses to marry him and thus to become the wife which the Victorian society idealizes through Bradshaw, whose view of women matches that which Rousseau offers in *Emile*; Bradshaw expects women to be submissive, gentle, clinging, uncomplicated, and, most of all, pure. Bellingham's defeat by Ruth, Watt claims, is almost a *fait accompli* even though her refusal is a source of agony (29). By making decisions for herself and for her son, Ruth acquires the characteristics of a strong and determined masculine agent. Corpron Parker remarks Ruth's male-like attitude, countering the view that Victorian women are passive victims suffering under patriarchal social structures (1–2). Ruth talks back to those who mystify her; she learns to speak up, albeit to herself, and comments on her own alienation from her symbolic place in the town's social sphere.

Despite her strong masculine traits, Ruth recreates her identity which, ironically, epitomizes Victorian femininity. Ruth's being, fixed in its syntactic and lexicological forms, "is not a primary and absolutely irreducible signified,.... It is still rooted in a system of languages and an historically determined 'significance'" (Derrida, *Of Grammatology* 23). Fundamental remains her capability of transforming the Victorian world, of absorbing it into her inner world. Convinced that no middle-class woman should appear in public with her hair streaming over her shoulders, gesture which would suggest intimacy and breaking down the barriers between private and public, Sally cuts Ruth's hair while the latter submissively accepts it. The maid's gesture clearly illustrates not only that gender is a construct, but also that the various types of the same gender, such as the womanly woman and the fallen woman, are artifices. Her cut hair does not diminish Ruth's beauty and, although she is not a "coquette" (Bayuk Rosemann 1), she (unswervingly) threatens Bradshaw's sexual frustrations.

In this way, the text does not present Ruth as a paragon of the Victorian woman, an almost genderless creature, and one which therefore stirs no sexual desire or frustration in men. Ruth has sexual desires as well, although she represses them, a gesture which the Victorian society expects from women. The night she meets Bellingham at Bradshaw's house, alone in her room in front of the window out of which she can see the storm, Ruth admits to herself that she still loves Bellingham. The strong wind gusts symbolize Ruth's (and the Victorians') struggle for chastity, her repression of her sexual desire. During the storm, Ruth evokes thoughts of her "darling" (Gaskell 274), which could denote her son, Leonard. However, the term "of old" makes room for ambiguity, suggesting that the child-like behavior may have characterized Bellingham; at the same time, the words "crept into her bed and clung to her" (Gaskell 274) signal Ruth's sexual arousal while reminiscing old events. Conscious of her sexual desire, Ruth prays, submitting to the Victorian decorum, in an attempt to repress her feelings: "Oh, my God, help me, for I am very weak" (Gaskell 274). Turning to religion, Ruth seeks help in a center valued by the Victorians' "logocentrism" (Derrida, *Of Grammatology* 11–12), God. Ruth has to act, not inside the home, but in society in order to redeem herself. At this point, the text presents her as more masculine.

Jemima, too, acts like a man when she voices anger and frustration at her father's mercenary attitude, which projects her as the future wife of his business partner, Mr. Farquhar. Rebellious, she defies her father by championing Ruth (Gaskell 338–339). However, Jemima seems to affirm her father's conviction that, even though she does have a fair amount of spirit, "something unruly in her, which might break out under a *régime* less wisely adjusted to the circumstances" (Gaskell 216), she is ultimately manageable.

As her father notes, nothing can be "more gentle and docile than she is when spoken to in the proper manner" (Gaskell 223). Although she accepts Farquhar only when she is sure of his love, Jemima's marriage to him signifies nonetheless that she succumbs to the Victorian social paradigm. At the same time, marriage does not crush her individuality. The text illustrates a complicated view of gender, exposing the artificiality of the dichotomous, simplistic Victorian perspective. Jemima Bradshaw is not submissive and uncomplicated, Ruth is not clinging and pure, Sally is not obsequious, and, like Faith, she is not a mother. Because the Victorian mindset attaches so much importance to wifehood and motherhood, marriage is deemed the apotheosis of a woman's fulfillment. Therefore, the issue of marriage develops into a source of anxiety for Jemima, who seeks to marry Farquhar. Unlike her, Ruth prefers to be single and rejects Bellingham's marriage proposal out of fear that he might hurt her again, without him even being aware of it: "The time that has pressed down my life like brands of hot iron, and scarred me for ever, has been nothing to you" (Gaskell 302). Throughout the novel, Ruth's signifieds change, to the Victorian reader's chagrin.

Ruth's religious signifieds, Eve, Madonna, Mary Magdalene, and Christ, represent different hypostases of the self, profoundly antithetical, but nonetheless supplementing each other, and at the same time they illustrate the movement of *différance,* "the formation of the form" (Derrida, *Of Grammatology* 63). They confer different meanings to the novel and to its presentation of gender construction in the Victorian society. The change of the signified in the religious imagery subverts the patriarchal fictions and proposes different stories. Precursor of sensational characters, Ruth recreates Eve through her seduction by Bellingham and subsequent fall, Mary Magdalene through her fall and costly atonement, and Virgin Mary through her giving birth to her son in a marginalized place. By presenting Ruth as both a Mary Magdalene and a Madonna figure, the text dismantles her culture's rigid and reductive, dichotomous view of women. Although she sinned, like Eve or like Mary Magdalene, "Ruth comes to embody Christ's love as a savior of her community, who even forgives and loves her betrayer" (Hatano 640). When she is attracted again to her former lover and father of her child, and is thus faced with genuine temptation, "Ruth, like Christ, must confront it, agonize over sacred and secular codes, and then firmly reject that temptation" (Jenkins 107). Swept by the wind and soaked by the rain, the heroine struggles with her own feelings for Bellingham, like Christ in the Garden of Gethsemane. The following day, under Donne's gaze at church she sees her agony as akin to that of Christ: "And when they prayed again, Ruth's tongue was unloosed, and she also could pray, in His name, who underwent the agony in the garden" (Gaskell 283). Furthermore, through her self-sacrificial act at the end of the narrative, the novel presents her as a Christ figure; having gained public forgiveness for her past, she does not need to nurse her seducer but does so, either out of Christian love or out of a strong ethics of care. Finally, Ruth's sacrifice/suicide becomes a symbolic reappropriation, her death becoming the movement of *différance,* which "produces what it forbids, makes possible the very thing that it makes impossible" (Derrida, *Of Grammatology* 143). While Ruth gains more and more signifieds in the novel, Bellingham's oscillate between male and female.

The spoilt, self-centered, and shallow Bellingham seems to be emblematic of masculine insensitivity. As a male, he seduces and abandons Ruth without being blamed by the society which holds double standards: it demands purity on the part of women, but merely asks for discretion on the part of men. Ruth sees him first as a powerful horseman, a symbol for the uncontrollable instincts of man, dashing into the river to rescue the child in distress. Perceiving Ruth as wild, that is, in need of being tamed, Bellingham compares her with game, with "timid fawns in his mother's park" (Gaskell 33). Consequently, the text conveys the idea that seducing Ruth represents a pleasurable game for Bellingham; he convinces the inexperienced, innocent sixteen-year-old girl that she cannot trust Mrs. Mason's sense of right and wrong because, as Ruth had told him, the dressmaker mistreats her apprentices (Gaskell 44).

Bellingham does not act as a male, in that he does not engage in analysis or self-reflection. Aware of the impression Ruth has made on him, the twenty-three-year-old Bellingham "did not analyse the nature of his feelings, but simply enjoyed them with the delight which youth takes in experiencing new and strong emotion" (Gaskell 31). Moreover, after Mrs. Mason forbids Ruth to go back so as not to spoil her apprentices' reputation, Bellingham asks Ruth to listen to "reason," a term which gains the meaning "emotion," and to accompany him, rather than to return to Thomas and Mary (Gaskell 61). Nonetheless, having asked his mother to rid him of Ruth, Bellingham does have a slight pang of remorse: he "feels," he does not reason, that "he was not behaving as he should do, to Ruth" (Gaskell 91). By submitting to his mother, he appears as a feminine character, almost impersonating the ideal femininity of the Victorians: "Mother, you are not helping me in my difficulty.... Dismiss her as you wish it; but let it be done handsomely, and let me hear no more about it; I cannot bear it" (Gaskell 90). Generally associated with women, the pallid trace of emotion which Bellingham experiences illustrates his feminine trait. The novel challenges not only the idea that female identity is expressed by emotion but also the notion that male identity is expressed by action.

The strategies that allow men to belong to a hegemonic idea of manhood are vigorous work, sexual activity, rigid duty, reserve, and straightforward speech. While Bellingham is idle and has no sense of duty, Bradshaw performs his duty toward the poor and the church but is sexually frustrated and incapable of expressing his feelings. The nineteenth-century women could speak of inner feelings, but men were defined by stoic silence. The text problematizes this view of stoicism as characteristic of men: both Mrs. Bradshaw and Ruth are silent and stoic. Benson, however, "a good angel in disguise" (Watt 31) does not act, but speaks. His first appearances in the novel, certainly surrounded by mystery, are the most striking aspects of Gaskell's text, as he is closer to a dwarf or the Welsh equivalent of a leprechaun than to a man (Watt 3). He appears like a fairy or a guardian angel at the very worst moment for Ruth, when she runs toward the mountain torrent, apparently with the intention of committing suicide. Unlike Benson, Bradshaw acts by sending gifts, donating money to the church, and becoming involved in politics. Lacking sympathy and self-perception, he illustrates what Shirley Foster calls "a kind of masculine deficiency" (154). Tyrannical and self-righteous, Mr. Bradshaw forces his wife and children into deceit or ill-suppressed rebellion.

Another deficient binary opposition dismantled by the text is fallen woman/angel. Watt sees that Ruth's fall is caused by her social class and her parents' death (22). Natalka Freeland points to gender construction in the text, contending that Ruth "debunks the ideal of domesticated female sexual purity as a solution to social problems" (810) and recalls that sexual morality itself is firmly rooted in the economic system which it promises to repair. Hatano acknowledges that although she is denied the position of the angel in the house, Ruth becomes an angel in the community through her self-sacrificial act. Having effaced her sin in the public sphere, she assumes the role of a saving angel in the community:

> The strong angelic imagery explicit in Ruth's tending the sick poor, and outcast is further conveyed by her insistence on nursing her seducer, who could easily obtain the care of first-rate nurses in London ... Ruth comes to embody Christ's love as a savior of her community, who even forgives and loves her betrayer [Hatano 640].

Using a deterministic approach which complements the constructed character of the world depicted in the text, Logan notices that Ruth has an unstable working-class background and becomes a seamstress, "an occupation popularly aligned with sexual falls" (20). Sexually betrayed and abandoned, she bears her child embracing maternity in spite of the illegitimacy.

The text uncovers different characters' ambivalent reactions toward Ruth, including the retort of the unsympathetic Bradshaw, who mistakes moral for material contamination. When he learns about Ruth's past, Bradshaw utters a catalogue of synonyms such as "profligacy," "wantonness," and "sin" (Gaskell 337). From his perspective, Ruth betrayed the morality of physical desire which the Victorian society invented. Viewing modesty as a supplement of natural beauty, Bradshaw equates sexual transgression with filth, and thus he forces Ruth's character into the category of the fallen woman. However, the term "profligacy" also conveys the idea of being abandoned, and the term "wantonness" means "undisciplined, unmanageable" as well. Therefore, the text undermines Bradshaw's view of Ruth as a fallen woman by emphasizing her status as an orphan lacking parental care, and at the same time it depicts the Victorian society's indifference toward young women. While Logan sees women's fall as caused by their social status, by the tensions within the society in which they live, Freeland regards Ruth's fall as "an individual failure of self-regulation" rather than as a societal failure of caring for orphan young girls (809). Jemima's question as to whether the fallen woman can be as pure as she knows Ruth to be suggests that the boundaries established by the Victorians between the fallen woman and the angel are fluid. The question also unravels the artificiality of the world portrayed by the text and opens new interpretations for the novel. Additionally, as in the case of other sensational novels, Jemima's question may shock the prejudiced Victorian reader who cannot establish any connection between the two terms of the binary.

The fallen woman/the angel binary entails another opposition utilized in the sensational novels, sinfulness/sinlessness, which corroborates the essentializing Victorian view. The sensational element on which the text centers, making a sinner "heroic [,] is essential to the newness of the novel" (Watt 21) and thwarts the Victorians' dichotomous view. By the end of the novel, Ruth frees herself from the cowed posture of debasement which she adopts as her destiny. Early in the text, her metaphoric journey to Wales signals her contact with the mores and the norms of respectable society. At first, she does not see her sexual relationship with Bellingham as a sin but as an expression of her love for him. Neither is she aware that she has been seduced because she has not internalized her culture's moral codes which display sexual double standard and punish only the woman, Ruth, and not the man, Bellingham, for their sexual relationship. Attempting to convince Ruth to accompany him to London, Bellingham speaks of himself in the third person as if to distance himself from the man he is talking about, proving thus his hypocrisy: "What is more natural (and, being natural, more right) than that you should throw yourself upon the care of one who loves you dearly — who would go through fire and water for you — who would shelter you from all harm?" (Gaskell 57). The verb which Bellingham utilizes, "throw [oneself] upon," may denote either "to beg the mercy or indulgency of," intimating Ruth's precarious condition as a mistress in case she accepts to go to London with him or "to rely on for support," implying that Bellingham would help her. Ruth's acquiescence ascertains her lack of experience and her gullibility.

The innocent, pure, and beautiful protagonist begins to comprehend her fallen state when a child calls her "a naughty girl" (Gaskell 71). Although she is innocent, the boy considers Ruth a prostitute, equating her inexperience with sin and revealing thus the way in which cultural plots shape people's understanding of the world. Albeit pure at heart, Ruth must redeem herself because she "can see her 'fall' only in terms of conventional sin and redemption" (Sutphin 5). Thus, her death may symbolize the demise of the distorted dichotomous view of the woman in Victorian times, sinless sinner and fallen angel.

The text shows that both the secular and the religious spheres that separated men and women and subjugated women in God's name are man-made and not a divine creation. At the same time, it expresses the idea that sin is also made and manipulated by man. Talking about the religious elements in the novel, Hatano remarks that, in order to conform to Evangelicalism, Ruth can only be redeemed by death (641). Logan, on the other hand, considers that Leonard's death "seems to be purchased at the price of the mother's life" (17). Finally, Morgan maintains that "*Ruth* is a novel about redemption and the transforming power of time" (90). The novel clearly depicts several sinners: Bellingham (who seduces Ruth), Bradshaw (who cannot forgive), Benson (who lies), and Sally (who prefers cleaning to religious activities). Despite the fact that all of them need redemption, only Ruth seeks and finds it. Her sacrificial act and death parallel those of Christ, impersonated in the novel by a woman who seems to pay for all the other characters' sins. Ruth's faith,

Christian mercy, and redemption change the opinion of the society that sanctifies her (Gaskell 456–458). By symbolically returning to childhood, Ruth regains her purity, conveyed by light, after a profane existence: "'I see the Light coming,' said she. 'The Light is coming,' she said. And, raising herself slowly, she stretched out her arms, and then fell back, very still for evermore" (Gaskell 448). From the Christian viewpoint embraced by the Victorian society, light represents a sign of divinity and of a beginning point as well, as the initial Logos is associated with the light. The light Ruth sees immediately before her death, a patristic symbol of the celestial world and of eternity, entails an elevation of her soul: she has paid for her sins.

Strongly connected with sin and belonging to the religious sphere is the binary faithful/unfaithful, which envelops another sensational element. Benson, who is a Dissenting minister, defends his efforts to help Ruth, the fallen woman, and work out her redemption, telling Mr. Bradshaw that he intends to stand "with Christ against the world" (Gaskell 351). Due to his use of the preposition "against," his words offer freeplay of signification. One interpretation would be that in Benson's view Ruth is a Christ-figure, with whom he will confront the Victorian society. Another reading may suggest that Benson does not really understand what Christianity is about, as Christians do not consider Christ *against* the world, but *for* it. Finally, the words can convey the idea that Benson obeys Christ's teachings in the New Testament that promote charity and love, and helps Ruth redeem herself, away from the non–Christian world's harm. To corroborate this last idea, the text illustrates Benson's sympathy and charity when he refuses to prosecute Bradshaw's son, Richard, for embezzlement.

Another sensational element is proposed by Bradshaw, who appears like Abraham of the Old Testament, ready to sacrifice his son. Only when faced with Richard's loss can he come close to understanding compassion. Although he claims to be a faithful Christian and, characteristically Victorian, shows common decency by donating money to the church, Bradshaw practices moral vengeance and, like most of the Victorian society, considers that fallen women should be ostracized: "The world has decided how such women are to be treated" (Gaskell 351). Gaskell's novel reveals the conflict created by the Victorian social codes of ethics especially by depicting the Bensons' interaction with the harsh and judgmental public:

> While Gaskell presents the Bensons as models of Christian charity, even they fear public admonition enough to misrepresent the truth of Ruth's condition, although out of compassion for the unborn child. In this way, both

> Ruth and the Bensons are at odds with their culture's ideology: Ruth falls
> from social grace, failing to fulfill its code for women; the Bensons refuse to
> comply with their culture's standards for dealing with such women [Jenk-
> ins 109].

The text dismantles the conflict between the law-abiding ethics of justice
with the charitable and compassionate ethics encouraging the reader to
reevaluate the standards considered divinely ordained and implicitly the Victorians' view of sentimentality.

Apparently equating the binary sentimental/non-sentimental with
weak/strong, the text illustrates their supplementary relationship. While
Bradshaw considers that Benson is weak because he is sentimental, the text
presents the minister as a strong, unselfish person who employs Christian
compassion and calls absolutes into question. However, Benson cannot forgive Bellingham after Ruth dies, and therefore he cannot be true to his pro-
fessed religion. Bradshaw, on the other hand, views himself a strong,
non-sentimental man but shows no compassion although he feels compassion toward Richard and Ruth. His weakness standing in his incapability of
expressing his feelings towards the people in his life, Bradshaw uses the term
"sentimental" pejoratively, mainly to dismiss Benson and his behavior.
Arguably, there is sentimentality in the unsentimental male Victorian —
Bradshaw helps society sanctify Ruth at the end of the novel. In contrast
with Bradshaw, Benson and Ruth see sentimentalism as positive, and they
prove to be strong characters, associated thus with masculinity rather than
with femininity, as one might expect. Watt states that Benson is one of
Gaskell's inversions in the novel: "He looks weak, yet he is strong. He looks
incomplete, yet he is whole" (30). Conversely, Bradshaw, the pillar of the
church and the embodiment of morality in the community, "appears strong
and dominating, yet as the novel progresses his insecurities become more
obvious" (Watt 30). These inversions in the text intimate a reevaluation of
the concepts of strength and weakness.

Ruth proves to be weak when she attempts to throw herself into the
river upon finding out that Bellingham has deserted her. Helped by the Bensons to find her strength, she becomes less constrained, imprisoned, and passive than the victim in a conventional gender-inflected world. However, her
decision to nurture Bellingham may illustrate her weakness, her incapability of denying her sexual desires as well as selfishness, as she makes on orphan
out of Leonard. Therefore, the text intimates that in the Victorian society,
Ruth's only fate is death because a woman cannot talk about her own sexu-

ality. Jenkins points out that Ruth is strong even three days after her death (a Christ-like strength), and mentions the heroine's final victory over Bellingham, who is exposed as her seducer and rejected by Benson. Thus, the end of the novel is a real *coup de theatre*, betraying the reader's expectations in that it appears to annul the double standards of the time, according to which only women are fallen. The text does not only empower the weak and sentimental fallen women, but it also avenges them.

Unlike Ruth, who seems to be weak and sentimental, Sally appears to be strong and non-sentimental. She cuts Ruth's hair as she perceives it as a sign of the fallen woman, mistakes spiritual purity for physical tidiness, and voices strong objections to Ruth, comparing her to dirt-spreading vermin. Sally stands for the arbitrary link between material and moral purity and illustrates a weakness which the Victorian society condemns: it seems that she lacks maternal instincts. While her housekeeping duties are very important, the prospect of marriage is not appealing to Sally. Nonetheless, the novel can be interpreted in different ways. Sally's lack of daring to live a married life of love, sympathy, and empathy, either proves her weakness or her strength, that is, her refusal to become a submissive, docile, silent, and obeying wife whose womanly virtues are best expressed in motherhood. She comes to care for Ruth and Leonard, becoming sentimental, a character trait which she despises, and fulfils her maternal instinct by taking care of Ruth's son.

Gaskell's seemingly simple novel proposes a fallen woman as its protagonist, employs sentimental and sensational elements. However, the novel contains multifarious intricacies that portray the Victorian society and, at the same time, demolish the image it tries to enforce, much as the sensation novels would later do: it exposes the Victorians' double standards toward males and females; it transforms binary relationships into supplements; and it calls into question the ethics practiced by the Victorians. The dichotomic views of the world merge into a single whole, and challenge the constructed values of the Victorian society, which establishes well-defined boundaries to not-so-well-defined realities. The novel presents Ruth to be more male than female, Jemima oscillating between male and female, Sally acting more like a male. Moreover, Benson acts more like a female and Bellingham illustrates both female and male characteristics. Jemima sees the fallen woman as pure as an angel; society sanctifies Ruth, the sinner, but it does not ostracize the seducer, Bellingham. Benson models his behavior mainly according to the Christian teachings, while Bradshaw behaves according to the Victorian mores and comes to understand the power of love and compassion. Several terms and concepts in the novel, such as gender, sin, sanctification, etc., shift their signifieds and allow the freeplay of interpretation. Moreover, by facilitating numerous interpretations, the text also encourages a reinterpretation of the Victorian society itself by identifying and analyzing the binaries, the supplements, and the *différance*.

Works Cited

Bayuk Rosemann, Ellen. "Fear of Fashion." *ANQ* 15:3 (Summer 2002): 1–7.

Corpron Parker, Pamela. "From 'Ladies' Business' to 'Real Business': Elizabeth Gaskell's Capitalist Fantasy in North and South." *The Victorian Newsletter* 92 (Spring 1997): 1–3.

Derrida, Jacques. *Of Grammatology.* Trans. Gayatri Chakravorty Spivak. Baltimore and London: The Johns Hopkins University Press, 1976.

_____. *Speech and Phenomena and Other Essays of Husserl's Theory of Signs.* Trans. David B. Allison. Ed. John Wild. Evanston: Northwestern University Press, 1973.

_____. "Structure, Sign, and Play in the Discourse of the Human Sciences." *The Critical Tradition. Classic Texts and Contemporary Trends.* Boston: Bedford Books, 1998. 878–889.

Dowling, Andrew. *Manliness and the Male Novelist in the Victorian Literature.* Burlington: Ashgate, 2001.

Foster, Shirley. *Victorian Women's Fiction: Marriage, Freedom, and the Individual.* Totowa: Barnes & Noble Books, 1985.

Freeland, Natalka. "The Politics of Dirt in Mary Baron and Ruth." *SEL* 42:4 (Autumn 2002): 799–818.

Gaskell, Elizabeth. *Ruth.* Oxford: Oxford University Press, 1985.

Hatano, Yoko. "Evangelicalism in Ruth." *Modern Languages Review* (July 2002): 634–641.

Held, Virginia. "Taking Care: Care as Practice and Value." *Setting the Moral Compass: Essays by Women Philosophers.* Ed. Cheshire Calhoun. Oxford: Oxford University Press, 2004. 59–71.

Jenkins, Ruth Y. "To 'Stand With Christ against the World': Gaskell's Sentimental Social Agenda." *Reclaiming Myths of Power. Women Writers and the Victorian Spiritual Crisis.* Lewisburg: Bucknell University Press, 1995. 93–117.

Johnson, Patricia. "Elizabeth Gaskell's North and South: A National Bildungsroman." *The Victorian Newsletter* 85 (Spring 1994): 109.

Langland, Elizabeth. "Nobody's Angel: Domestic Ideology and Middle-Class Women in the Victorian Novel." *PMLA* 107.2 (March 1992): 290–304.

Logan, Deborah Anna. "Victorian Silences." *Fallenness in Victorian Women's Writing.* Columbia: University of Missouri Press, 1998. 1–26.

Morgan, Susan. *Sisters in Time. Imagining Gender in Nineteenth-Century British Fiction.* Oxford: Oxford University Press, 1989.

The New Jerusalem Bible. Gen. Ed. Susan Jones. New York: Doubleday, 1985.

Schor, Hilary. "The Plot of the Beautiful Ignoramus: Ruth and the Tradition of the Fallen Woman." *Sex and Death in Victorian Literature.* Ed. Regina Barreca. Bloomington: Indiana University Press, 1990. 158–177.

Sutphin, Christine. "Human Tigresses, Fractious Angels, and Nursery Saints: Augusta

Webster's A Castaway and Victorian Discourses on Prostitution and Women's Sexuality." *Victorian Poetry* 38.4 (2002): 511–532.

Thompson, Joanne. "Elizabeth Gaskell's 'Lizzie Leigh.'" *The Victorian Newsletter* (Fall 1990): 22–25.

Watt, George. "Ruth." *The Fallen Woman in the Nineteenth-Century British Novel.* Totowa: Barnes & Nobles Books, 1984, 19–40.

Warhol, Robyn E. *Gendered Interventions. Narrative Discourse in the Victorian Novel.* New Brunswick: Rutgers University Press, 1989.

Violence as Patrimony in Le Fanu's *Uncle Silas*

STEPHANIE KING

In Le Fanu's 1864 Sensation novel, leering Uncle Silas is depicted as a violent, sexual predator. Silas is an accused murderer and an opium addict who has married below his class, thereby blurring his place in a British class hierarchy. Despite their deviance and isolation, Silas and his son Dudley remain the last male heirs to the aristocratic Ruthyn line. Both father and son are fallen men — characters who succumb to deviance and vice, thereby threatening their gentlemanly status. Silas is entrusted with the care of his niece Maud, when his brother dies suddenly. Status and wealth are important to Silas, yet he gambles with this last chance at genteel status when he commits heinous crimes under the blurred guise of opium. Just as fallen woman traditionally inherit moral blemishes from their mothers, so too do fallen men inherit a proclivity for vice and deviance. In Le Fanu's novel, the fallen men suffer miserable fates, while the young female victim narrates the tale. Gendered expectations are undercut when the seemingly powerless, naïve girl emerges triumphant and the threatening men fall helplessly to their demise.

When Le Fanu treats his male characters as fallen, he threatens tightly defined notions of Victorian masculinity. Silas reflects the Victorians' own affinity for vice, albeit with a darker and more sinister tinge. Silas sips laudanum at home quietly, a common enough pastime for a nineteenth-century gentleman. Silas, however, does not measure his laudanum, and he sometimes takes his opium in lozenges — a less seemly and more potent form. Silas partakes in the gambling fever of his times, but he gambles with more than just money when he murders Mr. Charke to avoid paying gambling debts. Silas is but one of many mid-century father characters who seek an advantageous match for their sons, yet Silas plots to murder Maud when his plan to marry her to Dudley fails. When Le Fanu's fallen man leaves a patrimony of deviance and doom for his son, he destabilizes, and even mocks the hierarchical system on which patriarchal lineages and masculine identities are built.

Throughout the novel, Silas sees his son Dudley as his last "hope — my manly though untutored son — the last male scion of the Ruthyns" (Le Fanu 331). Dudley, in fact, represents little hope, since he has already followed in his father's footsteps by marrying and abandoning a lower class girl, and he can therefore not redeem his family through marriage. Silas abuses his dead brother's final attempt to save him from a downward spiral. Instead of allowing Maud to spread gentility to Silas and his kin, he chooses instead to enlist his son in a ghastly murder plot.

Both Silas and Dudley receive narrative punishments that are absolute. To escape the law, Dudley flees to Australia — home to criminals, laborers, and outcasts in the Victorian times. Silas dies of an overdose, proving finally that his proclivity for vice will overpower any claims he might have to status and wealth. When Silas takes opium mostly in the acceptable form of laudanum, but does so in unmeasured doses, he represents the potential for deviance in all men. In a Victorian context, opium presents a representational conundrum. Wealthy Victorians imported opium to the detriment of the Chinese people whom they exploited. British opium merchants, often working for the government, induced addiction amongst British men, women and children. The middle and upper class Victorians attempted to establish a moral high ground, whereby opium taken as a medicine was sanctioned, while recreational use was not. The distinction between these two modes of ingestion was arbitrary and prejudiced by the vantage point of they who do the distinguishing.

When Silas and his son threaten the virtue and life of a young girl, they place themselves distinctly on the wrong side of even an arbitrary moral spectrum. Silas is given medical permission to continue taking opium; he then gives himself permission to commit violent crimes under its effects. This novel makes a direct link between opium ingestion and violent criminal activity, even though the drug itself is sanctioned by each doctor who appears on the scene. Later in the century, narratives such as Dickens's *The Mystery of Edwin Drood*, Conan Doyle's *Man with a Twisted Lip*, Collins's *The Moonstone*, and Wilde's *The Picture of Dorian Gray*— all link criminality to opium. Most of these writers send their criminals off to opium dens in the east side of London, where they smoke to forget their sins. In shifting addiction to the east, Dickens, Doyle and Wilde do not reflect the more likely scene of laudanum sipped quietly in an armchair. Julian North, in his article "Opium Eater as Criminal" notes another arbitrary distinction made by Victorian commentators; the racial composition of "bad" versus "good" opium eaters. North quotes an anonymous, though representative writer from 1853, who differentiates between British use of opium as medicinal, and Eastern use of opium as self-destructive and pleasure seeking. According to North, the English middle-class likes to see itself as being in control; both of opium intake and Eastern and British working classes (North 124). Writers of fiction transfer opium addiction onto the East End of town to separate themselves racially and economically from the villains. Dickens has been criticized for his melodramatic portrayal of Jasper's visits to the filthy opium dens, when, in fact, opium was readily available from West End chemists.

Collins and Le Fanu write Sensation fiction — meant to shock readers, and they do so by representing drug addicts who may pass as gentleman, even as they succumb to vice and become fallen men. In Collins's *The Moonstone*, the well meaning scientist Jennings is an opium addict who accidentally propels a motiveless crime by dosing a fellow dinner guest with the drug. As Alethea Hayter puts describes the novel as tightly plotted, controlled, and written under the heavy influence of opiates (259). In 1858, Collins famously said, "Who is the man who invented laudanum? I thank him from the bottom of my heart" (Berridge and Edwards 58). Taken in this context, the end of *The Moonstone* is anything but absolute. While the crime is solved, Collins's take on opium, crime, and responsibility is left open-ended.

In her critical look at violence in sensation fiction, Marlene Tromp finds that novels in this genre became "the site of a discourse that offered an alternative way of perceiving gendered relationships and the violence that may lie at their core" (10). In Uncle Silas, the fallen Ruthyn men try to seduce and frighten Maud, only to end up stripped of gentility, pride, virility, and power. Silas and Dudley are a threat because they represent the violent and deviant side of inherent masculinity.

In his recent study of Violence, Manliness, and Criminal Justice in Victorian England, Martin J. Wiener finds that violence indeed lies in the hearts of British men. Victorian laws reflected the need to suppress these historically consistent violent, masculine urges. During Victoria's reign, men were encouraged to channel their violent urges into military careers, since, as Wiener notes, the British were involved in some war or another throughout the Victorian era. With those men who were prone to violence off at war, the remaining members of the gentry were discouraged from carrying weapons, and both legal and cultural tools propelled a movement towards redefining ideal manliness. By the mid Victorian period, the British ideal of "the man of dignity"—who demonstrated prudence and self-command, replaced the earlier ideal of the "man of honour"—ready to avenge slights by violent means. Still, Wiener finds difficulty in interpreting and applying Victorian laws, which often used loosely defined terms of *violation* and *violence* to denote criminal responsibility. Debates in Victorian courtrooms raged on as to whether excessive drinking, for instance, was enough of a criminal defense. Lawyers and judges contemplated seriously whether a man might respond to a woman's angry words with physical assault, and be exempt from blame (Wiener 1–39). Sensation fiction exposes this same murky moral space that is evident most pronouncedly in Victorian legal conventions. In *Uncle Silas,* Le Fanu uses opium as a narrative tool to blur the boundary between criminal and gentleman, blame and forgiveness.

Silas, like his drug of choice, defies classification. At one point, Maud describes him as "martyr—angel—demon" (147). Maud alternates between wanting to share her dead father's belief in the man, and a sense of dread. Cousin Monica, an upright character, alludes to the unspeakable threat posed by Silas to his charge: "I *am* afraid of more than neglect" (142). The fallen man is a predator; he stands violent, drug-addicted and sinister. Female characters fear him, even though they must adhere to his role as guardian.

On the road to his demise, Silas demonstrates a tendency towards anger and violence which he tries to repress. When Monica tries to gain custody of Maud, Silas responds to her with characteristic fury, violence, and feigned religious sentiment:

> So my badinage excites your temper, Monnie. Think how you would feel, then if I had found you by the highway side, mangled by robbers, and set my foot upon your throat, and spat in your face. But—stop this. Why have I said this? Simply to emphasize my forgiveness [245].

Silas wants to hurt women; he also wants to impress upon them a false image of himself as a gentleman with noble intentions. Silas is a fallen man because he participates in the ceremonies of gentility, even as he plots to destroy innocent victims. He is neither lowborn nor truly destitute, yet he degrades himself and diminishes his status by exhibiting his violent fantasies.

This play between the roles of gentlemen and villain extends from Silas to his son. Dudley cannot fake refinement, and he does not share his father's ability to manipulate language. As he falls in love with Maud (and her fortune), Dudley tries to flatter and woo Maud as a gentleman might, and he pleads with her earnestly to consider him as a suitor: "I like ye awful, I do — there's not a handsomer lass in Liverpool nor Lunnon itself—*no* where" (293). While Dudley seems sincere in his approach, he still has a poor command of the English language, and moments later he demonstrates uncouth manners when he tries to grab Maud. Rejected by Maud again, Dudley resists assaulting his cousin, but suggests that in rejecting him, she risks being sexually victimized: "Another fellah'd fly out a' maybe kiss ye for spite!" (295). As he reveals his intentions, Dudley seems to have inherited the questionable sexual ethics of his father. He has ruined a country girl, and will not accept Maud's refusal of his marriage proposals and physical advances. He, too, is a fallen man, as he becomes a murderer by the novel's end, emanating Silas, and keeping his sinister values alive.

Fallen men are set up in contrast — though not in complete opposition — to more upright characters. Dudley is posited against Captain Oakley, as they fight for Maud's attention. However, these figures do not constitute an absolute dichotomy, as Oakley is somewhat fallen himself. He has a gambling past, but has partially redeemed himself through hard work. Oakley, though he acts like a gentleman, is still not "hero" material, as he loses the fist fight with Dudley, and, more significantly, loses his chance to win Maud's hand. As Captain Oakley speaks to Maud in poetic verse, Dudley comes up behind him, and "a smack was heard, and the Captain lay on his back, his mouth full of blood" (303). Brave Captain Oakley, who is described as "one great patch of blood," gets us and tries punching Dudley, who swiftly avoids the Captain's fist. The fight ends when Oakley is described as "the mangled captain," pleading with Dudley to "fight me as a gentleman" (303). Gentlemen are no longer supposed to fight, so Oakely represents the unstable values of gentrified behavior.

The overlap between upright and fallen men is evidenced in this scene. Neither man is a worthy suitor for Maud. The Captain may appear to woo Maud delicately with genteel gestures, yet he is swimming in debt, and wooing for his life. Dudley, who is high born, acts without gentility, and cannot marry Maud since he is already married to the lowborn Sarah Matilda Mangles. Indeed, Dudley, like Silas before him, "mangles" the class hierarchy by marrying and abandoning a low class woman. Like his father before him, the young Dudley "might have passed for a handsome man" (257), according to Maud, if only his behavior had been more refined. Indeed, just as opium blurs class boundaries with its wide range of users and abusers, so too do both Silas and Maud blur the categories of gentleman and scoundrel when they see the gentleman in Dudley.

Dudley wins the battle, but he loses the war, because, as a second generation fallen character, his future can only be bleak. When Maud rejects him for the last time, he walks off "with the countenance of a man who has lost a game, and a ruinous wager too" (352). For Dudley, as with fallen women such as Anne Silvester, Aurora Floyd, Tess D'Urberville, and Trilby O'Ferrall, ruin may easily be the result of a gamble gone wrong. Like a fallen woman, Dudley must leave England once scandal breaks, and he sets off for Australia soon after he accidentally murders the governess, Madame de la Rougierre, instead of Maud. Dudley stabs Madame violently, with a spiked hammer in "a scrunching blow" (426). The distinction between Dudley's and Oakley's violent tendencies is clear, even though the fact remains that both men, to varying degrees, turn to violence to solve their problems. Silas and Dudley, however, let go of the weak claim they have on gentility when they go overboard with everyday vice and urges. These fallen men are descendants of aristocrats. When they submit to their deviant cravings, Silas and Dudley threaten to shake up the very system of which they are an historical part.

In Victorian England, penniless aristocrats scrambled to maintain their prestige as they lived in debt, gambled with fervor, and tried to woo wealthy women. Still, many members of the fading gentility, both in and out of literature, maintained social status by grasping on to the appearance of wealth. Gwendolen Harleth in George Eliot's *Daniel Deronda* is the quintessential example of an impoverished gentlewoman, as she attempts to maintain appearances at all costs. Gwendolen, the spoiled child, gambles desperately for her status. Silas attempts no such social position. Rather than trying to fit into polite society, Silas isolates himself and his family, indicating that he has more to hide than fleeting genteel status. Lady Monica warns Maud that Silas'

> utter seclusion from society removes the only check, except personal fear — and he never had much of that — upon a very bad man.... But you know, Silas may be very good *now*, although he was wild and selfish in his young days [248].

Monica worries that Silas's moral behavior would deteriorate once he is removed from public scrutiny. Gentlemanly behavior, according to this statement, is an unstable construct that depends upon the opinions of others.

Silas is motivated by excessive greed, rather than by social appearances. He seeks Maud's inheritance above all else. Before reverting to murder to reach this goal, Silas tries to increase his status by appealing to Maud's social graces, by assuring her that she could have a real gentleman in the rough with Dudley, who has "the Ruthyn blood — the purest blood, I maintain in England" (318). When the despicable Dudley represents hope for aristocratic continuance, he begs the question as to whether circumstance is all that separates fallen men from gentlemen?

By the novel's close, Silas accepts his fallenness: "You may say I have no longer an interest in even vindicating my name. My son has wrecked himself by marriage" (348). If this fallen man novel is modeled, in part on the idea of a fallen woman narrative, then Dudley's trip to Australia is an appropriate fate for his depraved character. Still, to the end, Maud cannot quite accept Silas as deviant: "It is not possible that my uncle, a gentleman and a kinsman, can be privy to so disreputable a manoeuvre" (411). Silas' aristocratic heritage renders him, implicitly, among the masters of his land. He should, according to gender norms and conventions, be writing himself. Instead, naïve and innocent Maud writes her uncle's story, and presents his miserable fate as inevitable. The ending of *Uncle Silas* signifies a reversal between the powerful and the powerless characters, when Silas' intricate plan is foiled. Maud has been in the dark both literally and figuratively throughout the final scenes, but she emerges as a conveyor of knowledge and a complier of facts. Silas falls prey to his vice, and Dudley cannot remain in the country, for fear of detection. When fallen men get their dues, female characters are empowered.

Fallen women are often betrayed and controlled by men, while fallen men betray their ancestors by succumbing to vice and compromising their genteel familial standing. Within the novel's early focus on aristocratic lineage, bloodlines mark the rank and stature of the Ruthyn clan. By having his male characters' deviance also become a matter of lineage, Le Fanu emphasizes the role of fallen men as narrative disturbers. Though Silas, and to a certain extent, Dudley are born into the right sort of family, the son is marked for moral ruin because of his father's criminalities. While inherited titles mark status and denote responsibility well into the nineteenth century, they do not guarantee gentlemanly status or aristocratic behavior. Indeed, just as fallen woman narratives allow for destitute mothers to produce doomed daughter, so too do fallen men narratives place a negative value on inherited deviance. *Uncle Silas* disavows the traditional inheritance of title, as it demonstrates the more disturbing patrimony of deviance, violence, and doom.

Works Cited

Berridge, Virginia, and Griffith Edwards. *Opium and the People: Opiate Use in Nine-teenth-Century England.* New York: St. Martin's Press, 1981.

Braddon, Mary Elizabeth. *Aurora Floyd.* 1862. Peterborough: Broadview, 1998.

Collins, Wilkie. *Man and Wife.* 1870. Oxford: Oxford University Press, 1995.

_____. *The Moonstone.* 1868. Oxford: Oxford University Press, 1999.

Conan Doyle, Sir Arthur. "The Man with the Twisted Lip." *The Adventures of Sherlock Holmes and the Memoirs of Sherlock Holmes.* 1892. London: Penguin, 2002.

De Quincey, Thomas. *Confessions of an English Opium Eater.* 1821. New York: Penguin, 1997.

Dickens, Charles. *The Mystery of Edwin Drood.* 1870. London: Penguin, 2002.

Du Maurier, George. 1894. *Trilby.* Oxford: Oxford University Press, 1995.

Eliot, George. *Daniel Deronda.* 1876. London: Penguin Books, 1995.

Hardy, Thomas. *Tess of the D'Urbervilles.* 1891. London: Penguin, 1998.

Hayter, Alethea. *Opium and the Romantic Imagination: Addiction and Creativity in De Quincey, Coleridge, Baudelaire and Others.* Berkeley: University of California Press, 1970.

Le Fanu, J. S. *Uncle Silas.* 1864. New York: Dover, 1966.

Milligan, Barry. "'The Plague Spreading and Attacking Our Vitals': Opium Smoking and the Oriental Infection of the British Domestic Scene." *Victorian Literature and Culture* 20 (1992): 161–77.

North, Julian. "Opium Eater as Criminal." *Writing and Victorianism.* London: Longman, 1997.

Tromp, Marlene. *The Private Rod: Marital Violence, Sensation, and the Law in Victorian Britain.* Charlottesville: University Press of Virginia, 2000.

Wiener, Martin J. *Men of Blood: Violence, Manliness, and Criminal Justice in Victorian England.* New York: Cambridge University Press, 2004.

Wilde, Oscar. *Picture of Dorian Gray. Collins Complete Works of Oscar Wilde: Centenary Edition.* 17–159.

In the Company of Men:
Masculinity Gone Wild in Robert Louis Stevenson's The Strange Case of Dr Jekyll and Mr Hyde

Jennifer Beauvais

> We were full of the pride of life, and chose, like prostitutes, to live by a pleasure. We should be paid, if we give the pleasure we pretend to give; but why should we be honoured? We are whores, some of us pretty whores, some of us not, but all whores: whores of the mind, selling to the public the amusements of our fireside as the whore sells the pleasures of her bed (Stevenson 171).

As a self-described "sick whore" (Stevenson 171) who would probably be taken off the streets for possessing a "fatted brain and ... rancid imagination" (Stevenson 171), Robert Louis Stevenson playfully compares writers to prostitutes in the 1886 letter quoted above written to Edmund Gosse. The analogy reveals Stevenson's position on authors and their relationship with "that fatuous rabble of burgesses called 'the public'" (Stevenson 171). As "whores of the mind" writers find themselves choosing a way of life centered around "pretending" to give pleasure for financial gain. In the same letter Stevenson explains, "I do not write for the public; I do write for money, a nobler deity; and most of all for myself, not perhaps any more noble but both more intelligent and nearer home" (Stevenson 171). The writer certainly does not romanticize authorship, but he does make it clear that his devotion is to himself, in the form of money and personal achievement, and not to his public. He succeeds in creating an analogy that is both self-deprecating and empowering. The image of selling fireside pleasures to the public exposes the delicate balance between the public and private spheres, which the writer and prostitute must tread.[1] By relating to female prostitutes, Stevenson feminizes the writer and yet he avoids allusions to victimization and passivity. Instead, the public is construed as the senseless, passive consumer who is non-selective and more than willing to sacrifice his money for simple pleasures.

Stevenson conflates these issues in *Dr Jekyll and Mr Hyde* through his emphasis on a male-only community, the absence of female characters, and representations of class and gender, as well as the public and private spheres. The novella's principle characters are all professional men separated from the vacuous public by their class status, intelligence, and morality.[2] The male-only community harkens back to what Eve Kosofsky Sedgwick notes is the classical Spartan and Athenian models of virilizing male bonds by fully excluding the world of women (207). It is this exclusively male community of *Dr Jekyll and Mr Hyde* which allows for the exploration of issues of masculinity and the private sphere without the presence of the ideal of the domestic space — women. Through the absence of female characters, masculinity appears more fluid and mutable which is enhanced by the fact that these male professionals are all bachelors. Arguably, these men are not in traditional masculine roles since they are not husbands, and yet the position of the bachelor, by the late nineteenth century, has become an acceptable way of life for higher-class men. The bachelor demands attention for their redefining of masculinity and the remodeling of the domestic sphere.[3]

Nineteenth-century writers[4] have shown an interest in the bachelor by making him a central character, but it is Stevenson's 1886 novella and Wilde's *The Picture of Dorian Gray* (1891) that provide the best examples of these exclusively male communities. Katherine V. Snyder discusses how these works "encompass both the imaginary consolidation of charged relations between men within the figure of a single man and the imaginary distribution of a single man's self, driven by conflict, between two male figures" (105). The position of the bachelor as an accepted visitor in both the domestic and public spheres results in the creation of dual natures and double lives, which accentuates the delicate balance which the bachelor must preserve. This duality though has nothing to do with the bachelor's ability to maneuver between the worlds of women and men; instead, he must define himself in relation to other men. The dualism, which arises from the bachelor among men, involves questioning homosocial bonds and the possibility of being both bachelor and homosexual simultaneously. Here the bachelor figure defines himself in contrast to the acceptable Victorian status of the unmarried man through his public persona, while privately he is defined solely in relation to the male community no longer as "bachelor" but as "homosexual."

The bachelor's movements between the spheres question the concept of masculinity and a new understanding of manhood. Simultaneously living inside and outside the social circle gives the bachelor a unique perspective on society, especially its social mores, as Snyder states, the bachelor "confound[s] these ordering binarisms of masculine, bourgeois, and domestic life, at once demarcating and crossing the lines that mark the boundaries of these realms" (54). Crossing borders is what defines the bachelor and allows him to remain an ambiguous and fluid figure throughout literary history. His more extreme counterpart, the dandy, clearly discards any semblance of masculinity in his attempts to cross the boundaries and is clearly marked as a symbol of ridicule for nineteenth-century readers.[5] The masculinity that the bachelor maintains has the appearance of society's concept of maleness, but he also carries with him more feminine qualities that in his earlier incarnations allowed the bachelor to fully enjoy the company of women. This is not the case in the exclusively male community of *Dr Jekyll and Mr Hyde*. The feminine characteristics Hyde possesses serve to suggest a redefinition of *fin de siècle* masculinity and the possibility of indulging in the private sphere without encountering its primary inhabitants. Herbert Sussman observes the transformation of masculinity during the Aesthetic movement by commenting on Walter Pater's description of the expectation of the Victorian male in his "Conclusion":

> the normative Victorian masculinities-of reserve ... of manliness as the ... difficult discipline of desire; of the ... disciplined male self as analogue of the controlled flame of the steam engine and the forge; of psychic control as "success in life" similar to the mental discipline needed for victory within the commercial competitiveness of the male arena [202].

The bachelor does not promote this style of restrictive and repressive masculinity and it is exactly this type of repression and "psychic control" which Dr. Jekyll seeks to escape through the creation of Hyde. The bachelor possesses an amount of feminine qualities that allows him to move freely into the feminized private space, which is dark, mysterious, seductive, while at the same time he maintains a masculine appearance of a gentleman. This double nature is found in Dr. Jekyll when he recreates himself in Hyde, as well as in Mr. Utterson, who upon discovering his close friend's secret life is more open about his own double consciousness, but it is Mr. Hyde's ability to maintain a double nature that is mostly overlooked.

The male community in which Stevenson sets his novella allows for the exploration of masculinity, and possibly homosexuality, but it is in combination with the theme of duality and the creation of Hyde that a clearer understanding of the role of the public and private on issues of sexuality develops. In order to explore sexuality and masculinity Stevenson must create a character that has the ability to introduce what is considered the traditional masculine public into the private, creating a new space where the domestic can exist without a female presence. It is at this point that the late nineteenth-century bachelor separates himself from his earlier incarnations. By placing the bachelor within an exclusively male community he does not lose his ability to move between the public and private, except that these spheres are no longer categorized as the world of men versus women. Instead, the public and private in the male community become strictly masculine. The private and public within the male community do not lose their respective links to femininity and masculinity, but they are discussed in relation to male double consciousness.

Dr. Jekyll is the bachelor in his public life; he is a professional, reputable man, but is unable to participate in the private domain without losing his public identity. In this case, the bachelor of the male community cannot travel unscathed between the public and private spheres, and as a result Hyde is born. Mr. Hyde strips Dr. Jekyll of his profession, and grants him another identity through which he explores the secret world of the male private realm. The suggestion here is not that Jekyll represents the public persona, and Hyde the private; instead, Hyde is simultaneously both. Jekyll's creation is complete in that Hyde can penetrate both the public and private spheres without changing identities. While Jekyll appears unable to explore the private, his friend Mr. Utterson revels in it and finds it impossible to keep business and personal issues separate. The novella provides its readers with a variety of amalgamations of the public and private through the lives of its bachelor characters. In some instances the private dominates over the public as is the case for the lawyer Utterson, or perhaps as in Dr. Jekyll's case the public is all-consuming. While Utterson protects the traditional concept of the domestic, Dr. Jekyll creates Mr. Hyde in an attempt to escape the restrictive spheres. Stevenson's Hyde represents the new "bachelor" of the late-nineteenth century, who redefines the domestic sphere within an all-male society by replacing the traditional component of the Victorian family with the homosocial and masculine intimacy.

Dr. Jekyll attempts to describe his unique predicament to the inquisitive Mr. Utterson by explaining, "I am painfully situated, Utterson; my position is a very strange — a very strange one" (Stevenson 45). The bachelor in

Stevenson's novella masters the art of contortion and although this ability is "painful" and "strange" at first, he begins to embrace his situation and construct his own space. The bachelor is fluid and mutable, characteristics usually associated with the feminine, and he makes the most confining, and seemingly impenetrable space his own. This space is redefined from the traditional domestic sphere into one that includes the bachelor. Issues of exclusion and inclusion arise from this dichotomy, but there are no outsiders or outlaws here. The Other is redefined in *Dr Jekyll and Mr Hyde*; he finds his place within the public and private without transforming into the typical monster. Stevenson's novella champions the new bachelor and places him within a community of men who share similar characteristics. It also attests to the bachelor's evolution throughout the mid-to-late nineteenth century.

The New Woman[6] had been crossing boundaries and knocking down barriers for three decades prior to Stevenson's publication of *Dr Jekyll and Mr Hyde*. In Stevenson's novella the reader is struck by a different dissident, another bold boundary breaker whose gender, like that of the New Woman, undergoes a refiguring. Mr. Utterson holding the kitchen poker high, ready to break down Jekyll's cabinet door (Stevenson 62), is the epitome of the late nineteenth-century domesticated man. During a time when gender boundaries are blurring, here stands the domesticated gentleman armed with his weapon of choice: "The lawyer took that rude but weighty instrument into his hand, and balanced it. 'Do you know, Poole,' [Utterson] said, looking up, 'that you and I are about to place ourselves in a position of some peril?'" (Stevenson 63). Unlike Hyde's ability to cross boundaries with the agility of a ghost, Utterson is less discreet with his symbolic breaking down of the door.

Enfield's reactions to Hyde's trampling of the young girl and his ability to produce one hundred pounds in someone else's name at such an early hour reveal a familiarity with this process of blackmailing. Enfield's comment on Hyde's procuring of another man's check as "business" (Stevenson 34), which he considers unrealistic and "apocryphal" (Stevenson 34), demonstrates that he is aware of the real business which is at hand. The repetition of "my gentleman" and "my man" permeates Enfield's story of the door. When Enfield states, "For my man was a fellow that nobody could have to do with" (Stevenson 34), he clearly links himself with an established outcast of society. Arata believes that this statement demonstrates how Enfield "seems to be describing not a violent criminal but a man who cannot be trusted to respect the club rules" ("Sedulous Ape" 241). Enfield's rules alienate him from Utterson, who is ignorant of them, and from Hyde who does not follow them, yet Enfield still associates with Hyde based on his knowledge of the club despite his disrespect towards the rules. "My gentleman" is then contrasted with "one of [Utterson's] fellows who do what they call good" (Stevenson 34). This creates a barrier between Enfield and his domestic companion. Enfield and Hyde take one side as members of "the club," while Jekyll and Utterson are linked as outsiders.

Enfield's refusal to name names is described as a club "rule" (Stevenson 35). It appears that "delicacy" is an attribute for club members like Enfield: "The more it looks like Queer Street, the less I ask" (Stevenson 35). Although it would appear that the club simply requires that one be a professional male, Utterson's lack of knowledge in this area suggests there is more to it. Silence and discretion are key characteristics of club members, as Enfield states, "I knew what was in his mind, just as he knew what was in mine.... We could and would make such a scandal out of this as should make his name stink from one end of London to the other" (Stevenson 33). Silence unites Enfield and the doctor at the scene of the trampled girl. Their ability to read each other's minds and agree on the proper method for dealing with Hyde reveals many hidden signals. Not only does Enfield and the doctor identify with each other, they then determine that Hyde is one of them, and finally they agree on the appropriate punishment based on their "club rules," all of which is achieved in silence. Enfield's weapon against Hyde is to break club rules and expose him publicly. Enfield appreciates Utterson's silence: "The pair walked on again for a while in silence; and then 'Enfield,' said Utterson, that's a good rule of yours" (Stevenson 35). Enfield's use of silence differs from Utterson's. While Enfield's is a deliberate decision to keep quiet, Utterson's is a tendency towards effeminate passivity and a deep respect for the private.

Whereas Hyde represents the rebellious intruder of the public and private spheres, Utterson is reminiscent of the typical bachelor who finds himself unable to navigate between the two and suffers the consequence of embracing the one.[7] Although Utterson falls into this category of bachelor, he gains credit by evolving to meet late nineteenth-century expectations. Utterson is not completely domesticated and he makes an interesting figure in contrast to the violence of Hyde. Utterson attempts to balance his role as lawyer and friend, but without becoming both at once. Utterson is so fully in the private that he cannot trespass into the private space of others without feeling like an intruder. He then discovers the freedom of his professional and public self when he enters into the "business" of others and uses this to gain safe entry into the private. William Veeder notes, "Though he can only spy furtively on the domestic door of Jekyll the sleeping patriarch Utterson can break with impunity the professional door of Dr. Jekyll the errant scientist" (135). This leads to Veeder's argument that the entire male community *Dr Jekyll and Mr Hyde* uses "profession [as] a screen for the domestic" (135). Although this is indeed the case for the lawyer Utterson, it does not apply to Hyde. This is one of the attributes that differentiates these two types of bachelors. One is so deeply immersed in the domestic as its defender that he is unable to penetrate both spaces, while the other has the power to fully participate in both spaces simultaneously. As protector of the domestic, Utterson cannot bear to intrude on the private space of Jekyll. He does so occasionally, but mostly under the guise of his profession. Utterson, as domestic defender is confronted with Hyde who does not follow these rules, as Utterson imagines him sneaking into Jekyll's bedchamber and other sleeping houses at night (Stevenson 39). Why is Utterson interesting if he does not cross over these barriers? One reason is that he is associated with the improper sphere. Unlike previous studies of male characters who engage in domestic/feminine discourse, Stevenson's late nineteenth-century lawyer begins and ends inhabiting the domestic space. There is no question why he is there and whether he belongs; instead, his role is simple — to protect the domestic space from intruders like Hyde. Why is Utterson's presence in the domestic sanctified? Based on earlier male characters whose place within the domestic was challenged, by the 1890s the bachelor's position within the domestic has become acceptable. What is unacceptable is the roving, fluid and shifting figure whose place is nowhere, not within the public or private but within a newly-defined male sphere which excludes the purely domestic bachelor like Utterson. In fact, it would appear that Utterson is the "outcast" (Gaughan 193). Since Enfield hints towards having knowledge of this new space but chooses to no longer linger there, and Lanyon does cross over but is unable to survive the process; it appears that it is only Utterson who, even with a strong curiosity for this new frontier, remains loyal to the traditional domestic space.

The femininizing effects of inhabiting the domestic are evident when Utterson's affections are described like ivy (Stevenson 31), evoking the popular nineteenth-century image of the ivy and the oak used to describe a woman's role in marriage.[8] Immediately following this reference is a scene reminiscent of a marriage grown old. Utterson and Enfield's walks are permeated with suggestions of the tedious routine of married life: "They said nothing, looked singularly dull and would hail with obvious relief the appearance of a friend" (Stevenson 31). Yet, there is a sense of duty and commitment that is so strong that even "the calls of business [were] resisted" (Stevenson 31). This walk is a domestic duty for both involved, although it appears that Enfield also finds pleasure in other pursuits. His three o'clock stroll on a winter morning coming from "the end of the world" (Stevenson 32) supports Enfield's reputation as a "well-known man about town" (Stevenson 31). When Utterson chooses to retreat to his cozy fireside, Enfield has other plans. His encounter demonstrates how Enfield can relate more to Hyde than Utterson. The incident at the door reveals how in Stevenson's male community it appears that Hyde fits in better than the lawyer Utterson.

Hyde's first intrusion into the domestic is marked by the disturbance in Utterson's nightly regime. After hearing Enfield's description of Hyde, Utterson chooses his office over his bed, where he retrieves Jekyll's private document. Utterson as defender of the domestic is also the passive keeper of Jekyll's Will. The Will, as Utterson states, reveals either Jekyll's "madness" (Stevenson 37), or "how I begin to fear it is [his] disgrace" (Stevenson 37). Jekyll's reputation is in Utterson's safe-keeping. Under the veil of professionalism, Utterson recounts his emotional reaction to Jekyll's Will, which is made worse with the introduction of Hyde. It is Utterson's sleep or rather his "great dark bed" (Stevenson 38) which confirms the impact of Hyde, as the lawyer "toss[es] to and fro" (Stevenson 38). Utterson's domestic space is no longer a safe haven, which is what he imagines is also the case for Jekyll. Utterson is less concerned about the theft and deceit associated with the business of the Will, and instead puts more anxiety into Jekyll and Hyde's interactions in the bedroom. Utterson imagines how Jekyll's private space has been infiltrated by Hyde when he describes how the "curtains of the bed [were] plucked apart" (Stevenson 39). Interestingly, it is the power dynamics in the bedroom which concern the Lawyer Utterson. His second bedside image of Jekyll and Hyde reveals Utterson's obsession with the protection of Jekyll's domestic space: "It turns me cold to think of this creature stealing like a thief to Harry's bedside; poor Harry, what a wakening!" (Stevenson 43). Utterson is anxious about his friend's abandonment of the domestic in favor of this new space self-designed by the late-nineteenth-century bachelor.

Utterson's nightmares and the imagery surrounding Hyde are reminiscent of the discourse used to describe the New Woman. Utterson's rejection of Hyde is strongest when he trespasses into Jekyll's domestic space, especially his bedroom and the "pleasantest room in London" (Stevenson 42) — Jekyll's hall. The description of Jekyll's hall clearly idealizes the domestic: "a large, low-roofed, comfortable hall paved with flags warmed after the fashion of a country house, by a bright, open fire and furnished with costly cabinets of oak" (Stevenson 42). This space favored by both Utterson and Jekyll as a "pet fancy" (Stevenson 42) is chosen by Stevenson to emphasize Hyde's successful penetration of Jekyll's private space. Upon entering the hall Utterson "seemed to read a menace in the flickering of the firelight on the polished cabinets and the uneasy starting of the shadow on the roof" (Stevenson 42). Hyde is "both part of and an intrusion upon a scene" (Gaughan 193). Hyde is without and within simultaneously as spectacle and spectator, female and male.[9] The domestic defender is able to recognize the smallest signs of intrusion and he can see beyond the comforting firelight and identify the "menace" within.

As a guardian of the domestic, Utterson clings to what is left of the bourgeois gentleman's code of conduct. He struggles to maintain the performance of masculinity among a community of men who question these traditional gender foundations. Andrew Smith insists that Stevenson's male community "represents the bourgeois male in a state of terminal decline" (37).[10] I argue that although Stevenson's male community represents *fin de siècle* masculinity in crisis, it becomes clear that Utterson rejects this movement towards "degeneration."[11] Enfield appears as a character who has never completely embraced bourgeois masculinity, and Lanyon's scientific curiosity allows him to explore the possibilities while keeping his distance. Utterson is the only one who appears to completely embrace this brand of masculinity and defend it at all costs.

Utterson is confronted with Hyde's refusal to perform traditional masculinity, as Smith indicates, the "theatricality associated with the performance of the bourgeois gentleman is ostensibly threatened by the feral qualities of Hyde" (38). While Hyde functions as a disrupting force, Smith points out how "an alternative case can be made that it is the demands of performance that creates the possibility of this horror" (38). Although Utterson struggles to maintain the performance of masculinity, he indulges in moments of lapse similar to Jekyll's desire to create Hyde. Strangely, in a domestic scene with Guest, Utterson embraces the role of patriarch seeking advice from a Victorian icon of effeminacy, the clerk,[12] as opposed to placing himself in the role of the effeminate domesticated man. This is remarkably similar to a husband and wife relationship, where the professional lawyer seeks comfort by soliciting advice from someone he considers inferior. The scene is intentionally planned for Utterson's purpose and Guest plays the role of the Victorian wife fulfilling the patriarchal fantasy. The setting evokes the domestic as the two men sit on each side of the hearth and "midway between, at a nicely calculated distance from the fire, a bottle of a particular old wine" (Stevenson 52). In order to participate fully in this scene, Utterson requires the aid of wine, which is described using a combination of scientific and poetic diction. This draught of fermented acids aged to perfection is equivalent to Jekyll's potion.[13] Jekyll himself compares his dependence on the potion like that of an alcoholic (Stevenson 84). The wine allows the lawyer to melt insensibly (Stevenson 52), while Jekyll uses similar terminology to describe how the potion allows for "moral insensibility" (Stevenson 84). With the effects of the wine, Utterson is able to experience the same freedom as Jekyll with his potion.

Guest is accustomed to these domestic scenes and is the possessor of many of Utterson's secrets, "and he was not always sure that he kept as many as he meant" (Stevenson 52). As head clerk Guest fills the role of employee and confidante. The transition between these two roles is initiated by the staging of domestic accoutrements and especially the freeing effects of wine. The significance of this scene is that it calls into question traditional constructs of the bachelor. John Tosh describes the relationship between the bachelor and manliness, suggesting that "the appeal of all-male conviviality is probably greatest among young unmarried men who are temporarily denied the full privileges of masculinity" (38). Contrary to Tosh's image of the incomplete bachelor, the bachelors in Stevenson's all-male community are clearly exercising their full masculinity by successfully incorporating homosociality into the domestic. Guest needs only drop a remark, which Utterson might use to "shape his future course" (Stevenson 53). Like the angel in the house, Guest's advice must remain limited to a brief communication, which in the hands of the "patriarchal" lawyer, will be brought to its fullest potential. Within the comforts of a room made "gay with firelight" (Stevenson 52), these two male professionals engage in a completely domestic scene while exercising every aspect of Victorian masculinity. Although Stevenson practically banishes female characters from his novella, a tendency arguably shared with several other *fin de siècle* male writers,[14] the feminine and the domestic are clearly present. The evolution of masculinity and especially the bachelor has created a space where the private no longer requires a feminine presence and a family. The homosocial, which has been defined as belonging to the public sphere[15], becomes a vital component of the *fin de siècle* private sphere.

The exclusively male community in Stevenson's novella allows the bachelor to discover a new masculinity, one which is neither completely male nor female. The ambiguity and fluidity of the gender identity of the *fin de siècle* bachelor suggests that his sexuality also wavers. Hyde eludes the gaze and remains indescribable; while the narrative's attempts appear to fail, the discourse of writing is also employed for a similar purpose, but as M. Kellen Williams observes all attempts whether spoken or written will remain unsuccessful "so long as he eludes the proper name" (421). Williams follows the paper trail which he argues only leads to further discontinuities in the narrative discourse:

> Rather than any definitive depictions of Edward Hyde there are instead stories, handbills, and journal entries which fail to describe him; rather than any hard evidence for the connection between the two title figures, there are mysterious "enclosures," registered letters, "immodest" wills, and arcane notes; rather, in short, than some material, accessible referent there is always at least right up until the last dramatic scene, "nothing but papers, and a closed door" [420].

Although it would appear that the discourse of writing also fails to contain Hyde, it is the language of blackmail that provides the reader with insight into these seemingly disconnected written documents. The "unspoken" language of blackmail and homosexuality reveal that these male characters share a common understanding. Sedgwick identifies the Gothic genre as having "relatively visible links to male homosexuality, at a time when styles of homosexuality, and even its visibility and distinctness, were markers of division and tension between classes as much as between genders" (91). The Gothic tradition is evident in Stevenson's novella including murder, transformations, and potions, but also suggestions of sexual perversions, suicide, and homosexuality.

The language of *Dr Jekyll and Mr Hyde* involves secrecy, and unspoken insinuations which function as tropes of the Gothic genre, as Sedgwick outlines, "[s]exuality between men had, throughout the Judaeo-Christian tradition, been famous among those who knew about it at all precisely for having no name —'unspeakable,' 'unmentionable'" (94). Hyde appears to have more in common with Enfield and Utterson, rather than with his own creator, Jekyll. The unspoken words between Enfield and Utterson in the opening scene, and the clear understandings between Hyde, Utterson, and Enfield about scandal and disgrace reveal a secret language among the members of this exclusively male community, and Sedgwick remarks that there is a "defining pervasiveness in Gothic novels of language about the unspeakable" (94). The unspoken language becomes more concrete in the form of blackmail, which Sedgwick classifies as yet another example of a Gothic trope. "Homophobic blackmailability" (Sedgwick 90) finds a forum in the Gothic tradition where issues of homophobia and homosocial bonds can be worked out. Blackmail, secrecy, power, and control surround the male community in *Dr Jekyll and Mr Hyde* and suggest yet another variation of the bachelor as androgynous which Michel Foucault cites as an early understanding of homosexuality (43). The bachelor moves between the public and private spaces of the novella while transforming himself from an exemplar of middle-class patriarchy, to the model of fluid and elusive femininity, into his final transformation as the "man in the middle"—the homosexual.

Hyde as middle-class gentleman leading a public and private life is not exceptional, and his ability to perform these actions becomes part of the unspoken language between the men in Stevenson's work. Michel Foucault refers to understandings of the nineteenth-century homosexual in volume I of *The History of Sexuality*:

> [He] became a personage, a past, a case history, and a childhood, in addition to being a type of life, a life form, and a morphology, with an indiscreet anatomy and possibly a mysterious physiology. Nothing that went into his total composition was unaffected by his sexuality. It was everywhere present in him: at the root of all his actions because it was their insidious and indefinitely active principle; written immodestly on his face and body because it was a secret that always gave itself away [43].

The homosexual becomes an identity that is apparent in every aspect of his life, including his physical appearance. The body becomes the surface on which the secret of the homosexual is exposed. Anatomy, physiology, and phrenology were the methods by which Victorians categorized criminals, the insane, and the sexually deviant. Stevenson emphasizes Hyde's physicality and appearance using a unique combination of detail and uncertainty, which triggers Utterson's obsessive desire to see Hyde's face for himself. Hyde's physicality is described as repulsive, but no one is able to explain the reason for their disgust. This suggests that the reaction towards Hyde by the masses and the higher-class professionals is based on the vagueness of Hyde's sexuality and not a distinguishing feature.

The inability to pinpoint specific characteristics about Hyde demonstrates how feelings of disgust derive from Hyde's entire demeanor, or as Foucault states, "his total composition." Enfield's lacking description of Hyde titillates Utterson's interest in seeing Hyde for himself:

> He is not easy to describe. There is something wrong with his appearance; something displeasing, something down-right detestable. I never saw a man I so disliked, and yet I scarce know why. He must be deformed somewhere; he gives a strong feeling of deformity, although I couldn't specify the point. He's an extraordinary looking man, and yet I really can name nothing out of the way. No, sir; I can make no hand of it; I can't describe him. And it's not want of memory; for I declare I can see him this moment [36].

The ambiguity coupled with Enfield's certainty that he experienced feelings of disgust suggests Foucault's description of the nineteenth-century homosexual, and yet Hyde appears to succeed in maintaining some sort of mystery about him. Enfield's obscure picture of Hyde leads Utterson to believe that if he could only see Hyde's face he would know all:

> If he could but once set eyes on him, he thought the mystery would lighten and perhaps roll altogether away, as was the habit of mysterious things when well examined. He might see a reason for his friend's strange preference or bondage.... At least it would be a face worth seeing: the face of a man who was without bowels of mercy: a face which had but to show itself to raise up, in the mind of the unimpressionable Enfield, a spirit of enduring hatred [39].

Utterson's assumption that by seeing Hyde's face all will be clear is reminiscent of Foucault's description of the Victorian belief in the power of physical appearances to expose secrets. Utterson also suggests that he would be a better candidate than Enfield for deciphering Hyde's features.

Ronald R. Thomas also recognizes a strong link between Hyde and Utterson and refers to the dream Utterson has about Hyde sneaking into Jekyll's bedchamber. Alongside Utterson's obsession over Hyde's appearance is his fixation on Hyde as "Henry Jekyll's favourite" (Stevenson 48). As Thomas states,

> The images and action of the dream are characterized by power, stealth, and self-censorship. Hyde is as much Utterson's dream as Jekyll's here. His "power" is exercised over both of them. Utterson is "the law" to Jekyll's crime, and his response to the dream demonstrates that he is as subject to its bidding as Jekyll is [240].

Utterson's profession as a lawyer strengthens his belief that he, like Jekyll, is bound to the criminal, Hyde, as Utterson states in his well-known pun, "If he be Mr. Hyde ... I shall be Mr. Seek" (Stevenson 39). The unspeakable language fails to provide spectators with the appropriate image of Hyde as homosexual/criminal, but succeeds in delivering an overall impression of repulsion and, as it appears in the case of Utterson, attraction. Hyde's shroud of mystery relates back to his status as the *fin de siècle* bachelor and his ability to adapt, transform, and evolve to "fit into" a particular space, class, and gender. The language between the men in Stevenson's novella involves a codified structure with a variety of "dialects" including physical appearances, and the more threatening method of blackmail.

During a time when masculinity and concerns for the bachelors' increasing tendency to delay marriage[16] indicated a degeneration in nationhood, the new bachelor finds comfort in a domestic setting surrounded by his male companions. The Victorian bachelor appears to benefit from the *fin de siècle*'s "masculinity in crisis" by expanding his boundaries and pushing himself into the realm of the domestic. Whereas Arata argues that the bachelor sought to escape the isolation and repression of Victorian domesticity ("Sedulous Ape" 243), I argue that the bachelor finds within the private sphere a space where aspects of the homosocial broaden and reconfigure ideas of masculinity and its role in the domestic. The expansion and contraction of spaces comply with the fluidity and elasticity of Hyde as he moves through the streets of London, into the cabinet, hall, and bedchamber of Jekyll's house, Enfield's chambers, Hyde's own apartments, and Jekyll's Will. Although the streets of London seem a fitting place for Hyde to wander, he manages to "glide more stealthily through sleeping houses" (Stevenson 39), and particularly "steal ... like a thief to Harry's bedside." (Stevenson 43). His movements form the primary tension of the novella, fuelling Utterson's obsession. Space, whether in Soho or Jekyll's domestic Hall, communicates what the novel has difficulty expressing through narrative discourse.

Hyde is everywhere and nowhere — he is described as a ghost (Stevenson 39 and 49), who transpires and transfigures (Stevenson 42), and yet he can become earthly, animalistic, and quite concrete, especially when he tramples a little girl and clubs Sir Danvers Carew. This transformation from swift invisibility to "ape-like" (Stevenson 46) fury and deformity is the essence of Hyde as Other. In between these two extremes there is Hyde — the gentleman with furnished luxurious rooms and a knowledge of London and its customs. Hyde is no longer the traditional Gothic Other; instead, he is a hybrid who pushes the gender boundaries and forces the bourgeois professionals to explore their masculinity. Their stagnancy and failure to meet with the *fin de siècle*'s new definition of masculinity results in tragedy. The flexing of space is a silent commentary on the re-engineering of social order and gender roles. Space is controlled by Hyde, whether it be on the streets or within the intimate chambers of Jekyll's home, Hyde conquers all spaces in the novella. Since narrative discourse fails to contain Hyde, the discourse of space and of writing attempt to express the unspeakable.

Hyde's movement between the public and private spaces of *Dr. Jekyll and Mr. Hyde*'s exclusively male community is possible based on his ability to possess both masculine and feminine characteristics. His status as gentleman and defender of middle-class patriarchy, as Arata argues, provides Hyde with a social status that promotes the existence of dual natures and the need to keep secrets. Hyde's middle-class masculinity is the ideal mask to hide behind and allows him to penetrate into the male community. His feminine characteristics provide him with a fluid and elusive identity that cannot be categorized and, as Kane states, this signifies Hyde as the Other and Jekyll's discovery of his own feminine nature. Hyde is the ideal bachelor who, like Ik Marvel's bachelor narrator in *The Reveries of a Bachelor* (1850), finds a place within the domestic space through the exclusion of women. Hyde as bachelor flourishes in the male community of the novella and is able to move freely from the public realm of the masculine into the domestic space typified as feminine without any challenges. The unspoken language used by this male community reveals yet another transformation for the *fin de siècle* bachelor. Hyde as bachelor homosexual questions the delicate balance between pleasure and crime, sensuality and murder. The unspoken language of blackmail reveals a community familiar with homosexuality, but uncomfortable with the ambiguous and obscure sexual identity of Hyde. This becomes the essence for the *fin de siècle* bachelor who incorporates masculine and feminine characteristics as a tool for moving between public and private spaces. Hyde flourishes in Stevenson's male community by violently questioning Victorian masculinity and creating a new understanding of the nineteenth-century bachelor.

While Stevenson employs the discourse of writing and imprinting in an attempt to "capture" what is left unsaid, he is, in essence, engaging in a typically patriarchal scientific mode of defining the "feminine"— the ghost, the elusive. This discourse aims to bring a scientific method into the chaos which is *Dr Jekyll and Mr Hyde*. Although born from a laboratory potion, the science of Jekyll and Hyde ends there. Rather, the reader spends more time within the characters' parlors, halls, dining rooms, private offices, and bedchambers. The spaces within the novella leave the science fiction genre behind, and although this is a male-only community, it becomes clear that the themes do not stray from such familiar issues of identity, gender, and society associated with the marriage novel genre. The spaces in *Dr Jekyll and Mr Hyde* contradict its basis as an exploration of the moral issues affiliated with the progress of science at the *fin de siècle*. Instead, the exclusively male community and the wide array of private spaces suggest an emphasis on the re-evaluation of masculinity and the domesticity.

The argument here is not the unique ability for men to engage in both spaces, as Tosh confirms, "it is now widely recognized that constant emphasis on the 'separation of spheres' is misleading, partly because men's privileged ability to pass freely between the public and private was integral to the social order" (39). During the nineteenth century, a man's business and family often shared the same physical space in the home. A husband's impact within the private and a woman's contribution within the public has eliminated the argument that the spheres did not allow for movement (Tosh 69). The argument that requires attention in any discussion of the spheres, is how the domestic is being redefined by the *fin de siècle* bachelor. Men continued to cross between public and private, but the private is no longer Tosh's Victorian home consisting of a wife, children, and servants. Tosh argues that the bachelor's lack of a "proper" domestic space excludes him from "exercising [his] full masculinity" (38). As men begin to choose to marry later, at age thirty by the 1880s (38), it is debatable to suggest that these bachelors have not achieved masculinity. Although it is a man's "privilege" to move between the spheres, according to Tosh's definition of masculinity, it appears that there is a little freedom within the constraints of Victorian masculinity and the public and private spheres themselves, to the point where without engaging in one, you are denied a claim to the other. Does the private disappear when the family is not present? Are Stevenson's bachelors simply masquerading as men since, according to Tosh, they never fully engage in their masculinity? This is how the *fin de siècle* bachelor blurs the boundaries and pushes beyond the constraints of the spheres and gender. What is remarkable is that the result is a redefined domestic space that includes the bachelor.

The tension between male domesticity and homosociality (Tosh 71) is resolved by the reconfiguring of the domestic space. The bachelor is able to engage in every aspect of masculinity including issues of domesticity without the female presence. Stevenson's use of domestic space demonstrates how the bachelor not only transgresses private and public boundaries, he can also reshape the private to assume characteristics of the homosocial. Tosh uses the example of the London journeymen as "living out the dictates of 'separate spheres'" (71) by being married and yet still acting like bachelors, "according to a fraternal ethos of drunken misogyny" (71). This is a version of the bachelor as young, promiscuous, drunk, and exempt from the domestic. Stevenson's bachelors, on the other hand, perform as if they are married, and indulge in domestic bliss while exercising their claim to masculinity. Instead of being a source of male repression and isolation, Victorian domesticity expands to include the bachelor. Although male-only adventure fiction, the new genre of the mid–1880s, as Tosh points out, appears to do away with the marriage novel in favor of "bracing masculine fantasy of quest and danger, a world without petticoats" (107), it becomes clear that these domestic issues are still present, but have taken on a different and significant form in this *fin de siècle* male-centric genre.

Notes

1. The separation of the public and private spheres was strongly enforced against female authors who were often associated with prostitutes for exposing themselves publicly for financial gain.

2. Andrew Lang praises Stevenson's choice of an all-male society in his article in the *Saturday Review* dated 9 January 1886: "His heroes (surely *this* is original) are all successful middle-aged professional men ... we incline to think that Mr. Stevenson always does himself most justice in novels without a heroine" (200–01).

3. The bachelor has proven himself resilient and unique in his ability to maintain the crucial balance between the public and private spheres, as well as his position simultaneously outside and inside the social circle. An early example of the bachelor can be found in William Congreve's *The Way of the World* (1700), where "effeminate dandy" and the "delicate fop" Witwoud fails at his attempts to match the more courtly and witty bachelor, Mirabell. Mirabell possesses the right combination of fashion and wit, as the stage directions describe, he "is an extraordinarily handsome young bachelor whose habitual expression suggests a combination of worldly astuteness and tolerant humour which makes him adored by women and envied by men" (Congreve 63). Congreve places the bachelor in both the domestic sphere of women and marriage while being worshipped by men as representing the ideal of masculinity, and yet he remains elusive to both. This fluid and usually unhindered movement from the private sphere gendered female and the public sphere of men and masculinity makes the bachelor an interesting figure for successfully maintaining this crucial balance. His knowledge of women and their desires does not feminize the bachelor so long as he can simultaneously maintain a strong masculine connection through his position in the public sphere. What happens when the bachelor is removed from this position between the feminine and masculine world, and is forced into and exclusively male community? The term "bachelor" requires the female presence

in order to define himself in opposition. The early example of the bachelor does just that since he can dabble in both the world of the feminine and masculine, but in the late nineteenth century the bachelor is no longer defined by his rejection of marriage, but for his preference for the exclusively male community.

4. Nineteenth-century writers that have bachelor protagonists but do not limit themselves to male characters include Thomas Hardy, Anthony Trollope, Charles Dickens, George Gissing, Donald Grant Mitchell, Emily and Charlotte Brontë, George Eliot, Bram Stoker, Henry James, as well as the male adventure writers including Arthur Conan Doyle, Rider Haggard, and H.G. Wells.

5. Some examples of the emasculated and satirized dandy include Jos Sedley in Thackeray's *Vanity Fair* (1847–48) and Congreve's Witwoud in *The Way of the World*.

6. The term "New Woman" was coined by British journalist Sarah Grand, in an 1894 article for *North American Review*. The New Woman became the focus of magazines like *Punch* and *Yellow Book*; likewise, her American counterpart began to show up in such journals as *Puck, Judge, Life*, and *Chic* (Roberts 21). There were consequences to her popularity and over-exposure in journals, magazines, and novels; she was caricaturized as "bespeckled, bookish, and austere in dress, combin[ing] a Jane Eyre-like plainness with dandy-ish habits such as cigarette smoking. Garbed in bloomers, she was frequently depicted riding a bicycle" (Roberts 20–21). Overall, she represented women's rebellion against the stringent norms of the Victorian middle class and especially those of the institution of marriage.

Novelists writing in the 1890s such as Mona Caird, Emma Brooke, Sarah Grand, Olive Schreiner, Grant Allen, George Gissing, and Thomas Hardy explored in particular the New Woman's rejection of marriage for sexual freedom or her preference of intellectual stimulation over physical desires (Caine). Although the New Woman broke with conventional female roles, it was only Mona Caird, in *The Daughters of Danaus*, who went so far as to challenge "maternal instinct" (Weeks 166). Reaction to the introduction of the New Woman included the idealization and worship of the traditional female role. Elaine Showalter examines the New Woman in *Sexual Anarchy: Gender and Culture at the Fin de Siècle*. Showalter explores male anxiety surrounding the New Woman and the interplay between the sexes on issues of sexual freedom, marriage and education. Discussions between New Women and their male sympathizers, mostly socialists, took place in the Men and Women's Club, an organization that met in London from 1885–1889 (Showalter 47). While men were focusing on the Woman Question, women raised the Man Question (Showalter 49) and ideas of the New Man began to take shape.

Although the New Woman, also known as the "female *flâneurie*" (McCracken 58), was linked in the press with the decadent who shared similar interests in "challenging the institution of marriage and blurring the borders of the sexes" (Showalter 169), they did not always agree. While the aesthete promoted art and artifice, the New Woman was associated with the natural and physical (Showalter 170). After permeating the press and popular culture, Showalter notes how by the mid–1890s it was widely stated that the New Woman novel was passé (171).

For more on the New Woman in France see Mary Louise Roberts' *Disruptive Acts: The New Woman in Fin-de-Siècle France*. For examples of women's writing in the 1890s see Carolyn Christensen Nelson's anthology *A New Woman Reader: Fiction, Articles, Drama of the 1890s* and for literary criticism written by women see Solveig C. Robinson's anthology *A Serious Occupation: Literary Criticism by Victorian Women Writers*. Both collections include works by women pushing beyond the boundaries of their proper spheres into the "male" realm of literary criticism and exploring sexuality and the institution of marriage in their fiction. Elaine Showalter in *A Literature of Their Own: British Women Novelists from Brontë to Lessing* provides a thorough examination of women's literary tradition through the nineteenth century into the early twentieth century, including the brief but momentous interval of New Women's writing.

7. The consequence of secluding oneself in the domestic traditionally results in a form of feminization. The bachelor is a prime candidate for feminization, but, as John Tosh remarks, the family man is also susceptible: "the danger of domesticity to true manliness applied not just to sons, but to the head of the house himself; the man who spent too much time in the company of wife and daughters might becomes effeminized, at the expense of his manly vigour and his familial authority" (70).

8. "As the vine, which has long twined its graceful foliage about the oak, and been and been lifted by it into sunshine, will, when the hardy plant is rifted by the thunderbolt, cling round it with its caressing tendrils, and bind up its shattered boughs, so is it beautifully ordered by Providence, that woman, who is the mere dependent and ornament of man in his happier hours, should be his stay and solace when smitten with sudden calamity; winding herself into the rugged recesses of his nature, tenderly supporting the drooping head, and binding up the broken heart" (Washington Irving selection of "The Wife" in *The Sketch Book of Geoffrey Crayon, Gent.* [1820]). This passage refers to the popular nineteenth-century metaphor of man as oak and woman as vine.

9. Traditionally the female functions as spectacle submitting to the gaze of the male spectator. Judith Butler in *Bodies That Matter* and *Gender Trouble* examines gender performance and the role of the body in gender construction. Mary Russo analyzes the Gothic trope of female as grotesque spectacle in *The Female Grotesque: Risk, Excess and Modernity.*

10. Smith also reveals how he would prefer to move the debate beyond "readings of masculinity as a reactionary response to the women's suffrage movement" (4) and instead suggests that the crisis of masculinity in the *fin de siècle* arises from a "male tradition of writings on degeneracy" (4).

11. Max Nordau in *Degeneration* (1892) claims that decadence is "based on a model of a dangerous, potentially perverse and possibly infectious version of male effeminacy" (qtd. in Smith *Victorian Demons* 2). Nordau makes the link between masculinity in crisis and the decline of the nation during the *fin de siècle*.

12. A. James Hammerton examines the phenomena of Pooterism in "Pooterism or Partnership? Marriage and Masculine Identity in the Lower Middle Class, 1870–1920." Pooterism "refers to the dependent weakness and inflated social pretension of white-collar workers" (294). The clerk becomes an emasculated figure for his subordinate position at work, which was assumed to also carry over into the domestic sphere.

13. Daniel L. Wright in "'The Prisonhouse of My Disposition': A Study of the Psychology of Addiction in *J&H*" claims that the novella is "not just a quaint experiment in gothic terror but Victorian literature's premiere revelation, intended or not, of the etiology of chronic chemical addiction, its character and effects" (263). Wright links Jekyll's drinking of the potion to alcoholism, but he does not analyze the drinking habits of Mr. Utterson.

14. As Tosh points out, the "arrival of R. L. Stevenson and H. Rider Haggard on the literary scene in the mid–1880s signaled the rapid rise of a new genre of men-only adventure fiction, in which the prevalent concern of the English novel with marriage and family was quite deliberately cast aside in favour of a bracing masculine fantasy of quest and danger" (107).

15. Indeed Tosh puts the homosocial in opposition to the home, as belonging to two separate spheres (40).

16. Grace Moore explains in "Something to Hyde: The 'Strange Preference' of Henry Jekyll, how "with middle-class men often waiting until their thirties to marry, concerns extended to the continence of the bachelor" (150).

Works Cited

Arata, Stephen D. "The Sedulous Ape: Atavism, Professionalism, and Stevenson's *Jekyll and Hyde.*" *Criticism: A Quarterly for Literature and the Arts* 37.2 (Spring 1995): 233–59.

Butler, Judith. *Bodies That Matter: On the Discursive Limits of "Sex."* New York: Routledge, 1993.

Caine, Barabra. *English Feminism (1780–1980).* Oxford: Oxford University Press, 1997.

Congreve, William. *The Way of the World.* New York: Barron's Educational Series, 1958.

Foucault, Michel. *The History of Sexuality: An Introduction.* Trans. R. Hurley. 3 vols. New York: Vintage Books, 1990.

Gaughan, Richard T. "Mr. Hyde and Mr. Seek: Utterson's Antidote." *Journal of Narrative Technique* 17.2 (Spring 1987): 184–97.

Hammerton, A. James. "Pooterism or Partnership? Marriage and Masculine Identity in the Lower Middle Class, 1870–1920." *Journal of British Studies* 38.3 (July 1999): 291–321.

Irving, Washington. "The Wife." *The Sketch Book of Geoffrey Crayon, Gent.* (1820).

Kane, Michael. *Modern Men: Mapping Masculinity in English and German Literature, 1880–1930.* New York: Cassell, 1999.

Lang, Andrew. "Review of *The Strange Case of Dr. Jekyll and Mr. Hyde,* by Robert Louis Stevenson." *Saturday Review* 61 (9 January 1886): 55–56. Rpt. in *Robert Louis Stevenson: The Critical Heritage.* Ed. Paul Maixner. London and Boston: Routledge and Kegan Paul, 1981. 199–202.

Marvel, Ik. *The Reveries of a Bachelor: or A Book of the Heart.* New York: Home Book Company, 1850.

McCracken, Scott. "Embodying the New Woman: Dorothy Richardson, Work and the London Café." *Body Matters: Feminism, Textuality, Corporeality.* Ed. Avril Horner and Angela Keane. Manchester and New York: Manchester University Press, 2000. 58–?

Moore, Grace. "Something to Hyde: The 'Strange Preference' of Henry Jekyll." *Victorian Crime, Madness and Sensation.* Eds. Andrew Maunder and Grace Moore. Aldershot, England: Ashgate, 2004.147–61.

Nelson, Carolyn Christensen, ed. *A New Woman Reader: Fiction, Articles, and Drama of the 1890s.* Peterborough: Broadview Press, 2001.

Roberts, Mary Louise. *Disruptive Acts: The New Woman in Fin-de-Siècle France.* Chicago and London: University Chicago Press, 2002.

Robinson, Solveig C., ed. *A Serious Occupation: Literary Criticism by Victorian Women Writers.* Toronto: Broadview Press, 2003.

Russo, Mary. *The Female Grotesque: Risk, Excess and Modernity.* New York: Routledge. 1995.

Sedgwick, Eve Kosofsky. *Between Men: English Literature and Male Homosocial Desire.* New York: Columbia University Press, 1985.

Showalter, Elaine. *Sexual Anarchy: Gender and Culture at the Fin de Siècle.* New York: Penguin Books, 1990.

Smith, Andrew. *Victorian Demons: Medicine, Masculinity and the Gothic at the Fin de Siè-cle*. Manchester and New York: Manchester University Press, 2004.

Snyder, Katherine V. *Bachelors, Manhood, and the Novel 1850–1925*. Cambridge: Cambridge University Press, 1999.

Stevenson, Robert Louis. *The Letters of Robert Louis Stevenson*. Ed. Bradford A. Booth and Ernest Mehew. Vol. 5. New Haven and London: Yale University Press, 1995.

_____. *The Strange Case of Dr Jekyll and Mr Hyde*. Ed. Martin Danahay. Peterborough: Broadview Press, 1999.

Sussman, Herbert. "Masculinity Transformed: Appropriation in Walter Pater's Early Writing." *Victorian Masculinities*. Cambridge: Cambridge University Press, 1995. 173–202

Thomas, Ronald R. *Dreams of Authority: Freud and the Fictions of the Unconscious*. Ithaca: Cornell University Press, 1990.

Tosh, John. *Manliness and Masculinities in Nineteenth-Century Britain: Essays on Gender, Family, and Empire*. New York: Pearson Longman, 2005.

Veeder, William. "Children of the Night: Stevenson and Patriarchy." *Dr. Jekyll and Mr. Hyde after One Hundred Years*. Eds. William Veeder and Gordon Hirsch. Chicago: University Chicago Press, 1988. 107–55.

Weeks, Jeffrey. *Sex, Politics & Society: The Regulation of Sexuality since 1800*. 2d ed. London and New York: Longman, 1989.

Williams, M. Kellen. "'Down With the Door, Poole'": Designating Deviance in Stevenson's *The Strange Case of Dr. Jekyll and Mr. Hyde*." *English Literature in Transition (1880–1920)* 39.4 (1996): 412–29.

Wright, Daniel L. "'The Prisonhouse of My Disposition': A Study in the Psychology of Addiction in *Dr. Jekyll and Mr. Hyde*." *Studies in the Novel* 26.3 (Fall 1994): 254–267.

Ghostly Absence and Sexual Presence in James's "Owen Wingrave" and "The Jolly Corner"

NICHOLAS HARRIS

Critics have generally viewed Henry James's stories, "Owen Wingrave (1892) and "The Jolly Corner" (1907), as disparate examples of the author's work in terms of theme and effectiveness. However, despite the fifteen years that separate the publication of the stories, each employs Gothic elements that provide a sense of continuity within James's body of work. A postmodernist perspective can provide new interpretations of these similar works. By exploring sexual themes, narcissism, Gothicism, popular forms, and anti-interpretation, a postmodernist reading can offer evidence of James's explorations and critiques of hegemonic notions of masculinity.

In an example of the more traditional view of "Owen Wingrave," Louis Auchincloss writes:

> The concept of the ghost who kills the hero in "Owen Wingrave" is terrifying enough, but the horror is all confined to the final page. Up until then the story is about the troubles of a young man in a fanatical military family who refuses to go into the army. As such it is adequately interesting, but hardly a ghost story [94].

Auchincloss admires James's Gothic works, when he considers them Gothic. He sees *The Turn of the Screw* as one of the great uses of ambiguity to solve the dilemma of interpreting whether or not the ghosts are real (93). *The Turn of the Screw* questions whether the ghosts exist only in the imagination of an unreliable narrator. Generally, Auchincloss views this classic example from 1895, and the later ghost stories of James, including "The Jolly Corner," as fine examples of ghostly fantasy (100). In some of the earlier stories, such as "Owen Wingrave," traditional criticism, such as that of Auchincloss, misses the point of James's pervasive but subtle use of the Gothic.

Early postmodernist literary theory demonstrates how concerns with popular iconography and reactions against the predominance of structure in criticism can lead to a fuller understanding of literary content. Specifically, Roland Barthes uses popular iconography to lead the critic away from thinking in holistic structures by advocating the sense of immediate theatre as a viable and exciting force (*Mythologies*, 18–19). Commentators on Barthes, in particular Susan Sontag in her earliest writings, take his sense of the immediate to the level of "anti-interpretation" in which each moment of a literary work is enjoyed through its immediate effectiveness, what she terms an "erotics" of art (*Against Interpretation*, 14). For Sontag, artistic experience consists of a series of aesthetic moments, or "pure, untranslatable, sensuous immediacy" (9) that contain a concentration of bold popular excess. Terry Eagleton comments on the current popularity of the Gothic, noting "postmodernism's obsession with the deviant, exotic and grotesque" (17). This admiration of extremes is a part of Sontag's "erotics," the recognition of the immediate experience of excessive emotions from moment to moment, celebratory, suspenseful, horrific, or otherwise.

"The Jolly Corner" presents the story of an American who has lived in Europe most of his adult life. He returns home to live in the eponymous family house that has been empty for years, since the days of his grandfather's occupation of it. The returning Spencer Brydon describes himself almost in apology for having left America for so long:

> "I know at least what I am," he simply went on; "the other side of the medal's clear enough. I've not been edifying — I believe I'm thought in a hundred quarters to have been barely decent. I've followed strange paths and worshipped strange gods; it must have come to you again and again — in fact you've admitted to me as much — that I was leading, at any time these thirty years, a selfish frivolous scandalous life" [450].

Spencer is speaking to Alice Staverton, a woman who knew him in his youth and who has kept in contact with him. It is from Alice that Brydon first learns of the existence of a ghost in "The Jolly Corner," for it has appeared to her in dreams and she has faith that the dreams are reflective of a reality within the house (451–52). The ghost represents a replica of Spencer Brydon except for its stooped stature, "with his awful face" (483) and its missing fingers (476). Such Gothic images are well cataloged in studies such as that of Anne

Williams's *Art of Darkness* (1995). Williams describes how an innocent protagonist, usually a young woman, enters the domain of a dark old house and
falls prey to a patriarch. She is "intimidated by both his wealth and his forbidding manner" and eventually discovers some supernatural threat "emanating from this history-haunted place" (101). James puts Spencer Brydon
in the place of the innocent, and the supernatural threat is his distorted and
grotesque mirror image of what he may have become had he stayed at home.
As Auchincloss says of the ghost, its disfigurement represents the "the mutilation of the spirit caused by a life dedicated to mammon" in an increasingly
capitalistic America (100). Spencer Brydon assumes the role of the Gothic
innocent, and his ghost, his doppelganger, deformed as it is, represents the
Gothic patriarch with the terrible secret.

This grotesque figure presents what Julia Kristeva would call the
"abject": "one of those violent, dark revolts of being, directed against a threat
that seems to emanate from an exorbitant outside or, inside, ejected beyond
the scope of the possible, the tolerable, the thinkable" (*Powers of Horror* 1).
Brydon, in seeing himself as the abject figure, turns inward and experiencing a "dark revolt" within his self, signified by his confrontation with his
distorted mirror image. Brydon enters the abandoned "Jolly Corner" and the
specter leads him from room to room without showing its face. When finally
Brydon catches up to the figure and confronts it, he recognizes himself as
the abject and thus defines the pivotal moment of his story. In a traditional
view of the story, such as that of Terry Thomson (1998), the plot reaches its
climax at this point; at the moment of meeting with his doppelganger,
Spencer Brydon becomes both "the European gentleman combined with the
American capitalist" and he is "amalgamated into a unified and coherent
whole" (194). The exclamation of this culmination, from the James text,
reads:

> Horror, with the sight, had leaped into Brydon's throat, gasping there in a
> sound he couldn't utter; for the bared identity was too hideous as *his*, and
> his glare was the passion of his protest. The face, *that* face, Spencer Bry
> don's?—he searched it still, but looking away from it in dismay and denial,
> falling straight from his height of sublimity. It was unknown, inconceivable,
> awful, disconnected from any possibility—! [476].

James presents the theme of Narcissism positively by having Brydon identify his lifestyle as the positive, preferable image and his mirror reflection,
the doppelganger, as the distortion. Kristeva also declares Narcissism, both
positive and negative, as a foundation for the abject: "Unflaggingly, like an

inescapable boomerang, a vortex of summons and repulsion places the one hunted by it literally beside himself" (1). Through the mirror imagery of opposition, meaning turns inward into itself. The creation of this abject in literature emphasizes immediate effect, drawing the reader to "the place where meaning collapses" (Kristeva 2). In the case of the Gothic, the horrific comes to the front of the story and takes over the meaning of the piece. The Gothic innocent defines this horror by confronting it. "The Jolly Corner" presents a tale that unfolds with Kristeva's abject meaning, first by defining the hero as Narcissistic, then by presenting him as the Gothic innocent lured through the dark old house for the purpose of confronting the abject. Each moment of the story consists of immediate horrific exclamation.

In "The Jolly Corner" the recognition of unexplained sins as a reflected definition of self shows the influence on James of Oscar Wilde, especially *The Picture of Dorian Grey* (1890). Eric Haralson points out the influence of Wilde on James in this and several other instances (Haralson 81). James novel *The Tragic Muse* (1890) presents a personality who represents "James's closest approximation to the 'Wildean aesthete'" in a character named Gabriel Nash (54). This aesthete is delineated by Wilde in *The Picture of Dorian Gray*, a story that traces the life of a Narcissistic young man who enters into a demonic pact with a painting of himself, a pact in which the painting grows old and diseased while Dorian stays young and free from the outward effects of his dissipated activities. Wilde's prelude to the novel, filled with quips about artistry, demonstrates a complex aesthetic concerning the imitative nature of art. Describing the aesthete as delineated in Wilde, Haralson explains, "That stereotype would soon merge with another — the homosexual — through an intricate process of cultural articulation and social regulation" (54). A Victorian era stigma against the homosexual stereotype cast a dark shadow on the Victorian idea of masculinity. Specifically of James's character of Grahame Nash, Haralson writes: "Reviews in American newspapers ... did not hesitate to name Wilde outright as James's model, and thus to fortify the idea of Nash as Anglo-Irish or more importantly as *not* American" (56). British reviewers held opposite views, disowning Nash as having an American-like "social forwardness" (56). Clearly these reviewers were attempting to distance the Wildean stereotype from their own national character.

Like Nash, the character of Spencer Brydon in "The Jolly Corner" reflects the "Wildean aesthete." The American Spencer Brydon had lived a questionable yet self-defining existence as decadent exile. James, though, was torn between the two concerns of identifying Brydon with Wildean aesthetics and identifying him with the European gentleman.

Narcissism represents the secret element of the Gothic adventure here. Silent, narcissistic reflection is the key to the Gothicism of this story. The critic can turn again to Kristeva who, engaging in psychoanalysis, defines Narcissism as the underlying definition of love. The one who experiences love looks upon his or her self with a reflection that is "beyond narcissistic madness, of that western consciousness of self which might have nothing to do with an Ego in love with itself, but whose autoerotic jouissance is nonetheless striking" (*Tales of Love* 108). In light of Kristeva's ideas, Narcissistic stories such as *Dorian Gray* and "The Jolly Corner" show further parallels. In the final pages of the latter, Alice proclaims her love for Brydon. She loves him despite his hedonistic unexplained sins; she recoils in horror from the ghost, the man he could have become had he stayed in America. The longsuffering Alice is aware of the ambiguity in loving a man who proclaims to her that he "followed strange paths and worshipped strange gods." When she responds to Brydon concerning what the frivolous lifestyle has made of him, she tells him, "You see what it has made of *me*," implying that she has wasted her best years waiting for him to return (450).

Brydon's heterosexual relationship with Alice presents another ambiguity of theme in the story. As Haralson notes above, the Wildean aesthetic had become intertwined with a decadent stereotype of a homosexual long before the writing of "The Jolly Corner." So the fact that Spencer Brydon had adopted the European Wildean aesthetic as his preferred persona raises the question of homosexuality as a part of that persona. But mirror imagery plays a large part in this definition of Narcissistic self love as well as same-sex desire, for Spencer Brydon confronts himself in the ghost, in order to determine his true place in the world.

James here reflects work by other fin de siècle authors; his mirror imagery is reminiscent of Wilde's *Dorian Gray* and of Robert Louis Stevenson's *The Strange Case of Dr Jekyll and Mr Hyde*. The latter's hero journeys toward self definition; he creates and confronts a distorted view of himself and does so in order to define himself as a man, or at least partly for that reason. As Anne Williams points out, the Gothic elements used by each of these Victorian authors can be characterized as essentially feminine in nature. Early Gothic stories of a century before these told of female innocents suffering oppression at the hands of a domineering patriarchal figure, the male archetype who induced paranoia often through sadism or other cruelty. The male was often the cruel Other, but on occasion could be substituted for the innocent, who was usually a female. This sort of substitution creates the ambiguity of "apparent duality" (Williams 140–41). Gothic characters thus can combine a "masculine strength" with a "feminine capacity for intense feeling" (143–44). Depending on the role of the character, this duality held multiple meanings, sometimes with the masculine taking the role of heroic stance, and sometimes with the feminine taking the role of the good and true, but always with mystery involved.

The Victorian man, in an attempt to define masculinity, often confronts the Gothic motif of duality. The attempt to view himself as a good, true, gentleman accepted by society means looking at the qualities within the self that society perceives as bad, untrue or ugly, and often it is these horrid images that the man sees in his reflection. Stevenson foregrounds the duality of his story as Dr. Jekyll reflects his alter ego, and Wilde's Dorian mirrors his portrait. James takes these ideas and applies them directly to the Victorian ghost story, making the ghost a mirror image, and giving it a particularly Jamesian concern with defining American masculinity. Earl Roy Miner writes of James's criticism of *Jekyll and Hyde* in which he claims that Stevenson brings too much realism into a great romantic story (4). Simple reality is never enough for James. In part he took his idea of ambiguity from Wilde, especially concerning the transgressions of an individual whose sins are never entirely spelled out. Again Haralson writes, "James's manner of engaging the social and personal fact of same-sex passion ... was furtive and intermittent, vacillating between detection and deflection, flirtation and flight" (62). Homosexuality was not the only taboo that Wilde or James could have been writing about. But in questions of men searching for self-definition through mirror imagery, it is the taboo of most immediate interest.

Haralson also writes, "As the example of Wilde indicates, 'blanks' were not uncommon in Anglo-American fictional technique of the period, and they have proven to be as spacious and accommodating as the readerly imagination is large" (81). The sinner, whose injurious acts are "blank," or unstated, becomes the gothic monster who threatens the innocent. But the innocent can have unstated sins also. In the case of James, the evil resides in the dark old house in the form of the ghost, brought into existence by Spencer Brydon's guilt at having lived a hedonistic lifestyle, full of undefined evils.

Haralson's queering of James's work and the "blanks" that he describes in relation to sexual issues raises the question of the relationship of the gay man to Victorian Gothic literature. That Wilde was writing about homoerotic "vices" is not difficult to imply; that James was influenced by Wilde is probable (Haralson 81). These unspoken vices lead the reader to interpret the world that Spencer Brydon has left behind in Europe as a world of men, where his concern with selfish pleasures and probable homoerotic desires has been abandoned. But through assuming the feminine role of the innocent wanderer in the dark old house, Spencer Brydon eventually turns to the feminine world of Alice Staverton and the world of heterosexual alliance.

James's association with the "decadents" in the early part of the 1890's may have led to such concerns of same sex confrontations, even if he never crossed the line directly. Indeed, James was known to make offhand remarks against the homosexual friendly treatises of John Addington Symonds (Haralson 61). Still, according to John Auchard, the Wilde trials that began in 1895 "ended James's association with the decadents, but he had rubbed shoulders with them for some years, and much that he wrote accommodated itself to their *fin de siècle* refinement" (32). Though after the trials James distanced himself from Wilde, he held the decadents' preoccupation with horror and paradox and the ambiguity of hedonism.

Issues of gender are an important link between the various works of James, especially issues dealing with male to male confrontations and how these confrontations relate to same-sex desire. Unlike "The Jolly Corner," the story "Owen Wingrave" was written well before the Wilde sodomy trials. It was written only two years after Wilde's *Dorian Gray* and James's *The Tragic Muse*, but contains no character that can be likened to a "Wildean aesthete" in any direct sense. However, a transgressive sexuality remains an undercurrent in "Owen Wingrave"; same sex confrontations occur as the title character defines his manhood, as does a confrontation with a woman intended for his heterosexual match.

"Owen Wingrave" presents another study in Narcissism. The particular variety of Narcissism here concerns the man facing his patriarchal roots, the confrontation of a self as a product of a family that thrusts its patriarchal views upon its male members and forces them to question themselves in terms of those values. "Owen Wingrave" bears resemblance to *The Turn of the Screw* in that the ghosts are largely unseen. Psychological horror within the mind of the innocent may indeed be the very cause of the ghosts in both stories. The Wingrave family never questions the reality of the ghost, even though they can never discern its identity, or even if there is only one.

In James, ghosts are "real" in the pragmatic sense because they have an effect on the people who perceive them (Lewis 11). In "Owen Wingrave" there exists an evil in the Wingrave house, the result of the continual abuse of the children by their fathers. Generally this abuse is psychological in nature and takes the form of an adamant insistence on a military idea of courage and bravery that leads the Wingrave males to become military men when they reach adulthood. One instance of physical abuse stands out in the history of the family, the murder of a child by his father and the death of the father shortly thereafter (300). Every subsequent Wingrave who tempts fate by staying overnight in the room where the murder occurred dies of fright or goes insane and leaves the country in disgrace. So the family does not tempt fate in this manner, shutting up the room and avoiding it; yet they continue to oppress the male children with their sense of expected machismo or false bravado. This patriarchal evil, vaguely defined as it is, conjures up the presence of the ghostly occurrences. As a result of the emphasis on patriarchy as the cause of the family's problems, critics such as Roland Jordan and Emma Kafalenos (1989) interpret the ghost as the patriarchal father who murdered his son (137). They present a formalistic study dependent on a single patriarchal event that causes the family's troubles. Other possibilities, however, include the idea that the murdered son would take his revenge by haunting the haughty Wingrave males. Or possibly the ghostly horrors are the result of both ghosts caught in a cycle of creating the destruction of the family. Given James's penchant for the "pragmatic" use of ghosts, the ambiguous identity or identities is not as important as the effect the haunts have on the family members. The ghost is caused by the family's abusive patriarchy, and the effects of this patriarchy define why the ghost is present.

Jordan and Kafalenos, in their formalist analysis, emphasize ambiguity as a structural force, even comparing the story's form to that of a piece of music. But the concept of ambiguity can also represent what Susan Sontag refers to as "anti-interpretive." Sontag writes in *Against Interpretation* (1967) that what matters in dramatic scenes is "the pure, untranslatable, sensuous immediacy of some of its images" (9). These images solve problems of ambiguous form by bringing spontaneous contexts to the forefront as they occur, making the aesthetic transparent. As Sontag writes Roland Barthes's "ability to conjure up a vivacious duality: anything could be split either into itself and its opposite, or into two versions of itself" ("Writing Itself: On Roland Barthes" 428–429). James exposes Owen Wingrave's inner conflicts through such a conjuring. Wingrave's family manipulates him first toward the military, then towards the forbidden room. The ambiguity of his situation resonates from the first words of the story:

"Upon my honor you must be off your head!" cried Spencer Coyle as the young man, with a white face stood there panting a little and repeating, "Really, I've quite decided," and "I assure you, I've thought it all out." They were both pale, but Owen Wingrave smiled in a manner exasperating to his supervisor... [269].

These words express the resoluteness of Owen in his decision to abandon his military career despite his enjoyment of the all male society it provides. The decision also dismay's his captain, Coyle, and his friend Lechmere. Jordan and Kafalenos refer to this beginning as an ambiguous plotline, one that sets two contradictory lines in motion (139). But even in the spontaneous reading of the immediate moment, ambiguity is apparent. James's story represents a precursor of modernist concerns with ambiguity and psychology. Here is the exploitation of inner conflict that is immediate and visceral, the use of what John McGowan calls the "affective power of image" that postmodernism can embrace (586). Here is the moment by moment temporal form of "unmanageable" content (Sontag, *Against Interpretation* 12).

Within a few sentences James explains, "Mr. Coyle was a professional 'coach': he prepared aspirants for the army, taking only three or four at a time, to whom he applied the irresistible stimulus the possession of which was both his secret and his fortune" (270). James further explains Coyle in this way, "He was an artist in his line, caring only for picked subjects and capable of sacrifices almost passionate for the individual. He liked ardent young men ... and he had taken a particular fancy to Owen Wingrave" (270). The relationship of Coyle to Owen presents one of the primary ambiguities. Coyle takes a decidedly paternal tone with Owen from the beginning. Thus the reader knows that patriarchy will play a major role in the story's theme. But according to Kelly Cannon in *Henry James and Masculinity* (1994) a character, such as Coyle, in a James story who stands outside of the action trying to interpret it is a marginal narrator (13–14). As Canon notes, Coyle "explores the workings of the imagination, the first and last refuge of the marginal male" (8). Coyle has taken a paternal liking to Owen, as he does to all of his students, and he is shocked and disappointed to realize that Owen will have a life separate from his own. The text further describes Owen's effect upon Coyle: "This young man's particular shade of ability, to say nothing of his whole personality, almost cast a spell and at any rate worked a charm" (270). The charismatic magic of Owen's charm contrasts with the omnipresence of the theme of patriarchy, present the dominant themes of honor and masculinity. Owen offers pacifism as a legitimate alternative to life in the military. But Coyle and Lechmere cannot help but wonder whether cowardice, rather than pacifism, plays a part (289). The notion of cowardice held by many of the characters in "Owen Wingrave" may represent a fear, not on the part of the accused coward, but rather their own fear of the rejection of Victorian notions of manliness. These issues form the discussion as Owen returns home with Lechmere, Coyle, and his wife, as guests.

In contrast, the next scene of the story begins with the presence of Mrs. Coyle and her initial impression of the Wingrave house. "She characterized it as 'uncanny' and as looking wicked and weird, and she accused her husband of not having warned her properly" (291). Though moments of disquieting immediacy, eeriness, and unease have dropped hints, at this point the ghost finally appears in the conversation of the characters. Mr. Coyle tells the story of the ghost almost off-handedly to his wife at her insistence, startling her into a curiosity concerning the haunting. She confronts her husband: "Do you mean the house has a proved *ghost*?" Mrs. Coyle almost shrieked. "You brought me here without telling me?" (300–01). From this point in the story, Mr. Coyle interprets most of the actions through the observances of his wife as his marginal narrator status is reinforced. Owen echoes Mrs. Coyle's attitude of "weird" discomfort by expressing his own feelings unleashed by his decision to leave the army. "I've started up all the old ghosts. The very portraits glower at me on the walls.... It's what my aunt calls the family circle, and they sit, ever so grimly, in judgment" (297). Despite its patriarchal aura, the house is filled of women — Mrs. Coyle, Owen's aunt, his sister, a Mrs. Julian, and her daughter, Miss Julian, who through the years has been thought of as Owen's future wife — who appear simultaneously with talk of the family ghosts. Owen's unease at leaving the military life and the ghost story of the patriarchs in the Wingrave house, has been there from the story's beginning.

The silent presence of the ghosts is not unusual in James. Unheard and unseen, they lay dormant beneath the action. Major studies on the work of James confirm the importance of silence in his work (Auchard 1986, Johnson 2006). As a reader approaches "Owen Wingrave" scene by scene, the omnipresence of the silent collective of patriarchal concerns and its unsettling quality is present from the beginning.

Owen assumes the role of the Gothic innocent. As he wanders into the haunted family estate, his initial announcement of his departure from the military, the world of men, begins to acquire additional meaning. Little by little, through the eyes of Mr. Coyle, the reader witnesses Owen's journey into a Gothic edifice where he is taunted by the women who live there, especially his would-be fiancée, Miss Julian. The text provides the reader with a first impression of Miss Julian: "This young lady, who in plain terms was a mere dependent, would in effect be, as a consequence of the way she carried herself, the most important person in the house. Mrs. Coyle was already prepared to announce that she hated Miss Julian's affectations" (292). Miss Julian insists that Owen conform to the family's patriarchal code of honor and as such she insists that he return to his career as a soldier (307). She cruelly dares him to spend the night in the haunted room, in the presence of Lechmere (310) and Mrs. Coyle (315). Accused of cowardice by the ghosts of his patriarchal past and the women of his present, Owen acquiesces. Compromising with the ironic feminine insistence on adherence to the unwritten patriarchal law, Owen is defeated by these ghosts, first figuratively by succumbing to Miss Julian's demands that he spend the night in the cursed room; then literally by the supernatural agent that leaves him dead on the last page of the story. As the final sentence of the story reminds the reader, Owen's true battlefield was in his own home: "He was all the young soldier on the gained field" (319). He has gained the field of courage, but at the price of his life.

Mixed with patriarchal expectations, a false sense of masculinity is the definition of the ghost that haunts Owen Wingrave. He defies the ghostly specter of patriarchy by leaving the army, ostensibly for pacifist reasons. This bold defiance sometimes makes critics consider "Owen Wingrave" as primarily a story that advocates pacifism. For instance, the Benjamin Britten opera of 1971, *Owen Wingrave,* according to critic William Braun, emphasizes pacifism to the point where the supernatural elements are a distraction (Braun 72). Such a pacifist interpretation is quite appropriate for a work written during the period of the American War in Vietnam. But James's Gothicism addresses the notion of cowardice and male self identity, both Narcissistic and sexual, by setting up environments that are defined by gender, the male military and the female Gothic. Emphasizing only the pacifist message reduces the story to a single dimension that is not the usual domain of Henry James.

Lee McKay Johnson contends that James creates this visionary silence as his own particular method of holding together all of his fiction (3–6). Through silence, James could incorporate fantastic elements such as ghosts, unseen or questionable. Ambiguity of the influence of these fantastic elements is a major concern to James in his Gothic stories and indeed elsewhere in his fiction (Lewis 33). The Gothic element, the fantastic, and the super-natural, indicative of James, hold "Owen Wingrave" together. The author emphasizes the iconography of the dark old house and the innocent who jour-neys within in both the major ghost story, "The Jolly Corner," and the story of questionable genre, "Owen Wingrave."

Narcissistic reflection links the two stories as the Wingrave family cre-ates for Owen a patriarchal looking glass whereby he constantly defines him-self in comparison to his father and the generations of Wingrave men before him. Moreover, gendered meanings issue from the combination of feminine Gothicism and the patriarchal motif of "cowardice" as an unmanly charac-teristic, implying sexual otherness. As Neill Matheson writes of Henry James's use of the gothic:

> The intimate connection between sexuality and the supernatural horrors of Gothic is mediated by a chain of related words indicating a turning from norms, including "perverse," "queer," and "unnatural," which are available for both supernatural and sexual meanings [722].

This wordplay is a part of what Matheson calls improvisation and spontane-ity in linking sexuality with the Gothic. Owen Wingrave's concern with sexuality involves his turn from the masculine world of the army back to the feminine world of his ancestral home and the family's ironic insistence on patriarchal values. Their reaction to Owen's perceived cowardice, "unnatu-ral" to the Victorian gentleman, reflects the obfuscation of gender roles in Owen's family and in his individuality. As the Gothic innocent, returning to the dark old house for a journey into the sinister unknown, confronting the patriarchal monsters within, Owen puts himself into a position of fem-ininity as he leaves the masculine world of the soldier. James as an author wants to keep the sexual themes obscure, silent even. As Auchard notes, in a "good" ghost story, according to James, "the focus of vitality is that which is missing" (39). Haralson writes of James's work in general, "The queer desire that is apparently implied gets filtered in the very process of implica-tion" (64). In James's best ghost stories, the presence of the sexual subtext lies just beneath the surface and is never truly absent.

In both "The Jolly Corner" and "Owen Wingrave" James shows an implied desire by the main character to live in the male oriented company from which he has turned, Brydon's circle of European libertines and Wingrave's military friends. In both stories, James uses Gothic iconography, particularly the innocent protagonist wandering through the dark old house, in order to obfuscate the sexual themes inherent in the characters defining

204

themselves. The reader discerns a common method of storytelling in which Gothicism and Narcissism lend themselves to an "anti-interpretive" method in which form is not paramount. Each moment of each story has an immediate impact, a satisfaction in the realm of suspense, horror, joy, or beauty. The point of these stories is not the appearance of the ghost on the ultimate or penultimate pages. Rather, the ghost is always there. Owen Wingrave in his story and Spencer Brydon in "The Jolly Corner" realize they have spent their lives trying to overcome that which the ghost symbolizes, an obfuscated and unwanted version of their identities.

Works Cited

Auchard, John. *Silence in Henry James. The Heritage of Symbolism and Decadence.* University Park: Pennsylvania State University Press, 1986.

Auchincloss, Louis. *Reading from Henry James.* Minneapolis: University of Minnesota Press, 1975.

Barthes, Roland. *Mythologies.* 1957. Trans. Annette Lavers. New York: Hill and Wang, 1972.

Braun, William R. "Britten: Owen Wingrave." *Opera News* 69. 12 (June 2005): 72.

Cannon, Kelly. *Henry James and Masculinity. The Man at the Margins.* New York: St. Martin's, 1994.

Eagleton, Terry. "The Nature of Gothic." In *Figures of Dissent: Critical Essays on Fish, Spivak, Zizek and Others.* New York: Verso, 2003.

Haralson, Eric. *Henry James and Queer Modernity.* New York: Cambridge University Press, 2003.

James, Henry. "The Jolly Corner." 1907. In *The Altar of the Dead, The Beast in the Jungle, The Birthplace and Other Tales.* New York: Scribner's, 1909.

_____. "Owen Wingrave." 1892. In *The Altar of the Dead, The Beast in the Jungle, The Birthplace and Other Tales.* New York: Scribner's, 1909.

_____. *The Tragic Muse.* London: MacMillan, 1890.

_____. *The Turn of the Screw.* 1898. In *The Portable Henry James.* Ed. Morton D. Zabel. New York: Viking, 1979.

Johnson, Lee McKay. *Finding the Figure in the Carpet. Vision and Silence in the Works of Henry James.* New York: iUniverse 2006.

Jordan, Roland, and Emma Kafalenos. "The Double Trajectory: Ambiguity in Brahms and Henry James." *19th Century Music* 13. 2 (Autumn 1989): 129–144.

Kristeva, Julia. *Powers of Horror. An Essay on Abjection.* Trans. Leon S. Roudiez. New York: Columbia University Press, 1982.

_____. *Tales of Love.* Trans. Leon S. Roudiez. New York: Columbia University Press, 1987.

Lewis, Pericles. "'The Reality of the Unseen': Shared Fictions and Religious Experience in the Ghost Stories of Henry James." *The Arizona Quarterly* 61. 2 (2005): 33–66.

Matheson, Neill. "Talking Horror: James, Euphemism, and the Specter of Wilde." *American Literature* 71. 4 (1999): 709–750.

McGowan, John. "Postmodernism." In *The Johns Hopkins Guide to Literary Theory & Criticism.* Baltimore: Johns Hopkins University Press, 1994.

Miner, Earl Roy. "Henry James' Metaphysical Romances." *Nineteenth-Century Fiction* 9. 1 (June 1954): 1–21.

Sontag, Susan. *Against Interpretation and Other Essays.* New York: Farrar, Strauss & Giroux, 1967.

_____. "Writing Itself: On Roland Barthes." In *A Susan Sontag Reader.* New York: Farrar, Strauss & Giroux, 1982. 423–446.

Stevenson, Robert Louis. *Dr Jekyll and Mr Hyde.* 1886. New York: Signet Classic, 1978.

Thompson, Terry. "James' *The Jolly Corner.*" *Explicator* 56. 4 (Summer 1998): 192–196.

Wilde, Oscar. *The Picture of Dorian Gray.* 1890. Ebook, New York: Modern Library, 2000.

Williams, Anne. *Art of Darkness: A Poetics of Gothic.* Chicago: University of Chicago Press, 1995.

About the Contributors

Elizabeth Anderman, Ph.D., is a lecturer at the University of Colorado at Boulder. Her dissertation was entitled "Visible Sensations: Illustration and Ekphrasis in Sensation Fiction." She is also a community activist and fundraiser whose non-profit involvement has included serving as chair of the ACLU of Colorado Board of Directors, development committee chair for the Board of Directors of KBDI Channel 12, and secretary of Theater in the Park.

Julie M. Barst is a Ph.D. candidate in literary studies at Purdue University. Her dissertation, "Transporting Conviction: The Narrative Power of Australia in Nineteenth-Century British Literature," analyzes the relationship between Great Britain and the colony of Australia from 1788 until 1901. She argues that the geographic space of Australia, initially colonized via convict transportation, was significant in transporting convictions (transforming ideas and beliefs) within British society. Her essay included here was originally published in the *Australasian Victorian Studies Journal* in 2004, and she also recently published an essay in *European Romantic Review* entitled "Transporting the Picturesque: Australia Through the Claude Lorraine Glass."

Jennifer Beauvais is a doctoral candidate in the English department at the University of Montreal. Her areas of expertise include nineteenth-century masculinity and social boundaries. Her dissertation is "In Between Spheres: Male Characters and the Performance of Femininity in Five Victorian Novels, 1849–1891," which questions the definition of masculinity and the public and private spheres by focusing on the domesticated man in Victorian fiction. She has published "Domesticity and the Female Demon in Charlotte Dacre's *Zofloya* and Emily Brontë's *Wuthering Heights*" in *Romanticism on the Net* (November 2006), as well as "Approaches to Teaching Emily Brontë, George Eliot, and Mary Shelley" in the *Instructor's Guide to the Broadview Anthology of British Literature* (2008). She currently teaches English at Marianopolis College in Montreal.

Marilyn Brock is a literary critic and fiction writer. She has a Ph.D. in English and comparative literature from the University of Cincinnati, where her studies focused on Victorian literature, psychoanalytic, feminist and race theory and twentieth century American literature with an emphasis on the Gothic. She has published short fiction in *Miranda Literary Magazine*, *Starry Night Review*, *Planet Magazine* and other literary journals. She presented "The Vamp and the Good English Mother: Female Roles in Le Fanu's *Carmilla* and Stoker's *Dracula*" at the 2004 NEMLA conference.

Richard Fantina is a professor of graduate studies in the Literature and Writing program at Union Institute and University. His most recent publications are the edited collection *Straight Writ Queer: Non-Normative Heterosexuality in Literature* (McFarland, 2006) and *Victorian Sensations: Essays on a Scandalous Genre* (Ohio State, 2006), co-edited with Kimberly Harrison. He is also author of *Ernest Hemingway: Machismo and Masochism* (Palgrave-Macmillan, 2005).

Nicholas Harris is a jazz pianist with an M.A. in music theory from the University of Iowa. Long a devotee of nineteenth century and modernist American literature, he is currently pursuing a graduate degree in literature and writing at the Union Institute and University.

Kate Holterhoff is currently in the University of Cincinnati's master's degree program studying English and comparative literature. Her interests include British Victorian literature with an emphasis on cultural studies, especially as they relate to science, aesthetics, and anthropology.

Stephanie King is currently a lecturer at Concordia University in the Department of English. She earned her Ph.D. from McGill University, where her research revolved around questions of masculinity and narratology in Victorian fiction. King's dissertation, "Devious, Dashing, Disturbing: Fallen Men in Victorian Fiction, 1860–1900," questions Victorian conventions of narrative and gender by introducing the character of the fallen man as an identifiable nineteenth-century persona. She has published an article on the fallen man in *Nineteenth Century Gender Studies*. King's current research links patrimony to violence and disfigurement in Victorian and Edwardian literature.

Judith Sanders teaches English at Shady Side Academy in Pittsburgh, where she lives with her husband and son. She has a B.A. in literature from Yale, an M.A. in writing from Boston University, and a Ph.D. in English from Tufts. She has taught literature and writing at Bowdoin, Tufts, MIT, and Boston University, as well as in France on a Fulbright fellowship. She has also worked as a freelance editor, writer, and writing coach. She has published articles in *The American Scholar*, the *Journal of Popular Film and Television*, *Modern Jewish Studies* and *Film Quarterly*, and in the anthology *Mama, Ph.D.*, from Rutgers University Press. Her poems have appeared in *Poetic*, anthologies, and the *Pittsburgh Post-Gazette*.

Saverio Tomaiuolo is a lecturer in English literature and language at Cassino University, Italy. He has published a monograph on Alfred Tennyson (*Tennyson e il senso del narrare*, 2003), as well as articles and essays on postmodernism (Robert M. Pirsig, Antonia Byatt) and Victorian literature (Alfred Tennyson, G. M. Hopkins, Henry James, Ellen Wood, Charles Dickens, Wilkie Collins, R. L. Stevenson and Mary

Elizabeth Braddon). He has recently published a book on translation theory titled *Ricreare in lingua: La traduzione dalla poesia al testo multimediale* (2008) and he is working on a monograph on Mary Elizabeth Braddon provisionally titled *In Lady Audley's Shadow: Mary Elizabeth Braddon and Victorian Literary Genres.*

Laurence Talairach-Vielmas is an associate professor in English at the University of Toulouse (UTM), France. She is the author of *Moulding the Female Body in Victorian Fairy Tales and Sensation Novels* (Ashgate, 2007) and *Wilkie Collins, Medicine and the Gothic* (University of Wales Press, forthcoming), as well as numerous articles on Victorian literature. She is also the editor of Mary Elizabeth Braddon's *Thou Art the Man* (Valancourt Books, 2008).

Maria Granic-White is originally from Iasi, Romania, where she obtained a bachelor's degree in Romanian and English language and literature, and a master's degree in poetics and stylistics. She also obtained a master's degree in English from Sam Houston State University. Currently, Maria is enrolled in a Ph. D. program in theory and cultural studies in the English Department at Purdue University. Her essay "Teaching as Acting and Directing" was published in the spring 2006 edition of *Academic Exchange Quarterly*. Maria is also co-author of "Discoveries in Chemistry and Textiles: The Development of a Two-Week Elective Chemistry Course in Germany and Paris," which will be published by *Chem. Educator* in December of this year. Maria's current research centers on theatricality as well as on visualizations of temporality in Victorian novels.

Index